diffordsguide
GIN
THE BARTENDER'S BIBLE

SIMON DIFFORD

FIREFLY BOOKS

"For me as a novice, gin is either 'AJ' (after Jared) or 'BJ' (before Jared): prior to meeting Jared Brown, master distiller at Sipsmith, gin mostly signalled my second-favourite Martini. Who knew it could be delicious neat and drunk like good whisky? That it would signal a shift to superior spirits, summer cups, fizzes, slings. I was still rooted in the days of dangerous women, ice and lemon. Now there are dozens of craft distilleries and companies such as Plymouth and Beefeater have woken up to new opportunities and appetites. And now gin has its own geek's bible, diffordsguide Gin, a heady cocktail of information, enthusiasm and authority. Welcome to the spirit world. Gin is it."

Allan Jenkins
Editor, Observer Food Monthly

"For me, tracing the ebb and flow of humanity's love affair with different types of booze is nothing less than fascinating, which is why this book so draws me in. Taking in the social history of gin, alongside the backgrounds of some of the most interesting brands available today, this is partly a reference book and partly a collection of short stories – tales of the lengths people will go to get their beloved gins to market. You don't need to work in the drinks industry to like this book – although appreciating a well-made gin and tonic would certainly help – and it is perfectly timed, coming at a moment when drinkers are taking more of an interest than ever in the ingredients that go into their glasses."

Rebecca Seal
food and drink writer

A FIREFLY BOOK

Published by Firefly Books Ltd. 2013

Copyright © 2013 Odd Firm of Sin Limited

First printing

Publisher Cataloging-in-Publication Data (U.S.)
A CIP record for this title is available from the Library of Congress

Library and Archives Canada Cataloguing in Publication
A CIP record for this title is available from Library and Archives Canada

Published in the United States by
Firefly Books (U.S.) Inc.
P.O. Box 1338, Ellicott Station
Buffalo, New York 14205

Published in Canada by
Firefly Books Ltd.
50 Staples Avenue, Unit 1
Richmond Hill, Ontario L4B 0A7

Printed in China

Don't Blame Us
The views expressed in this publication are not necessarily the view of Firefly
Books or Odd Firm of Sin Limited. While every effort is made to ensure the
accuracy of information contained in this publication at the time of going to
press, no responsibility can be accepted for errors or omissions and Odd Firm
of Sin Limited specifically disclaim any implied warranties of merchantability or
fitness for a particular purpose. The advice and strategies contained herein may
not be suitable for your situation.

Contents

Introduction

As a born-and-bred Londoner, I feel something of a patriotic affinity for gin. Although the Dutch can rightly lay claim to having created the first popular juniper-flavoured spirit, what is unquestionable is that the modern style of gin mostly enjoyed around the world today has English origins, in London to be specific. And what a journey it has had – a veritable rollercoaster ride over three centuries.

When gin first hit the capital, it was popular with the masses but shunned by the gentry. Over the years, it struggled to find acceptance by the upper classes, but by the days of the British Raj, polite society had properly accepted and adopted it into its noble ranks, peaking in the 1930s cocktail era.

During the dying decades of the 20th century, gin then suffered in the fashion stakes as vodka's star shone ever more brightly, but the turn of the millennium seems to have heralded a new enthusiasm for gin once again. Today, gin might be considered the most fashionable and dynamic spirit category of the moment.

Despite my patriotic affinity for the spirit, I also feel sad that the term 'London Dry Gin' is not protected by an appellation and can be adopted by gins made all over the world. It also pains me that precious little gin is now produced in our great capital.

This book is a celebration of gin, and I hope that it helps gather support for the idea of creating a protected appellation that finally acknowledges the city's role in today's drinking culture and affords it the recognition it deserves. Just as the 'New Western Dry' category articulates a trend for New World gins, so the London-born old-school tradition of gin-making should now be properly protected.

Thankfully, trend-setters are now calling for their gin of choice and the great British G&T is arguably more fashionable than it was when it was first created during Queen Victoria's reign. Long live gin, and long live the G&T!

Cheers,

Simon Difford
simon@diffordsguide.com

"Although the sale of gin was officially outlawed, consumption was equivalent to every man, women and child drinking two pints every week."

Gin History

1100s
ORIGINS OF DISTILLATION

Distillation originated in the Arab world, moving to Europe in the middle ages courtesy of the Moors and their rule of Sicily. It is thought that Benedictine monks in Salerno, Italy used this newly acquired distilling knowledge to make alcohol which they used to dissolve and preserve medicinal plants, including juniper which grows abundantly in the nearby hills.

A collection of treatments compiled around 1055 under the name Compendium Salernita includes a recipe for a tonic wine infused with juniper berries.

In the 12th century monks and alchemists across Europe joined the quest for an 'aqua vita', or water of life. These early distillers made spirits by heating wine hence the word 'brandy' emerged from the term 'burnt wine'.

1269
EARLY MEDICINES

Physicians through the ages used juniper in their preparations due to its reputation as a diuretic (a diuretic is something that increases the excretion of urine). For centuries, juniper-infused compounds would be used to treat conditions of the stomach, kidneys and liver.

An oft-quoted written reference to a juniper-based tonic lies within a 1269 Dutch publication, 'Der Naturen Bloeme' (the "flower" of nature or the book of nature), by Jacob van Maerlant te Damme. This early natural history encyclopaedia includes a chapter on medicinal herbs including juniper.

1340s-1700s
THE PLAGUE & JUNIPER

During the 14th century the bubonic plague originated in Central Asia and by the late 1340s had spread to Europe. Also known as the Black Death, this deadly pandemic is estimated to have killed one- to two-thirds of Europe's population.

People across Europe consumed juniper cordials and elixirs in the misguided belief they would ward against the Plague. It was also common to wear masks filled with juniper berries as a barrier to the pathogen.

EARLY 1500s
SPREAD OF DISTILLATION

Distillation spread from Italy through the southern grape-growing regions and eventually through the rest of Europe, when, over the course of the 16th century, the art of distilling from mash made from grain was mastered.

The spread of distillation knowledge was helped by the invention of the printing press in the 1440s by the German Johannes Gutenberg. By 1500, printing presses were in operation throughout Western Europe. Published by Hieronymus Braunschweig, an Alsatian physician in 1500, the 'Liber de Arte Destillandi' ('The Book of the Art of Distillation'), describes distilled spirits as "the mistress of all medicine".

Early distillates would have been comparatively low in alcohol and rough tasting due to the impurities that primitive distillation failed to remove. The Dutch are usually credited for perfecting the art of turning these

'low wines' into a stronger, and so purer, spirit through a further secondary distillation process. However, Cognac and other centres of early European distillation also make creditable claims.

MID-1500s
SPREAD OF JUNIPER FLAVOURED SPIRITS

There is much conjecture as to who first made 'genever/jenever' with malt wine and juniper distillate – it could well have been those 12th century monks in Salerno, Italy but is thought to date from the 1400s. However, the first written evidence of genièvre is found in the 1552 'Constelijck Distilleer Boek' ('Constelijck Distiller Book').

There is also evidence suggesting juniper-flavoured distillates where made in the 1560s by Hugenot refugees in Flanders, on the northern border of France. And by this time juniper-flavoured spirits were also available throughout the Low Countries (Holland, Belgium and parts of Northern France).

1572
PROFESSOR SYLVIUS DE BOUVE

Professor Sylvius de Bouve is widely credited with the creation of what we would recognise today as genever, and so, by extension, gin. He was a chemist, alchemist, renowned scholar and one of the founding professors of the oldest academic institutions in the Netherlands, Leiden University (founded in February 1575).

He added oil of juniper to grain spirit to make what he called genièvre to be used a stimulant, diuretic and treatment for lumbago. It is presumed by many that it

was Dr Sylvius's recipe that was later commercialised by Bols. In records dating back to 1595, Sylvius de Bouve sold a juniper-flavoured distilled moutwijn (malt wine), but it is likely he was selling this many years earlier, possibly as early as 1572. However, he was belatedly miscredited as while he undoubtedly made a juniper flavoured 'medicinal' spirit, such spirits almost certainly originated in the 1400s with the first written reference to genièvre appearing more than 20 years before Leiden University was founded in 1551.

It is perhaps worth mentioning that Sylvius de Bouve is often confused with a German doctor, Franciscus Sylvius, born François dele Boë (1614-1672), also known as Dr Sylvius, who was Professor of Medicine at the University of Leyden some ninety years later (1658 1672).

1575
BOLS WAS ESTABLISHED

Well, 1575 is the first documented date for when the Bulsius family set up their distillery in Amsterdam, in the process also shortening their name to the more Dutch sounding Bols. It is believed they ended up in Amsterdam after first fleeing from Antwerp as religious refugees to Cologne were protestants were welcome. They then settled in Amsterdam, which was independent from the rule of the Catholic Spanish king and a haven for religious refugees.

They may well have done this slightly earlier but even the 1575 date makes Bols the world's oldest distilled brand. Evidence of the date is found in the front of a 1763 Bols family bible where the writer talks about his great grandfather starting the family distillery in 1575.

Sadly the grandfather is not named, just referenced.

Bols is believed to have started producing juniper-flavoured spirits as well as liqueurs soon after arriving in Amsterdam in 1575 and was certainly the first to establish a genever 'brand'. Bols may not have been the first to make it but it was the first to commercialise genever. Presently in many markets it appears that history is repeating itself.

1585
DUTCH COURAGE

In 1585 English soldiers were sent by Queen Elizabeth I of England to help the predominantly Protestant Dutch revolt against Philip of Spain and their Spanish Catholic rulers. In 1618 the Low Countries once again became the battlefields of Europe as France, England and Spain fought the Thirty Years War which would last until 1648.

English troops fighting these wars discovered genever and returned home with tales of the spirit that had given them "Dutch Courage".

1602
THE DUTCH EAST INDIA COMPANY (VOC)

The 'Vereenigde Oost-indisch Compagnie' (VOC), the Dutch East India Company was established in 1602, when the States-General of the Netherlands granted it a 21-year monopoly to carry out colonial activities in Asia. Europe's first stock exchange in Rotterdam opened that same year and the VOC is considered the world's first multinational corporation and the first to issue stock.

The VOC quickly became a huge operation with 5,000 ships and 50,000 employees handling some

2,500,000 tonnes of spices and other goods over the course of the 17th century – more than two-and-a-half times that of the English East India Company.

Bols developed a close relationship with the VOC and their relationship gave them preferential access to exotic herbs and spices shipped to Amsterdam by the VOC. In return Bols supplied spirits and liqueurs to major shareholders in the VOC.

EARLY 1600s
GRAIN SPIRIT DISTILLATION

Early distillation was from fermented grapes (wine) but producing spirit on a large scale is easier and more cost effective when distilled from fermented grain (beer). Distillation allowed farmers to preserve surplus grain and turn it into a concentrated, more-easily moved and traded commodity.

The first major centres of grain spirit distillation were the coastal cities of the Low Countries, drawing upon the abundant plains of northern and central Europe. After 1618, the Thirty Years War interrupted the supply of French cognac so boasting international demand for Dutch grain spirits.

Schiedam, close to Rotterdam in the Netherlands, at the mouth of the great river Maas and its North Sea shipping port, turned from being a small fishing village to the most important centre of grain distillation with one of Europe's largest grain auctions. The handling, processing and distillation of grain dominated the local economy with supporting trades such as millers, maltsters, glass blowers and coppers. Schiedam remains the Dutch centre of genever production to this day.

SEMPER IDEM

1638
THE WORSHIPFUL COMPANY OF DISTILLERS

In 1638 Theodore De Mayerne, a noted physician and alchemist who would later be dubbed 'The Father of English Distilling', joined Thomas Cademan, physician to the Queen, to found The Worshipful Company of Distillers, one of the City of London's livery companies to this day. Its royal connections secured a Royal Charter issued by Charles I giving the Company exclusive rights to distil grain within the Cities of London and Westminster, and 21 miles around them. This granted a virtual monopoly on the production of spirits and vinegar. The duo set minimum quality and production standards which they documented in a pamphlet called 'The Distiller of London'. This banned the sale of 'low wines' and specified that spirits must be rectified.

Like Dutch genever, English gin went through two stages of production (and in most cased still does). In the first, 'malt distillers' distilled malted barley and other cereals to produce what are known as 'low wines'. These tended to be large-scale operations and there were only a few of them, most being situated in greater London and represented by the Worshipful Company of Distillers.

In the second stage of production the malt distillers supplied low wines to 'compound distillers', so called because they compounded or flavoured these spirits before diluting them to drinking strength. These compounders tended to be small operations.

1652
LUCAS BOLS

Lucus Bols, the man who the modern Lucas Bols

Company is named after, was born in 1652. (He is not to be confused with Louis de Bils, the son of a wealthy Dutch merchant who supported the work of Boë Sylvius, a physician whose name is often connected to the development of genever). Lucas Bols took over the management of his family's business during the Dutch Golden Age. Dutch products, especially genever, became very fashionable in England after the Dutch King William III, became William I of England.

Lucas turned Bols into an international brand and expanded the range of liqueurs to more than 200 recipes, many designed specifically for important customers. After his death in 1719, his two sons, Hermannus and Peter, took over the business.

Few records survive from this period and the first written proof that Bols distilled juniper is a 1664 record of Bols purchasing juniper berries.

1663
SAMUEL PEPYS

By the early 1600s crude gin was being distilled in the port cities of London, Plymouth, Portsmouth and Bristol and its early consumption was under the pretext of its supposed health benefits.

Samuel Pepys diarised his bodily functions in as much detail as he did the events of the age. On 9 October 1663 he records suffering from "My great fit of cholic" and the next day reports being constipated and suffering "pain in making water ... Sir J. Minnes and Sir W. Batten [his work colleagues], did advise me to take some juniper water, and Sir W. Batten sent to his Lady for some for me, strong water made of juniper. Whether that or anything else of my draught this morning did it I cannot tell, but I had a couple of stools forced after it." Possibly a little too much information but proof of the regard juniper held as a diuretic at the time. When Pepys refers to 'strong water' you should read this as being 'alcohol'.

1689
WILLIAM OF ORANGE/KING WILLIAM III
It was the arrival of a Dutchman to the English throne that drove the popularity of genever in England and turned it from a medicine to a fashionable drink.

The succession of James II was controversial but the new Stewart king's less-than-diplomatic support of Catholicism made him unpopular to both his English protestant subjects and Parliament alike. The king's opponents forced his eventual flight to France in 1688 and leading English political figures (the 'Immortal Seven') took the unprecedented step of inviting the Dutch protestant William of Orange, who was married to James's daughter Mary, to invade and establish a protestant alliance between England and the Netherlands against Louis XIV's Catholic France.

William's invasion fleet was bigger than the Spanish Armada of a century before but met no resistance from the English and on 11 February 1689 Parliament declared that, by fleeing the country, James had abdicated as king. His daughter Mary was declared queen, to rule jointly with William who adopted the name William III.

This led to a constitutional monarchy and the 'Bill of Rights', the crowning of William and Mary as King and

Queen of Scotland and the Irish battle of the Boyne. But I digress, back to gin.

As part of the conflict with France, William naturally sought to weaken his enemy's economy, so started the English blockade against French goods. At that time French brandy was the most popular spirit in Britain; rum was not established; whisk(e)y was only enjoyed by the Scots and the Irish; and vodka was hundreds of years away from breaking out of Poland and Russia. Genever was starting to flow from Holland and due to gin being grain-rather than wine-based it could also be produced in England. Thus genever, and by extension, gin quickly took the place of dwindling French brandy supplies.

Genever naturally became the fashionable drink at William and Mary's court in Kensington and amongst the gentry who viewed its consumption as showing their patriotism to the new king and supporting the Protestant faith.

1690
THE DISTILLING ACT
Gin was further helped in 1690 by the British Parliament passing 'An Act for encouraging the distilling of brandy and spirits from corn', enabling anybody to distil grain spirit. This Act was intended to encourage English distillers to fill the demand left by French brandy's sudden disappearance, and charging a low excise duty on the spirits produced help fund the war.

Fortuitously, the new act also helped English farmers who by, selling surplus grain to the distillers were able to pay higher rents to the landowners who dominated both houses of Parliament and whose support the king needed for his war.

1691
KETEL ONE

The Nolet family's distillery was established in the Dutch city of Schiedam in 1691 when Joannes Nolet started his distillation business. The Dutch refer to their pot stills as 'ketels', thus their genever (and latterly their vodka) is named after the Nolet's original Distilleerketel #1'.

1694
TONNAGE ACT

Yet another war helped the rise of gin – the War of the Grand Alliance (a.k.a. the League of Augsburg). Like the previous war it also left the British government short of funds. In 1694 this led to the founding of the Bank of England and the Tonnage Act. This Act established the concept of National Debt and enabled the Government to levy duties on ships according to their tonnage, and upon beer and other liquors.

The taxing of beer dramatically increased its price to the extent that there was little difference in the price of beer and gin. This encouraged many to try the juniper-flavoured spirit for the first time and many found they preferred it.

The act also allowed anyone who wanted to distil alcohol to legally do so by simply posting a public notice giving at least ten days' notice of their intention to start distilling.

1695
DE KUYPER FOUNDED

Famous for its genever and liqueurs, the Dutch firm of De Kuyper was established in 1695 when newlywed Petrus de Kuyper founded the firm in Horst in Limburg, in the south of the Netherlands. Originally De Kuyper was a manufacturer of 'kuipen'; wooden barrels for transporting genever and beer. The direct translation of De Kuyper refers to this trade in the same way 'Cooper' does in English.

In 1729 Jan de Kuyper, third son of Petrus and his wife Anne Custers moved to Rotterdam and became shopkeepers. There are no records to indicate whether this shop was a liquor store but in 1752 Jan de Kuyper took over a distillery in the Genever manufacturing centre of the time, Schiedam, just outside Rotterdam, but sold it again only two years later.

The family were destined to be distillers and in 1769 two of Jan's sons, Johannes and Pieter de Kuyper, who up to this point, had individually traded brandy, joined forces setting up a partnership to buy an existing distillery in Rotterdam. It was from this base that De Kuyper rapidly expanded and today the De Kuyper family are the 10th generation to run the business.

1702
BRANDY NAN

In 1702 William III was succeeded by Queen Anne who earned the nickname 'Brandy Nan' due to her penchant for drinking brandy mixed with cold tea dispensed from an apparently innocent tea pot.

Queen Anne inadvertently encouraged increased gin production by cancelling the charter which Charles I had issued to the Worshipful Company of Distillers granting them sole rights to distil within the Cities of

NOLET Anno 1691

Westminster and London and 21 miles around. Hundreds of back-street distilleries sprung up and within a generation London's slum dwellers were drowning themselves with gin. By revoking the Distillers Company Charter she also abolished their ability to ensure the quality of spirits produced.

1714
FIRST RECORDED USE OF THE WORD 'GIN'

The first known written use of the word 'gin' appears in a 1714 work, 'The Fable of the Bees, or Private Vices, Publick Benefits' by Bernard Mandeville. He wrote, "The infamous liquor, the name of which deriv'd from Juniper-Berries in Dutch, is now, by frequent use... from a word of middling length shrunk into a Monosyllable, intoxicating Gin."

Although this is the first recorded use of the word it is of course likely to have been in colloquial use sometime earlier. Incidentally, the Dutch term 'jenever' or 'genever' was borrowed from Old French 'genevre' (modern French genièvre) meaning 'juniper tree', which in turn comes from the Latin word for the tree 'juniperus'.

1700-1770
THE GROWTH OF GENEVER

Heavily subsidised English malt exports provided the basis for the rapid expansion of the Dutch distilling industry during the early 18th century. Genever production was centred around the town of Schiedam near the mouth of the great river Mass, on the North Sea, close to the vast grain port of Rotterdam and its large grain actions. The botanicals needed to flavour the genever were supplied by the Amsterdam-based Dutch East India Company, the world's first multinational.

The number of distilleries in Schiedam increased from 34 in 1700, to 121 in 1730. By the early 1770s some 85 per cent of the genever produced in Schiedam was exported to markets such as England, France, Spain, the East and West Indies and North America. At its height, in 1881, there were 394 distilleries in Schiedam. Today there are only four.

1720
BRITISH MUTINY ACT

The British Mutiny Act of 1720 absolved tradesmen engaged in distilling from having to billet soldiers. The term 'tradesmen' included innkeepers, and they were the ones most likely to be forced to house unwanted soldiers. So, unsurprisingly, this legislation was enough to persuade many innkeepers to start distilling their own gin, thus making them tradesmen engaged in distilling and so absolved from having to house the unwanted guests.

1726
DANIEL DEFOE & COMPANY OF DISTILLERS

Now most famous for his novel 'Robinson Crusoe', Daniel Defoe (1660-1731) was the greatest hack of his time and extremely influential. In 1726, he wrote a pamphlet on behalf of London's Company of Distillers entitled, 'A Brief Case of the Distillers, and the Distilling Trade in England, Shewing how Far it Is the Interest of England to Encourage the Said Trade'. In this catchily

named document he writes, "the ordinary people are now so very satisfied with malt spirits, and especially with their new compositions, that they do not seek French Brandy in such manner that they formally did".

Despite Defoe's biased protestations the gin produced by London's distillers at the time was poor compared to the quality of Dutch genever and it was common for 18th century English distillers to add sugar, glycerine, large amounts of herbs and far worse to their gin in order to make their poorly made spirits more palatable. Some distillers tinted their gins to resemble brandy.

The quality of English gin, even towards the end of the 1720s, may have been dubious but it was cheap and readily available. London's population went on a drunken bender which was to last until the end of the 1750s.

1717-1757
LONDON'S GIN CRAZE

Daniel Defoe must have regretted his support of the Company of Distillers, for just two years after writing its pamphlet he publicly blamed gin for most of London's problems. In 1728 he writes, "in less than an Age, we may expect a fine Spindle-shank'd Generation".

The impact of gin on London's deprived inner-city population, unused to anything stronger than beer, has been compared to the effects of crack cocaine on American inner-city ghettos. The period during which gin had its greatest impact in Britain has since become known as the 'Gin Craze'. Today we use the term 'drug crazed', but back in the 18th century London the poor were 'gin crazed'. This period is generally perceived to have covered 1720 to 1751 – these were the dates

between which people publicly expressed their concern over the craze.

London's gin consumption peaked in 1743 and despite the Gin Act of 1751 these high levels lasted until 1757 when a series of crop failures forced distillation of grain to be banned.

Gin allowed the 18th century poor to forget the squalor and hardship in which they lived. It was a powerful drug that was cheaply and easily available. A much-quoted gin shop sign from Tobias Smollett's 'History of England' reads: "Drink for a penny, dead drunk for two pence, clean straw for nothing".

Street vendors peddled cheap gin from carts and back street compounders used lethal ingredients such as turpentine and sulphuric acid to flavour their product. In the back rooms of gin shops, men and women spent the night unconscious on straw surrounded by the aroma of gin and vomit.

1723-1757
MOTHER'S RUIN

In 1723 the death rate in London outstripped the birth rate and it remained higher for the next decade, and as many as 75 per cent of those babies that were born died before the age of five. Gin was blamed for lowering fertility.

Women addicted to gin neglected their infants or quieted them with gin; babies were born deformed by foetal alcohol syndrome. More women than men fell foul of gin so the spirit gained a feminine identity and earned itself nicknames like 'Ladies' Delight', 'Mother Gin' or 'Madam Geneva'. One other, the term, 'Mother's Ruin', survives to this day.

1726
BOORD'S GIN FOUNDED

The London firm of Boord's was founded in 1726. Over a century later this brand would become famous for its Old Tom gin and distinctive Cat & Barrel trademark.

1729
THE FIRST GIN ACT

The rising level of drunkenness among the poor and the shocking effects of poorly distilled gins in 1729 led parliament to introduce the first of eight Gin Acts. These acts were given more official names and some were clauses inserted into other legislative acts, but they have become universally know as the 'Gin Acts'.

The 1729 Gin Act was intended to restrict gin sales by increasing duty on its sale and raising retail licensing fees. A major flaw in the act defines gin as spirits to which "juniper berries, or other fruit, spices or ingredients" had been added. Thus the act was circumvented by simply not adding these ingredients and the result was known as 'Parliamentary Brandy'.

Legitimate distillers were heavily penalised by this act while illicit distillers thrived. This first Gin Act was the start of a battle between those calling for temperance, the land owners, farmers and distillers, and successive government exchequers. (Nothing much seems to have changed). Duty raised from gin helped fund the building of the British Empire.

1733
THE SECOND GIN ACT

The ill conceived first Gin Act of 1729 failed to check the growth of gin and was repealed just four years after it became law. Its 1733 replacement sought to end sales of gin by street hawkers and general stores and encourage sales from taverns. The act was as flawed as the one it replaced and merely resulted in thousands of houses being turned into gin shops. This new act was the first to rely on professional informers for enforcement.

1734
JUDITH DEFOUR THE KILLER

The effects of gin on those addicted to it were as profound as modern-day hard drugs and anti-gin campaigners of the day in particularly latched onto the shocking case of Judith Defour as an example of its evil affects.

Judith, who made a living twisting silk into thread, was the single mother of two-year-old Mary and both lived in Bethnal Green Parish Workhouse. In January 1734 she collected Mary for a day out. The workhouse had dressed the child in new petticoats and Judith promised the warden to return the child by the afternoon that same day. Instead she turned up for work that evening a little worse for drink and with no sign of the child.

After continuing to drink gin at work, something that was not unusual, she told a colleague that she had left the child in the field. Mary was discovered dead and it transpired that Judith had strangled her with a hand-kerchief and stripped the child to sell its cloths to buy gin. She was tried and found guilty at The Old Bailey on 1 March 1734. The trading of her own child's life for gin greatly influenced the introduction of a further gin act.

1736
THE THIRD GIN ACT

In 1736 the previous ineffectual 1733 Gin Act was replaced by a new Gin Act, officially named, 'The Act for Laying a Duty upon the Retailers of Spirituous Liquors'. This practically prohibited gin sales by imposing a two gallon minimum unit of sale and swingeing duties of £1 per gallon. It also required retailers to purchase a £50 annual licence (then equivalent to 14 months' wages for a skilled craftsman) with heavy fines for the unlicensed sale of spirits.

Like the previous act of 1733 this new act relied heavily on professional informers. It succeeded in putting many of the more respectable retailers of gin out of business but the act merely forced the sale of gin, or spirituous substances purporting to be gin, underground and the bootleg spirits peddled in the streets blinded and killed many of those who drunk them.

The highest proportion of gin shops lie in the poverty-stricken narrow lanes and alleys of East London. These were hard for the authorities to control as these shops were little more than a plain room within a house or behind a shop front. These served as makeshift meeting places from where it was common for prostitutes to operate. Infamous addresses included Crock Lane in Holborn, Rosemary Lane and Hog Lane near Tower Hill, while the main arterial routes in and out of The City such as Mile End Road, Kingsland Road and Whitechapel Road were lined with street vendors operating from small stalls.

1737
THE FOURTH GIN ACT

The Gin Act of 1737 was not actually an act in its own right but a clause inserted into the so-called 'Sweets Act'. This served as a revision to the 1736 act in that it plugged the previous acts loophole allowed the gin trade to continue via back street gin shops and makeshift stalls. This new act also allowed informants of even the most petty of gin sellers to be rewarded.

The 1737 act led to a surge in informants and convictions. Thousands of Londoners were prosecuted for flouting the Gin Act – mostly women. Despite this gin sales continued to rise. This Gin Act stoked a backlash against not only the Gin Act but also the rule of law and government itself.

1738
THE FIFTH GIN ACT

Hardly a day passed without a gin informer being attacked or killed, sometimes by mobs of hundreds. Magistrates read the Riot Act but were ignored as the rabble hit out at both informers and authority.

The Gin Act of 1738 virtually outlawed gin and made attacks on informers a felony. It also dealt with the problem of excise officers refusing to arrest friends and neighbours by empowering individuals to arrest gin sellers. Gin distilling was forced further underground and illegal stills and drinking dens proliferated, particularly in London's unruly east.

1738
CAPTAIN DUDLEY BRADSTREET

Captain Dudley Bradstreet researched the intricacies of the Gin Act and took advantage of a loophole that said an informer must know the name of the person renting a

property from which gin was illegally being sold, for the justices to have the authority to break into the premises in order to arrest the transgressors of the act.

In 1738, Dudley had an acquaintance rent a house in the City of London on Blue Anchor Alley and nailed a sign of a cat in the window, under its paw he concealed a lead pipe. He let it be known that gin would be available from a cat in the alley on the following day and moved in with supplies of food and £13 worth of gin purchased from Mr. Langdale's distillery in Holborn before barricading himself into the house.

His patrons pushed coins though a slot in the cat's mouth and Bradstreet would in return pour gin down the pipe to trickle out from under the cat's paw. Customers would hold a cup or simply their mouth under the paw to receive their gin. The authorities found themselves powerless to act and Bradstreet apparently profited from his scheme for three months before so many copied him that competition caused him to move on.

Years later, in 1755, Bradstreet wrote about his exploits in a book entitled 'The Life and Uncommon Adventures of Captain Dudley Bradstreet'.

There is no evidence linking Bradstreet to the term 'old tom'. It is my belief that Bradstreet's cat and the term 'old tom' are coincidental and that 'old tom' originated in the 1830s in deference to the distiller Thomas Chamberlain (see 1830s). He did, however, start the trend for what became known as Puss and Mew houses. Vendors would sit concealed within a premise and customers wanting to buy gin would say 'puss'. The vendor would respond with 'mew' and push out a drawer into which the customer would deposit payment. The

vendor would recover the coins from the drawer and push it forward filled with a measure of gin. These human vending machines where found all over London and for a short period the subterfuge succeeded in stifling attempts to enforce the 1738 Gin Act.

1740
BOOTH'S GIN ESTABLISHED

The Booth family, who moved to London from north-east England, were established wine merchants as early as 1569. By 1740 they had added distilling to their already established brewing and wine interests and built a distillery at 55 Cowcross Street, Clerkenwell, London. This date is referenced on Booth's label and makes Booth's the oldest gin brand still in existence.

1740
FINSBURY GIN ESTABLISHED

The Finsbury name was founded by Joseph Bishop back in 1740 and is possibly a reference to Clerkenwell springs, which was once the centre of London's gin industry and part of the Borough of Finsbury.

1743
THE SIXTH GIN ACT

Attacks on informers continued despite the measures introduced in the 1738 Gin Act. Matters were made worse by corruption within Excise Office and crooked informers. Few of those convicted could pay the £10 fine but informers were still due their £5 reward. The Act was running at a huge loss and by 1739 the commissioners had run out of money to pay informers.

Over the years the various Gin Acts had been in force, production of spirits had risen by over 30 per cent to eight million gallons a year. Although the sale of gin was officially outlawed, consumption was equivalent to every man, women and child drinking two pints every week.

England was at the height of the War of Austrian Succession (1740-1748) and a New Act was sought to reduce gin consumption, settle public unrest and raise revenue for the war effort. The Gin Act of 1743 was the first to target distillers rather than retailers and it reduced the retail licence fee from £10 to just £1. This was a level that legitimate publicans could afford to pay so ending the career of informers. The 1743 Act also forbid distillers to sell gin direct to the public and increased the excise duty payable by them. However, because the level of duty was relatively low, the distillers did not revolt against paying it – they had little choice as there were relatively few of them, making this new act much easier for the authorities to enforce.

This was the first Gin Act to actually cause consumption of gin to drop.

1747
THE SEVENTH GIN ACT

The War of Austrian Succession (1740-1748) still raged causing a government funding crisis. The response was the Gin Act of 1747 which increased the excise duty payable by the gin distillers but appeased them but allowing wholesale distillers to buy £50 licences allowing them to sell directly to the public.

The increase in duty further dampened demand for gin and government revenues from the spirit fell. Beer tax was reduced in the hope of raising revenue from increased beer consumption so levels of insobriety changed little.

1750
HOGARTH'S GIN LANE

In 1750 William Hogarth released his print, 'Gin Lane', depicting the excesses and resulting hardship brought about by gin consumption. In his engraving a man is depicted gnawing on one end of a bone with a dog chewing the other, while on the opposite side of the picture a mother pours gin down her baby's throat. Above her, a suicidal bankrupt hangs from a beam within his crumbling house while the undertaker's house next door, marked by its hanging coffin, is pristine due the prosperity of its owner at the gin drinker's expense.

The picture is set in the heart of St. Giles, an area at the eastern end of Oxford Street then notorious for its gin houses and where Centre Point stands today. Hawksmoor's St. George's church in Bloomsbury and its spire can be easily identified in the background of Hogarth's work, which he tops the with a statue of George I as a symbol of the crown being above the church. But above all else is the pawnbroker's sign, actually forming a cross on top of the church, illustrating how society's values had been inverted by the effects of gin. The mother sprawled on the steps in the picture's foreground is thought by many to be the artist's personification of Judith Defour (see 1734). The women, pictured with marks on her legs denoting illness, is neglecting her child as it falls from the steps, meanwhile her gin influenced expression is one of blissful ignorance.

Left: *Gin Lane* **Right:** *Beer Street*

Gin Lane is one of a pair of engravings by Hogarth; the other, 'Beer Street', is in stark contrast. In this picture the church rises above all and a drooping pawnbroker's sign is below the level of the royal standard flying from the spire to mark the king's birthday. Only the artist is thin and gaunt in Beer Street. The rest are depicted has happy and plump, many enjoying their ale. Quite different to the unhappy depraved souls of Gin Lane.

These works of propaganda are thought to have been commissioned by the magistrate Henry Fielding.

1751
THE EIGHTH GIN ACT

The end of the War of Austrian Succession in 1748 brought with it a new threat to London's society that was even worse than gin: crime. The returning soldiers had no trade and were not given any support by the state so many simply started stealing and mugging. The 1750s saw the moral reformers blame the still-growing crime wave on the excesses of gin and they used this as ammunition in their lobbying for prohibition.

In 1751 a Westminster magistrate, Henry Fielding, also a respected playwright and novelist, published a scare-mongering paper titled 'An Enquiry into the Causes of the Late Increase in Robbers'. This links cheap gin with the rising crime wave and was timed to coincide with the start of the 1751 parliamentary session. It formed part of a well orchestrated lobby calling for gins prohibition.

Fortunately for the distillers, the Gin Act of 1751, known as the Tippling Act, which inevitably followed in the wake of the anti-gin crusade only modestly increased duties on distilled spirits. It doubled the price of a retail licence to £2 and specifically made that licence only available to inns, alehouses and taverns. The act also granted immunity from prosecution and a reward of £5 for any unlicensed retailer that informed upon a distiller supplying them.

Although the duty increase was small, the 1751 act practically ended all back street gin sales so dramatically affecting its availability. By 1752 the volume of spirits produced on which duty was paid had fallen by over a third.

1757
ENGLISH GRAIN DISTILLING BANNED

In 1757 the harvest failed and, fearing a bread shortage, exports of corn and malt were banned, as was all distillation of wheat, barley, malt or any other grain. This was intended to be a temporary measure but when the 1758 harvest proved little better, the ban was extended.

Spirits were still being made from imported sugar molasses but due to the high cost, production was comparatively small, and so the spirits that were available were priced beyond the reach of the poor.

Sobriety prevailed and London enjoyed growing prosperity and many civil improvements to its infrastructure with the construction of new roads and the introduction of street lighting. London's standard of living rose for both rich and poor alike.

1760
GRAIN DISTILLING RESTORED

The bountiful harvest of 1759 led distillers and farmers to lobby for distillation to be legalised once again.

However, their demands were countered by those of moral reformers, a stronger church and the growing middle classes who argued for out-and-out prohibition. However, the lack of availability of gin was causing rum imports to rise and this, along with the preference for the government to earn excise duty from domestic distillers, led to a compromise. In March 1760 a bill restored corn distilling but with double the levels of previous excise duty. Britain's distillers also benefitted from the introduction of subsidies for all spirits exports.

The cost of getting drunk on spirits was now greater than that of getting drunk on beer so the urban poor simply returned to beer and by the 1760s a proliferation of dingy back street pubs had sprung up, most remaining open throughout the night. Meanwhile the more expensive gin found new respectability and regulation of distilling led to an improvement in quality and the growth of a handful of dominant distillers.

1761
GREENALL'S GIN ESTABLISHED

Thomas Dakin built his distillery on Bridge Street in the Cheshire market town of Warrington in 1760, finally commissioning and producing his first gin in 1761. Dakin's Warrington Gin was a great success and his son, Edward, took over the business in due course.

The Greenall family had been brewers in St Helens for some time when Edward Greenall bought the Dakin distillery in 1870. The 'G' & 'J' of the now familiar G&J Greenall comes from his two younger brothers, Gilbert and John.

1769
FOUNDATION OF GORDON & COMPANY

In 1769 Alexander Gordon established Gordon & Company in London's Bermondsey. He was born in Wapping, London but at the age of four, after his father's death, was brought up by his grandfather in Glasgow, also Alexander.

As an adult he moved back to London and lived on Charterhouse Square, Clerkenwell where he moved his distilling operations from their original Bermondsey location in 1798 due to the superior quality of the Clerkenwell water available from the plentiful wells after which the area is named.

The establishment of Gordon & Company and the others which followed in the subsequent years heralded the start of a regulated and reputable English distilling industry which produced quality spirits. London was at the centre of this industry, partly due to the River Thames and its docks and quays which supplied distillers with exotic raw ingredients such as oranges, lemons and spices from British colonies in the Caribbean. London was the world's largest city and its docks the busiest.

1770
BURNETT'S WHITE SATIN ESTABLISHED

It is claimed that Burnett's White Satin was first made in 1770 by the Lord Mayor of London and that the originator and Lord Mayor was Robert or Thomas Burnett: according to my research, neither a Robert nor a Thomas Burnett has ever held this office.

My understanding is that Robert Burnett joined the

company that came to bear his name in 1770, established his gin, then became Sheriff of London in 1794 and was knighted the following year. There is a requirement for a Lord Mayor of London to have previously served as a Sheriff but Robert Burnett never went on to hold the mayoral office.

1777
CANNY SCOTS

The Haigs and Steins started exporting grain alcohol to London for rectification into gin in 1777. Much to the upset of the English distillers this was the start of a flow of cheap, quality grain alcohol from Scotland which has grown over the centuries to the extent that what little gin is still produced in London today is more often than not made with Scottish grain alcohol. Formerly London-distilled brands such as Gordon's and Tanqueray are now made in Scotland.

1793
PLYMOUTH GIN ESTABLISHED

The Black Friars distillery where Plymouth Gin is made was set up in 1793 when the Coates family joined the established distilling business of Fox & Williamson and converted the old Black Friars monastery.

The Coates family made a gin that was fuller-flavoured with less citrus and more pungent root flavours than its typical London dry counterparts. The Royal Navy purchased large quantities of gin for its officers (ratings were issued with rum, not gin) and as Plymouth was a naval dockyard much of Coates business was to the officers' mess. Other naval towns such as Bristol and Liverpool also had distilleries supplying the navy with the town's particular style of gin but Plymouth is the only one to survive. Plymouth is also the only British gin still being made at its original distillery.

Although Plymouth gin is still made in the same distillery in which it was created, Coates has been owned by a range of different companies. It is said by some that when it was owned by Seager Evans, a company based in London's Deptford but controlled by Schanley of New York, the recipe was changed so the gin fell more in line with the predominant London Dry style and with American tastes.

1794
LONDON TRADE DIRECTORY

A 1794 trade directory for the cities of London and Westminster and the Borough of Southwark lists over 40 distillers, malt distillers and rectifiers. This proves that the production of gin production was an established industry.

1767-1803
COCKTAIL FRIENDLY TRIO

The development of cocktail culture and, by default gin-based cocktails, were much aided by three developments: artificial carbonation of water (1767), commercially traded ice (1800) and refrigeration (1803).

Seltzer water had long been available but back then the term referred to effervescent mineral water obtained from the natural springs near the village of Niederseltsers in South West Germany. Artificial

GORDON'S DRY GIN

Report on Gordon & C⁰ˢ "*Dry Gin*" London.
Dec. 22ⁿᵈ 1908

On several occasions (in 1892, 1899 and 1904)
I have analysed samples of Gordon's Dry Gin.
The results invariably have been excellent. I have
at the present time again submitted to analysis a
sample of this Spirit, with results entirely
corroborative of the previous analyses. The analytical
data which accompany this certificate show that the
Gin is absolutely dry, not the least trace of sugar
being present and the proportions of secondary
constituents are extremely minute, indeed from all
practical points of view these may be regarded as absent.
The alcoholic strength of the Gin is high and
I have no hesitation in once more expressing

carbonation was first introduced in 1767 by an Englishman, Joseph Priestley. Then Johann Jacob Schweppe, a watchmaker and amateur scientist, developed his process to manufacture carbonated mineral water and founded the Schweppes Company in Geneva in 1783 before moving to London's Drury Lane (1790). On the other side of the Atlantic in 1807 Benjamin Silliman, a Yale University chemistry professor, started bottling his brand of 'seltzer water'.

Today's soda water (club soda) is also artificially carbonated but contains other additives as well, including sodium bicarbonate, sodium chloride, sodium phosphate, sodium citrate and sometimes light flavouring.

By 1800 ice was for sale in America in the form of slabs hacked from frozen lakes. Ice harvesting became big business in America, mainly due to New Englanders Nathaniel Wyeth and Frederic Tudor, the latter eventually became known as the 'Ice King'. Tudor developed better insulation products which allowed him to ship ice even to the tropics and then store it in purpose-built ice houses. Wyeth devised a method of quickly and cheaply cutting uniform blocks of ice thus making handling, storage and transportation more efficient.

In 1803 Thomas Moor of Maryland, USA patented his refrigeration process which was later developed and introduced chiefly for the benefit of brewers as it regularised the fermentation process regardless of season.

John Gorrie (1802-1855) studied tropical diseases while a physician at two hospitals in Florida. His experiment with iced cooling rooms to aid his patients' recovery led him to experiment with making artificial ice. On 6 May 1851 Gorrie was granted a Patent for his ice machine.

1805
SEAGER'S DISTILLERY ESTABLISHED

Seager's Deptford distillery was established in 1805, a date better remembered for The Battle of Trafalgar (21-October-1805) where Admiral Lord Nelson defeated the combined fleets of the French and Spanish Navies.

1806
FIRST DEFINITION OF 'COCKTAIL'

The first written definition of a cocktail appears on 6 May 1806 in a New York newspaper, 'The Balance, and Columbian Repository', though the word 'cocktail' had appeared in print, though undefined, in a London newspaper in 1798. In the previous edition a politician who has just lost a local election presents a tongue-in-cheek account of his fruitless pursuit of victory. Under a list of 'loses' he includes "25 do. cock-tail".

In the following edition, a response followed a reader's query for a definition of cock-tail, "Cock tail, then is a stimulating liquor, composed of spirits of any kind, sugar, water and bitters it is vulgarly called a bittered sling, and is supposed to be an excellent electioneering potion inasmuch as it renders the heart stout and bold, at the same time that it fuddles the head. It is said also, to be of great use to a democratic candidate: because, a person having swallowed a glass of it, is ready to swallow any thing else."

PINK GIN

Glass: Martini
Garnish: Lemon zest twist
Method: Stir all ingredients with ice and strain into chilled glass.

2 shots London dry gin
2 shots Chilled mineral water (reduce if wet ice)
1 dash Angostura aromatic bitters

1815
WELLINGTON HELPED BY GIN

One story from the The Napoleonic wars (1800-1815) is often cited in the history of gin. In 1815 Marshal Blücher was marching his Prussian army to support Wellington at the Battle of Waterloo but progress was halted when Blücher was badly thrown from his horse. It is recorded that he was revived by a rub of gin and onions enabling him to go on and help Wellington defeat Napoleon. Hurrah.

1830
DYSLEXICS CAN'T BE WRONG

Bols spells genever with a 'g', while De Kuyper seems to prefer spelling jenever with a 'j'. Both spellings are correct. Prior to 1830 it was mostly written with a 'g' and subsequently with a 'j'.

1840
PIMM'S (POSSIBLY) LAUNCHED

Pimm's, the quintessential English summer tipple, is usually accredited to James Pimm, who in 1823-4 began trading as a shellfish-monger in London's Lombard Street. He later moved to nearby number 3 Poultry, also in the City of London, where he established Pimm's Oyster Warehouse. It is here, in 1840, that he is said to have first served this drink. (Formerly a pub called the Three Graces, the premises were mentioned by Samuel Pepys in his diary of August 1661: "We drank a great deal of wine, I too much and Mr Fanshaw until he could hardly go.")

However, some (myself included) dispute Pimm's origins, claiming that the drink is named after the establishment, not its founder, and the true credit lies with James Pimm's successor, Samuel Morey who is recorded as taking out a retail liquor licence in 1860. Many establishments of the day mixed house spirits to serve with liqueurs and juices as 'cups', a reference to the tankards in which they were sold. Naturally the gin based 'cup' made at Pimm's Oyster Bar was named after the establishment, which retained its founder's name.

Pimm's restaurant became very popular and changed hands a couple more times before eventually being sold to Horatio David Davies, a wine merchant and owner of cafés in London. Horatio Davies became Sir Horatio, a Member of Parliament and, between 1897-1898, Lord Mayor of London. He formed Pimm's into a private company in 1906, which after his death was controlled by family trusts for another 57 years.

The precise date that the drink Pimm's was first sold outside restaurants and bars controlled by the Pimm's company is unknown. However, it is certain that the original product, No. 1, was based on gin and flavoured with numerous botanicals including quinine. Therefore it is one of the most famous gin cocktails of all time, albeit a premix.

1824
ANGOSTURA AROMATIC BITTERS INVENTED

Johann Gottlieb Benjamin Siegert (1796-1870) was a German doctor who had settled in Venezuela where he was Surgeon-General of a military hospital in the town of Angostura (now called Ciudad Bolivar). In 1824 he created the now famous bitters, which he originally called Amargo Aromatico and used it to treat stomach disorders and indigestion of his fellow settlers.

Siegert soon changed the name of his creation to Angostura, after the town where he was working (not, as is often presumed, after Angostura bark, which is not an ingredient). When the doctor died in 1870, production of the bitters was taken over by his sons who, in 1875, due to unrest in Venezuela, moved to Trinidad.

Henry Workshop was a ship's surgeon serving on H.M.S. Hercules, which was patrolling the Caribbean on the watch for slave trader vessels, in 1826. The British Admiralty already prescribed the use of chinchona bark (quinia) to ward against tropical diseases and as a medical man he was interested in Angostura as he had heard the preparation included this and many other herbal remedies. While on shore leave in Georgetown he procured a couple of bottles. Back on ship, he and the ship's captain, Jack Bristow, mixed a small amount of the medicinal bitters with their gin ration and found the pink drink it made to be very agreeable. They served their new creation to the other officers on the ship. Word spread and 'Pink Gin' as it became known, became popular with officers of his Majesty's Navy.

1826
BOKMA GRAANJENEVER LAUNCHED
Bokma, the famous Dutch genever, was first created by the Bokma family in 1826 in the Frisian capital of Leeuwarden. 'Bok' means a male goat, hence the goat emblem on the crest. Klaas Bokkeszoon owned a corn mill and a public house and so it was almost natural that his son Freerk Klaaseszoon Bokma established his own distillery, which he named 'The Source'.

Convinced that the full-bodied contents of a Bokma bottle were already 'round' enough, in 1894 Freerk's son Pieter designed a unique square bottle, predating other famous quadrilaterals.

1828
FIRST GIN PALACE
The 1820s saw the establishment of the first licensed public houses selling beer. Their numbers quickly multiplied and many streets boasted one on every corner and several in-between. These early pubs were simply converted homes (hence the term 'public house'), most in a very poor state of repair, and this led magistrates to start demanding improvements before issuing licences. It became commonplace for landlords to receive money from brewers to renovate their pubs on condition that they signed a sole supply contract with that brewer. These became known as 'tied houses'.

In 1825 the government slashed spirit duties with the dramatic affect that within a year, spirit production more than doubled to hit levels not seen since 1743. The distillers were doing well and sought to compete with the growing number of up-market pubs. They replaced the traditional gin shops with opulently decorated establishments which soon became known as 'Gin Palaces'. Lit by gas lights their interiors were furnished with polished carved mahogany and embellished with brass, engraved glass and mirrors.

Henry B. Fearon is credited with being the pioneer of the gin palace. It is said that he opened the first near St. Andrew's Church at 94 Holborn Hill, London circa 1828 under the name of his wine merchant company

'Thompson and Fearon's'. Obviously a forward thinking man he was also one of the founders of London University.

In his 'Sketches by Boz', Charles Dickens famously writes of a gin palace, "perfectly dazzling when contrasted with the darkness and dirt we have just left … ".

John Buonarotti Papworth (1775-1847) a prolific Victorian architect designed Thompson and Fearon's and many other early gin palaces. Their design was based on the style of upmarket shops of the era and would influence that of pubs throughout the rest of the eighteenth century.

By the late 1840s there were more than 5,000 such 'palaces' in the London area alone – remember in those days this did not include areas such as Kensington and Mayfair which then were still country villages yet to be engulfed by the city. These establishments sold much more than gin and some still survive to this day. Examples in London include:

The Argyll Arms, 18 Argyll Street, W1F 7TP.
King's Head, 84 Upper Tooting Road, SW17 7PB.
Prince Alfred, 5a Formosa Street, W9 1EE.
Princess Louise, Holborn, WC1V 7EP
Red Lion (built 1821), St. James's SW1Y 6JP.
Red Lion, 48 Parliament Street, SW1 2NH
The Salisbury, 90 St. Martin's Lane, WC2N 4AP

One of the finest surviving examples of a Victorian Gin Palace is Crown Liquor Saloon, Great Victoria Street, Belfast, Northern Ireland. This is now owned by National Trust and a full restoration was completed in 1982.

1830s
TRUE ORIGINS OF 'OLD TOM' NAME

Old Tom, as it became known, was a sweet style of gin that was overwhelmingly popular in the 18th and 19th centuries. Prior to the invention of the column still gin was more pungent due to the limited rectification (purification) of the base spirit possible in copper pot stills. The rough tasting fermentation congeners no doubt present in the gin were masked by flavouring (most commonly with lemon or aniseed) and or sweetening with sweet botanicals such as liquorice. The addition of liquid sugar came later as this previously expensive commodity became more affordable.

Old Tom probably started as a general term but it became associated with a particular sweet style of gin. One story has it that a cat fell into a vat of gin at an unnamed distillery, giving the gin a distinctive flavour. However, the creation of this style of gin more likely lies with Thomas Chamberlain, an early gin compounder.

During my research I have found references to one Thomas Norris, otherwise known as 'Young Tom' who was a former apprentice to Thomas Chamberlain, or 'Old Tom', at Hodges' distillery in Church Street, Lambeth. It would appear that Young Tom left the distillery to open a gin palace in Great Russell Street, Covent Garden where he sold gin from casks purchased from his former employers. He labelled the casks of gin according to their flavour or style with one, marked 'Old Tom', apparently concocted by Thomas Chamberlain.

More compelling evidence links the term 'old tom' with Thomas Chamberlain and Boord's of London. The company appear to be the first to bottle a gin with a label

illustrated with a tomcat sat on a barrel this went on to become by far the best known brand of this sweetened style of gin.

In 1903 Boord & Son went to court against Huddart & Company to defend their 'Cat Brand' trademark under 'passing-off laws'. They presented evidence to Mr Justice Swinfen Eady that they had introduced the term in 1849 and that the brand was named after "old Thomas Chamberlain of Hodge's distillery" and presented an old bottle label with a picture of "Old Tom" the man on it, and another label with a picture of a young sailor aboard ship named "Young Tom."

In the 1830s it was common for gin distillers to finance the opening of gin palaces as tied houses for the sale of their gin. I would guess that Thomas Norris was a loyal and trusted employee who the company backed to open his gin palace. Norris would have bought several styles of gin from Boord's including lemon, unsweetened and sweetened. It is not implausible that he named a style perfected by 'old' Thomas, his former boss, 'Old Tom's Gin' and that Captain Dudley Bradstreet's cat is purely coincidental (see 1738).

1829
CHELSEA DISTILLERY LICENSED

The origins of Beefeater Gin lie in the Chelsea Distillery operated by John Taylor & Son which was built during the 1820s and licensed in 1829. In 1863 James Burrough paid £400 to purchase the distillery and renamed the firm 'James Burrough, Distiller and Importer of Foreign Liqueurs'. Burrough did not create the Beefeater Gin brand until circa 1876.

1823
BOLS SHIPS GENEVER TO USA

In 1823, Gabriël Theodorus van 't Wout, (a financier from Rotterdam who had acquired the Bols Company five years earlier) exported the first shipment of liqueurs and genevers to the United States. He was an astute business man and also became an accomplished distiller. Fortunately, the accountant in him compelled him to make detailed notes and in 1830 he embarked on a seven year undertaking to compile four volumes entitled 'Distillateurs- en Liqueurbereiders Handboek door een oude patroon van 't Lootsje' ('Distillers and Liqueur makers Handbook by an old patron of The Little Shed'). The beautifully written books detail recipes, the origin and specifications for botanicals and production methods. Bols still refers to these journals when they want to revive a long-forgotten recipe and one of the four volumes is on display at the Bols visitor centre.

1830
TANQUERAY GIN ESTABLISHED

The Tanqueray family were originally silversmiths who left France for England early in the 18th century, where three successive Tanquerays became rectors in Bedfordshire. In 1830 Charles Tanqueray, then aged twenty, broke the mould: rather than become a clergyman, he established his Bloomsbury Distillery in London's Finsbury, then noted for its spa water.

Tanqueray is distilled by the traditional one-shot process in a copper pot still nicknamed 'Old Tom': the No. 4 still which has moved location a number of times in its long career. In fact, like most other 'London Dry

gins' Tanqueray is no longer made in London – or even, any longer, in England. The distillery in Laindon, Essex, closed in 1998 and the site is now a business estate named Juniper Park: production and Old Tom were both relocated to Cameronbridge Distillery in Fife, Scotland.

1831
AENEAS COFFEY PATENTS COFFEY STILL

The beginning of the 19th century saw attempts to develop a still to speed and improve the distilling process and 1826 Robert Stein invented a still consisting of two columns. An Irishman and patent office cleric, Aeneas Coffey, considerably improved the design and patented his 'Coffey' still in 1831.

Column stills are also known as 'continuous stills' because, as its name suggests, they can be run continuously without the need to stop and start between batches as in pot stills (aka: alembic stills). This coupled with the higher concentration of alcohol in the final distillate makes column stills much more economical to operate than pot stills.

1831-1870
DRY GIN

The Coffey still enabled distillers to produce a much purer spirit, and on a larger scale than was previously possible. By the middle of the 19th century the quality of gin produced using clean spirits from the new continuous stills was close to the standard to spirit we enjoy today and distillers reduced or omitted the sugar previously used to soften the harshness of the old style gins.

This new style of gin eventually became known as dry gin, then London Dry Gin. The first London dry gins were more aromatic than is typical of today's style.

1833
NORTH WEST PASSAGE

During the 19th century Sir Felix Booth set up another distillery at Brentford and grew Booth's Distillers into the largest distilling company in England. In 1829-33 he financed John Ross's expedition to chart the North West Passage: Ross failed to do this but did succeed in locating the true position of the magnetic North, and named some newly discovered areas after his patron, notably Boothia Peninsula in Canada.

King William IV gave the Royal Arms to Booth's distillery in 1833 and from then on the gin was sold under the strap line 'King of gins'.

1847
BOODLES GIN ESTABLISHED

This old British brand of gin dates back to 1847 but is now only sold in the United Sates. The brand is named after Boodle's gentlemen's club in St. James's, London, founded in 1762 and originally run by Edward Boodle. Unusually Boodles contains no citrus botanicals.

1850
EXPORTS, THE RAJ AND THE G&T

In 1850 Sir Felix Booth of the Booth distilling family succeeded in pushing a private Members Bill through Parliament which removed duties on export gin. London's distillers were quick to seize the opportunity and pushed their new quality dry gin style to new markets.

Quinine, extracted from the pungent bark of the South American cinchona tree, gives tonic its distinctive bitterness. It was first used to treat malaria in Rome in 1631 and the first known quinine-based tonic was launched by Erasmus Bond in 1858. Tonic was very popular in British colonies, especially India so when Schweppes launched its first carbonated quinine tonic in 1870, they branded it 'Indian Tonic Water'. The ladies and gentlemen of the Raj also drank phenomenal quantities of gin. It is therefore accepted that gin and tonic emerged in India during the second half of the nineteenth century and was drunk partly for its anti-malarial properties.

London Dry Gin became a respectable drink: the preferred tipple of officers on board ship, and gentlemen of the Raj, mixed with medicinal flavourings such as tonic (Gin & Tonic) or bitters (Pink Gin). Gin and soda, garnished with lemon, was known as 'the British soldier's delight' while gin and ginger beer was called 'Hatfield'.

1850s
US SALOONS

Wild West saloons weren't all the swing-door-and-sawdust emporia portrayed in Westerns. Some, like the El Dorado in San Francisco, were elaborate, fantastical places, decked out in expensive art, antiques, opulent fabrics and mirrors. They offered everything from gambling to live music to prostitutes (some, just like in the westerns, had a brothel upstairs) – essentially, anything that could convince a miner to part with his bag of gold dust.

Over the second half of the nineteenth century, the US enjoyed phenomenal wealth, transformed by gold rushes, oil booms and the coming of the railroad. The new rich sought places to socialise and spend their money, so grand hotels and clubs sprang up to accommodate them, places like the Astor House, the Hoffman House, the Manhattan Club, the Jockey Club and the Metropolitan Hotel. Their elaborate décor, gilt murals and even the bars, owed much to the saloons of the west.

It was in these saloons that American bartenders started combining different drinks to create some of the first cocktails – many featuring imported genever and gin.

1862
JERRY THOMAS

An American, Jerry Thomas (1830-1885) is credited for creating the modern-day bartending profession and for publishing the first known bartender's guide in 1862. He was a raconteur and his career stretched from the Occidental hotel in Gold Rush San Francisco to New York via London and New Orleans, and encompassed stints as a showman, gold miner and sailor.

Thomas's book, 'How to Mix Drinks or The Bon-Vivant's Companion', brought a new professionalism to the bar industry and featured a range of different styles of drinks – the cocktail was then a subset of mixed drinks, rather than the general catch-all term for mixed drinks it has become. Besides Cups, Sangarees, Flips and Pousse-Cafés, there were Cobblers, Crustas, Cocktails, Fixes, Toddies, Sours, Slings, Smashes and even a section of Temperance Drinks.

Interestingly, it is commonly accepted that except where he specifically mentions 'old tom gin', Thomas is actually referring to genever, which at that time would have been 100 per cent malt wine genever. To quote David Wondrich, the respected cocktail and drinks historian: "In the nineteenth century, Holland or genever gin was imported [to the USA] at the ratio of 5 or 6 gallons to every gallon of English gin."

Although the Martinez cocktail (see 1884) appears in the 1887 edition of Jerry Thomas's 'Bartenders' Guide' as a variation, there is no evidence that Jerry Thomas invented the Martinez and significantly it is omitted from the earlier 1862 edition of his 'Bartender's Guide'. (Jerry Thomas died in 1885 before the last edition of his book came out).

1863
PHYLLOXERA STRIKES FRENCH WINE

Phylloxera Vastatrix, a louse that attacks the roots of grape vines eventually causing the death of the plant, was discovered in French vineyards in 1863. Phylloxera devastated 90 per cent of Frances vines and quickly spread through much of Europe.

This crippled the European wine, and also the brandy industry, for over a decade. American grapes, where the pest originated from, were found resistant to the creature so European vines were grafted to American rootstock so making the new hybrid vines resistant to Phylloxera attack. Although this solved the problem in the intervening years, sales of gin greatly benefited.

1867
(SOMETIME AFTER) - GIMLET COCKTAIL CREATED

In 1747, James Lind, a Scottish surgeon, discovered that consumption of citrus fruits helped prevent scurvy, one of the most common illnesses on board ship. (We now understand that scurvy is caused by a Vitamin C deficiency and that it is the vitamins in citrus fruit which help ward off the condition.) In 1867, the Merchant Shipping Act made it mandatory for all British ships to carry rations of lime juice for the crew.

Lauchlin Rose, the owner of a shipyard in Leith, Scotland, had been importing limes from the West Indies to sell the juice to the Navy. He recognised the need to solve the problem of keeping citrus juice fresh for months on board ship and in 1867 he patented a process for preserving fruit juice without alcohol and so created the world's first concentrated fruit drink. To give his product wider appeal he sweetened the mixture, packaged it in an attractive bottle and named it 'Rose's Lime Cordial'.

Once the benefits of drinking lime juice became more broadly known, British sailors consumed so much of the stuff, often mixed with their daily ration of rum and water ('grog'), that they became affectionately known as 'Limeys'. Naval officers mixed Rose's lime cordial with gin to make Gimlets.

A 'gimlet' was originally the name of a small tool used to tap the barrels of spirits which were carried on British Navy ships: this could be the origin of the drink's name – "sharp as a gimlet". Another story cites a naval doctor, Rear-Admiral Sir Thomas Desmond Gimlette (1857-1943), who is said to have mixed gin with lime 'to

GIMLET

Glass: Martini
Garnish: Lime wedge or cherry
Method: STIR all ingredients with ice and strain into chilled glass.

2½ shots London dry gin
¾ shot Rose's lime cordial

Tom Collins

Glass: Collins
Garnish: Orange slice & cherry on stick (sail)
Method: Shake first three ingredients with ice and strain into ice-filled glass. Top with soda, lightly stir and serve with straws.

2 shots Tanqueray No. TEN
1 shot Freshly squeezed lemon juice
¾ shot Sugar syrup (2 sugar to 1 water)

Top up with Soda water (club soda)

help the medicine go down'. Although this is a credible story it is not substantiated in his obituary in 'The Times', 6 October 1943.

1868
COCKTAIL (RE)-CROSSES ATLANTIC

During the latter half of the 19th century, American-style grand hotels and clubs, complete with American bars, began to open in London, Paris, Rome and summer resorts such as the South of France. American bartenders arrived to run many of these bars, although the bar at London's Savoy (opened late 1890s) was staffed for some time by a British woman, Ada Coleman.

The first such American bar in London opened in 1868 close to the bank of England followed by the Criterion in London's Piccadilly Circus in 1874. However, the most famous European cocktail bar, Harry's American Bar in Paris, did not open until 1911.

1870
FIRST AMERICAN DRY GIN

The Fleischmann Brothers establish their distillery in Ohio in 1870 and produce the first American dry (unsweetened) gin.

1872
GILBEY'S GIN ESTABLISHED

In 1857 Walter and Alfred Gilbey returned from service in the Crimean War and set up a wine importing business in London's Soho. Trade grew so much that by 1867 they had moved to the famous Pantheon building on Oxford Street – five years later they set up a gin distillery in Camden Town.

Business boomed and the Gilbey family acquired several whisky distilleries in Scotland as well as foreign concerns such as Crofts port: by the 1920s the company had gin distilleries in Australia and Canada.

During Prohibition, consignments of Gilbey's gin were shipped to just outside the legal twelve-mile limit off the American coast then smuggled into the States. As a result, Gilbey's was widely counterfeited by the US underworld: the company introduced distinctive square bottles with sandblasting on three sides in an attempt to protect its intellectual property, only reverting to the original clear glass style in 1975. By this time it had distilleries in New Zealand, Uruguay, Namibia, East Africa, Swaziland, Mauritius and Mozambique.

The dragon-like creature featured on Gilbey's label is a Wyvern, a mythical winged animal often seen in medieval heraldry.

1874
TOM COLLINS

In England, this gin-based drink is traditionally credited to John Collins, a bartender who worked at Limmer's Hotel, Conduit Street, London. The 'coffee house' of this hotel, a true dive bar, was popular with sporting types during the 19th century, and famous, according to the 1860s memoirs of a Captain Gronow, for its gin-punch as early as 1814.

John (or possibly Jim) Collins, head waiter of Limmer's, is immortalised in a limerick, which was apparently first printed in an 1892 book entitled 'Drinks of the World'.

"My name is John Collins, head waiter at Limmer's.

Corner of Conduit Street, Hanover Square,
My chef occupation is filling of brimmers
For all the young gentleman frequenters there."
In 1891 a Sir Morell Mackenzie had identified John
Collins as the creator of the Tom Collins, using this
limerick, although both the words of the rhyme and the
conclusions he drew from it were disputed. But,
according to this version of the story, the special gin-
punch for which John Collins of Limmer's was famous
went on to become known as the Tom Collins when it
was made using Old Tom gin.

Others say that the Tom Collins originated in New
York, and takes its name from the Great Tom Collins
Hoax of 1874 (the theory I favour), a practical joke
which involved telling a friend that a man named Tom
Collins had been insulting them, and that he could be
found in a bar some distance away, and took the city by
storm. This is supported by the fact that the first known
written occurrence of a Tom Collins cocktail recipe is
found in the 1876 edition of Jerry Thomas' 'Bartender's
Guide'. Three drinks titled Tom Collins are listed:
Tom Collins Whiskey, Tom Collins Brandy and Tom
Collins Gin.

An alternative story attributes the drink to a Collins
who started work at a New York tavern called the
Whitehouse in 1873. Another identifies a different Tom
Collins, who worked as a bartender in the New Jersey
and New York area. There are apparently also versions
of its creation in San Francisco and Australia, and it is
not impossible that the drink evolved in two or more
places independently.

1876
BEEFEATER GIN LAUNCHED
Originally established as John Taylor & Son in 1820, the
company papers of what became known as James
Burrough Ltd (eponymously named after the new owner
who acquired the company in 1863) first record
Beefeater gin in 1876, alongside other brands then made
by the company such as James Burrough London Dry
and Ye Old Chelsey gin.

1883
ORIGINS OF SEAGRAM'S GIN
It is often claimed that the Seagram family crest on the
gin's label dates back to 1857 and this date features
prominently on the packaging. A claim substantiated by
the founding of a whiskey distillery in Waterloo,
Ontario, Canada that year. However, gin was not
distilled there at this time and Joseph E. Seagram did not
become a partner until 1869, and only assumed sole
ownership in 1883: this was when the company became
known as Joseph E. Seagram & Sons. Joseph died in 1928
and a few years later the Distillers Corporation, founded
by Samuel Bronfman, acquired Joseph E. Seagram &
Sons, and took over the Seagram name.

When Seagram's gin first launched it was named
'Seagram's Ancient Bottle Distilled Dry Gin' and the
bottle was embossed with seashells and starfish.
Although successive marketers have modernised the
bottle, the bumpy surface remains a trademark: so much
so that someone came up with the strap line "The
smooth gin in the bumpy bottle". Bizarrely, 'The Perfect
Gin' logo which graces the shoulder of the bottle bears a

MARTINEZ

Glass: Martini
Garnish: Orange zest twist
Method: Stir ingredients with ice and fine strain into chilled glass.

1½ shots Genever
1½ shots Sweet vermouth
⅛ shot Orange curaçao liqueur
2 dashes Angostura aromatic bitters

scary resemblance to the Salvation Army's logo.

Unusually, Seagram's gin is "mellowed" for "several weeks" in charred white oak barrels which have previously been used for maturing whiskey. The golden hue this gin once had is now barely noticeable, probably as a response to the dominant consumer perception that gins should be clear.

1884
MARTINEZ/DRY MARTINI

The Martini and its origins is a topic that can raise temperatures among drinks aficionados and, as so often, no one really knows. Today the drink is a blend of dry gin or vodka with a hint of dry vermouth. Yet it seems to have evolved from the Manhattan via the Martinez, a rather sweet drink based on genever with the addition of sweet vermouth, curaçao and orange bitters. The first known recipe for a Martinez appears in O.H. Byron's 1884 'The Modern Bartender' where it is listed as a variation to the Manhattan. Its first written standalone listing in a recipe book appears in Harry Johnson's 1888 'Bartender's Manual'.

Many claim that one Julio Richelieu created the drink in 1874 for a gold miner and that the drink is named after the Californian town of Martinez, where that unnamed gold miner enjoyed this libation.

Another myth attributes the creation of the Dry Martini to one Martini di Arma di Taggia, head bartender at New York's Knickerbocker Hotel, in 1911, although this is clearly too late. It is also no longer believed that the name relates to Martini & Henry rifles, the first of which was launched in 1871.

The Martini, like the Martinez, was initially sweet and very heavy on the vermouth by modern standards. In 1906 Louis Muckenstrum wrote up a Dry Martini Cocktail which, like the Martinez, benefited from curaçao and bitters as well as vermouth. Yet, unlike earlier versions, both the gin and the vermouth were dry. According to gary regan, the marketeers at Martini & Rossi vermouth were advertising a Dry Martini cocktail heavily at that time.

1884
PLYMOUTH APPELLATION CONTRÔLÉE

London distillers clearly envied the Black Friars distillery and its 'Plymouth' name and reputation. On 13th March 1884 and 10th February 1887 Coates successfully obtained injunctions preventing London distilleries from making 'Plymouth gin'. Today the gin enjoys Appellation Contrôlée protection and only gin made in the town of Plymouth can have the name Plymouth on its label. (It is a shame London Dry gin is not equally protected.)

1888
RAMOS GIN FIZZ COCKTAIL

The gin-based Ramos Gin Fizz cocktail was the secret recipe of Henry C. Ramos, who opened his Imperial Cabinet Bar in New Orleans in 1888. At the onset of Prohibition his brother, Charles Henry Ramos, published the previously closely guarded secret recipe in a full-page advertisement. Since 1935, the Roosevelt (now named the Fairmont) Hotel, New Orleans, has held the trademark on the name Ramos Gin Fizz.

RAMOS GIN FIZZ
Glass: Small Collins (8oz)
Garnish: Half lemon slice & mint sprig
Method: 1/ Flash BLEND first eight ingredients without ice (to emulsify mix). Then pour contents of blender into shaker and SHAKE with ice. Strain into chilled glass (no ice in glass) and TOP with soda from siphon. ALTERNATIVELY: 2/ Vigorously DRY SHAKE first eight ingredients until bored/tired. Add ice to shaker, SHAKE again and strain into chilled glass (no ice). TOP with soda water from siphon.
2 shots London dry gin
½ shot Freshly squeezed lemon juice
½ shot Freshly squeezed lime juice
¾ shot Sugar syrup (2 sugar to 1 water)
1/8 shot Orange flower water
3 drops Vanilla extract (optional)
1 fresh Egg white
1 shot§ Double (heavy) cream
Top up with Soda water from siphon

1898
TANQUERAY & GORDON'S MERGE
In 1898 what are now two of the biggest names in gin, Alexander Gordon & Company and Charles Tanqueray & Company, merged to form Tanqueray Gordon & Company.

1890s
FIRST BOTTLED GINS
Gin was originally sold in casks or earthenware crocks of the type still used for some genevers today. Bols then developed an elongated heart-shaped green glass bottle which was widely copied by other Dutch genever distillers and English gin distillers. It was not until the 1890s that improvements in glass technology allowed production of the first clear glass bottles showing the clarity of the liquid inside.

1902
LANGLEY DISTILLERY ESTABLISHED
Originally a brewery, distillation started at Langley Green (near Birmingham) in 1902 as a result of the Victorian gin boom when local publicans clubbed together to purchase the brewery and install stills.

This distillery is now owned by W H Palmer Group, a family-owned company whose main activity is not distillation but chemical compounding and wholesale. Indeed the group only began distilling when they took over these premises and its dormant gin distillery in 1955. Langley now produces its own Palmer Gin as well as contract distillation of Martin Miller's, Finsbury and Whitley Neill gin amongst others.

1906
BRONX COCKTAIL CREATED
The classic gin-based Bronx Cocktail was created in 1906 by Johnny Solon, a bartender at New York's Waldorf-Astoria Hotel (the Empire State Building occupies the site today), and named after the newly opened Bronx Zoo. This cocktail is reputedly the first cocktail to use fruit juice.

BRONX NO.1
Glass: Martini
Garnish: Maraschino cherry
Method: SHAKE all ingredients with ice and fine strain into chilled glass.
1½ shots London dry gin
¾ shot Dry vermouth
¾ shot Sweet vermouth
1 shot Freshly squeezed orange juice

1907
GORDON'S EXPORT LAUNCHED
Until around 1900 only green glass could be produced in volume, so until this time Gordon's green livery had remained effectively unchanged. The distinctive clear bottle and yellow Gordon's export guise was first created in celebration of a large, prestigious Australian export order placed in 1907.

1909
CLOVER CLUB COCKTAIL
The Clover Club is one of the best-known gin cocktails but little is known about its true origin. In his 1931 'Old Waldorf Bar Days', Albert Stevens Crockett credits the creation of this cocktail to the Bellevue-Stratford Hotel, Philadelphia. The earliest known recipe appears in the 1909 'Drinks – How to Mix and Serve', by Paul E. Lowe in which Lowe omits the lemon juice but this is thought to be a mistake.

CLOVER CLUB COCKTAIL (LOWE'S RECIPE)
Glass: Martini
Garnish: None
Method: SHAKE all ingredients with ice and fine strain into chilled glass.
1 shot London dry gin
1 shot Dry vermouth
1 shot Freshly squeezed lemon juice
1 shot Raspberry syrup (1 juice to 1 sugar)
½ fresh Egg white

1911
SINGAPORE SLING COCKTAIL
This famous gin-based cocktail was created some time between 1911 and 1915 by Chinese-born Ngiam Tong Boon at the Long Bar in Raffles Hotel, Singapore.

Raffles Hotel is named after the colonial founder of Singapore, Sir Stamford Raffles, and was the Near East's expat central. As Charles H. Baker Jr. wrote in his 1946 'Gentleman's Companion', "Just looking around the terrace porch we've seen Frank Buck, the Sultan of Johor, Aimee Semple McPherson, Somerset Maugham, Dick Halliburton, Doug Fairbanks, Bob Ripley, Ruth Elder and Walker Camp – not that this is any wonder". Raffles still sticks out of modern-day Singapore like a vast, colonial Christmas cake.

Although there is little controversy as to who created the Singapore Sling, where he created it and (roughly) when, there is huge debate over the original name and ingredients. Singapore and the locality was colonially known as the 'Straits Settlements' and it seems certain that Boon's drink was similarly named the 'Straits Sling'.

Singapore Sling

RAFFLES
HOTEL

SINGAPORE SLING (BAKER'S FORMULA)

Glass: Collins (10oz max)
Garnish: Lemon slice & cherry on stick (sail)
Method: SHAKE first three ingredients with ice
and strain into ice-filled glass. TOP with soda,
lightly stir and serve with straws.

2 shots Old Tom gin
¾ shot Bénédictine D.O.M. liqueur
¾ shot Heering cherry brandy liqueur
Top up with Soda water (club soda)

The name appears to have changed some time between 1922 and 1930.

Not even the Raffles Hotel itself is sure of the original recipe and visiting the present-day Long Bar in search of enlightenment is hopeless. Sadly, the Singapore Slings now served there are made from a powdered pre-mix, though which is also available in the gift shop below.

While contemporary sources are clear that it was cherry brandy that distinguishes the Singapore Sling from another kind of sling, great debate rages over the type of cherry brandy used. Was it a cherry 'brandy' liqueur or actually a cherry eau de vie? Did fruit juice feature in the original recipe at all? We shall probably never know but there is no debate over the fact that this famous cocktail was, and still is, based on gin.

1912
PINK LADY COCKTAIL

The classic gin-based Pink Lady cocktail is named after a successful 1912 stage play and is basically a Gin Sour sweetened with pomegranate syrup.

PINK LADY

Glass: Martini
Garnish: Lemon zest twist
Method: SHAKE all ingredients with ice and fine strain into chilled glass.
2 shots Tanqueray London dry gin
½ shot Freshly squeezed lemon juice
½ shot Pomegranate (grenadine) syrup
½ fresh Egg white (optional)

1914-1918
WORLD WAR I

By early 1915 The Great War was rightly causing much concern in England as the Anglo-French forces, bogged down in Flanders, had failed to beat the Germans by Christmas 1914. There was also a demoralising shortage of shells and the Prime Minister, Herbert Asquith, outrageously sought to deflect the scandal by blaming production shortcomings on workers drinking too much rather than a shortage of raw materials. With this in mind he instigated an amendment to the Defence of the Realm Act (known by the acronym DORA) mandating the obligatory maturation of whisky (and other aged spirits) for at least three years before sale. Up to that time expensive periods of aging had only been applied to deluxe blends and straight malts: the majority of whisky comprised of inexpensive grain whisky with minimal age.

Gin, being a rectified spirit requiring no maturation, was unaffected by the new law and immediately benefited (as did the quality of whisky in the long term). The Great War also caused British licensing laws to be restricted to ensure munitions workers were fit and ready for an early start. As a result, and despite recent reforms, many British publicans still call last orders at 11pm and 10.30pm on Sundays.

Although a human tragedy, The First World War did not dent the thirst for cocktails or gin.

1919
FRENCH 75 COCKTAIL

The French 75 cocktail was named after the 75mm

FRENCH 75

Glass: Flute
Garnish: Lemon zest twist (knot)
Method: SHAKE first three ingredients with ice and strain into chilled glass. TOP with champagne.

1½ shots London dry gin
½ shot Freshly squeezed lemon juice
¼ shot Sugar syrup (2 sugar to 1 water)
Top up with Perrier Jouet brut champagne

Howitzer field gun used by the French army during the First World War. Its origin is often credited to Harry's American Bar, Paris but like other drinks in the first (1919) edition of Harry's own book, 'The ABC of Mixing Drinks', he credits the drink to Macgarry of Buck's Club, London, England.

However, its creation is now commonly attributed to the USA and although the Howitzer was mounted on American tanks, I question whether an American, now or then, would name a drink after a metric measurement. Being a Brit, I favour The French 75 being an English drink that gained in popularity in France during the Prohibition era and found its way to the US with returning officers.

1919
NEGRONI COCKTAIL

The Negroni cocktail was created in 1919 by Fosco Scarselli at Caffè Cassoni, Florence, Italy. This drink takes its name from Count Camillo Negroni who was said to have asked for an Americano "with a bit more kick".

NEGRONI

Glass: Old-fashioned
Garnish: Orange zest twist
Method: POUR all ingredients into ice-filled glass and STIR.
1½ shots Tanqueray London dry gin
1½ shots Campari
1½ shots Martini Rosso sweet vermouth

1920-1933
USA PROHIBITION

Oh dear. The combination of a spirits-based drinking culture where men often worked away from home for months at a time did not please the campaigning Women's Christian Temperance Union. Saloons even offered free lunches, which could lure in the unsuspecting worker to spend his wages on booze rather than feeding the family, and functioned as a Mecca for violence and prostitution. In an attempt to cure the nation's growing drink problem, American senators signed the Volstead Act, prohibiting recreational consumption of any beverage stronger than 0.5% alcohol by volume.

` In 1919, America embarked on the 'Noble Experiment', and those distilleries which could not switch to production of 'medicinal' alcohols shut down. Most skilled bartenders left the country – Harry Craddock came to the Savoy's American bar this way – and many headed to Cuba, to which luxuriously outfitted ferries would transport American citizens for weekends of drinking and debauchery.

Many of those who chose to stay in the US turned for booze and entertainment to the wonderful world of the speakeasy, beautifully designed venues which combined, bar restaurant and club in one. Although firmly illegal – and often shut down – these places drew women as well as men, unlike the old saloons which had been, but for the odd hooker, all-male haunts.

These underground venues were often decorated far more luxuriously than their legal predecessors, and featured elaborate systems to conceal all signs of boozing within seconds of the alarm being raised.

Prohibition was not kind to cocktails. It made economic sense to smuggle in good quality gin, yet Al Capone and his ilk were not really interested in bootlegging volumes of vermouth or bitters. Long, fully stocked back-bars would take time to clear away if a venue was raided. So most places served drinks by the bottle.

Although the better speakeasies used smuggled spirits, there was plenty of toxic home-made hooch around. As well as illicit stills, industrial alcohol such as antifreeze was denatured to remove poisons from the ethyl alcohol. If the purification process was not handled by a skilled chemist the results could be deadly and this is where the phrase 'to die for' originates.

This is the period when 'Bathtub gin', made by mixing 'purified' industrial alcohol with juniper oil and glycerine originated. The term could be due to old bath tubs being used for the mixing process or some say because the vessels it was made in were usually so tall that the only tap they would fit under was that of the bath tub. Whichever, the end result at best had a raw taste, which benefited from masking with fruit juice or cream. The taste of alcohol, which had been central to mixed drinks, understandably receded from centre stage and drinks such as the Alexander began their ascent.

Perversely Prohibition proved to be good news for British distillers as thirsty Americans were prepared to pay dearly for English gin which they recognised as being a premium product, the 'Real McCoy'. English distillers sent regular shipments to islands in the West Indies and Canada, the favoured routes for the smugglers.

Incidentally, William (Billy) McCoy was a Canadian boat builder who smuggled whisky from Nassau and Bimini in the Bahamas to the east coast of the United States on his British registered schooner named Tomoka (after the name of the River that runs through his hometown of Holly Hill). McCoy was known for the authenticity of his smuggled liquor giving rise to the phrase, 'it's the real McCoy'.

When Prohibition was finally repealed on 5 December 1933, demand for London dry gin was many times what it had been at the beginning of Prohibition. Post Prohibition it boomed. In a world mired in first depression then world war, gin and cocktails became synonymous with glamour.

1923
WHITE LADY COCKTAIL
In 1919 Harry MacElhone created his First White Lady Cocktail whilst working at Ciro's Club, London, England. This consists of triple sec, white crème de menthe and lemon juice. He went on to create his second, rather better, and famous version with gin in 1923. By this time he is the owner of the equally famous Harry's New York Bar in Paris, France.

WHITE LADY
Glass: Martini
Garnish: Lemon zest twist
Method: SHAKE all ingredients with ice and fine strain into chilled glass.
1 ¾ shots London dry gin
1 shot Cointreau triple sec
1 shot Freshly squeezed lemon juice
1 fresh Egg white

1920s
MONKEY GLAND COCKTAIL

This gin-based cocktail was created sometime in the 1920s by Harry MacElhone at his Harry's New York Bar in Paris. The Monkey Gland takes its name from the work of Dr Serge Voronoff, who attempted to delay the ageing process by transplanting monkey testicles.

MONKEY GLAND COCKTAIL

Glass: Martini
Garnish: Orange zest twist
Method: SHAKE all ingredients with ice and fine strain into chilled glass.
2 shots Plymouth gin
¼ shot La Fée Parisian 68% absinthe
1½ shots Freshly squeezed orange juice
¼ shot Pomegranate (grenadine) syrup

1930
SAVOY COCKTAIL BOOK

Having moved to England during Prohibition, Harry Craddock set up behind the stick at the American Bar at London's Savoy Hotel, quickly becoming the UK's most famous bartender. In 1930 the hotel published the regarded 'Savoy Cocktail Book' with some 750 recipes compiled by Craddock and illustrations by Gilbert Rumbold. The book has been republished several times since: 1952, 1965, 1985, 1996 and 1999, latterly with additional text and cocktails by his 'heir' at the American Bar, former head bartender (for 38 years) Peter Dorelli.

1933
RED LION COCKTAIL

A red lion was already an established icon for Booth's gin and appeared prominently on the label. When the company opened its new distillery in 1959 it was naturally named the Red Lion Distillery. The Red Lion gin-based cocktail is said to have been created for the Chicago World Fair in 1933. However, it won the British Empire Cocktail Competition that year and was more likely created by W J Tarling for Booth's gin and named after the brand's Red Lion Distillery in London.

1933
GORDON'S DISTILLED IN USA

When Prohibition was repealed in 1933, Gordon's owners, Tanqueray Gordon, established a huge distillery and bottling plant in New Jersey. Another followed in Illinois in 1965 and a third hit California in 1971. The campaign to produce and sell large volumes of Gordon's to the lucrative US market continues to this day.

1939-1945
WORLD WAR II

After the Great Depression, Europe slipped with barely a pause into World War II: America joined in 1941 (but I note has since been more punctual where wars are concerned).

In Britain, spirits were not officially rationed but in reality were practically unobtainable unless via the black market. Those purchased through legitimate channels were subject to excise duties that had been doubled and even if you could procure gin, mixers were an even rarer commodity.

Hardly any of London's distilleries escaped damage during the heavy bombing of the blitz and there are stories of incendiary bombs falling into vats of gin but failing to explode. Plymouth was a major naval base and consequently regularly the target of German bombing raids. Although the distillery was hit it only suffered minor damage and production continued throughout the war.

The Tanqueray distillery was almost completely destroyed during the great Battle of Britain air raid of 1941 and only one of the stills, known as "Old Tom", survived. It is still used today at the Cameronbridge Distillery in Scotland.

After the war, gin availability recovered much quicker than that of Scotch whisky and consequently sales quickly soared to levels far above pre-war heights.

During the war, frivolities such as cocktails were hardly appropriate – even if the ingredients to make them were available. Britain's post-war austerity saw food rationing continue till 1953 and cocktails were not properly revived until well into the 1990s. Conditions were better in the USA where the gin cocktail was kept alive in the form of the Dry Martini.

1950s
DRY GIN DOMINATES

In the second half of the 19th century unsweetened or 'dry' gin grew in popularity, partly led by the growing fashion for dry champagne at the time. Old Tom gin had gradually become lighter in style as the quality of the base spirit had improved thanks to inventions in distilling technology and sugar had replaced more flavoursome botanicals such as liquorice previously used to sweeten the gin. The new dry gins were even lighter in style with little or no added sugar and much closer in style to what we know as 'London dry gins' today.

During the 20th century Old Tom gin which had typically contained between two and six per cent sugar practically died out with what little continued to be made in England mainly exported to Finland, Japan and parts of the USA. In response to this trend Tanqueray introduced the name 'Special Dry' to its brand in 1950.

1953
CORONATION OF QUEEN ELIZABETH II

The Coronation of Queen Elizabeth II on 2 June 1953 heralded a new start for a Britain that had finally put the war behind it with petrol rationing finally ending that same year. Britain was also celebrating Sir Edmund Hillary successfully reaching the summit of Mount Everest.

The new-found feeling of prosperity helped gin sales in Britain and the fact that the coronation was televised also drove record sales of televisions. In America sales of gin also soared as the coronation drove a craze for all things British.

1955-1990
DEMISE OF GIN & COCKTAILS

Gin boomed well into the mid-1950s but vodka was about to have its moment and as it became more fashionable so gin appeared old-hat and past it. Gin's running partner, the cocktail, was also doomed.

The wartime and post-war period saw the birth of convenience foods: highly processed ingredients such as powdered mash potato or jello mixes that were easy to store, quick to prepare and, apparently, the modern way forward. In 1937 an enterprising American invented the first cocktail premix, a powder that could deliver the sought-after balance of sweet and sour without the need to painstakingly juice fresh citrus and balance it with sugar. Soda guns arrived, and the syrup dispensers were stocked not only with cola, soda and lemonade but with tonic, ginger ale and even "fruit juices". Finally, ice-making machines arrived, that could produce small cubes of ice extremely quickly. These tiny, fast-melting ice cubes replaced the chunkier cubes and slabs of ice from earlier days, leaving drinks watery.

Faced with these trends, the vast majority of bar owners opted for mechanical solutions to the bartending skills deficit. Rather than train their staff to make a balanced, fresh drink, they chose to teach them to produce a chemically balanced, mediocre drink, using premixes. By the early 1980s bartending, cocktails and gin were at an all time low.

1962
CORENWYN BRAND REGISTERED

The Brand 'Corenwyn', a specific type of genever with more than 51 per cent malt wine, was registered by Bols in 1962. Like all genevers it is a blend of malt wine and botanical distillates, but Corenwyn is differentiated by the high percentage of malt wine, the botanicals used and the period of aging after the three ingredients are blended together.

1964
CALVERT GIN LAUNCHED

Calvert gins origins are connected to Calvert whiskey which was produced by the Calvert Distillers Company in Relay, Maryland, USA. The Calvert name was in memory of Lord Calvert, the first governor of Maryland. This was one of two large distilleries purchased by the Canadian Joseph E. Seagram & Sons Inc. immediately after the repeal of Prohibition in 1933.

Seagram's marketed various whiskies under the Calvert brand name and in 1964 launched Calvert Gin. The brand name was sold to Jim Beam Co in December 1991 along with five other brand names for $375 million.

1988
BOMBAY SAPPHIRE

Throughout the Eighties, gin's fortunes and sales plummeted as vodka's rose. This was particularly so in its home market, the UK, also the base for the massive conglomerate Independent Distillers & Vintners (IDV), owners of Gordon's, Tanqueray and Bombay Dry. This was a multinational with a new product department that had ability, balls and big budgets with a successful track record that included Bailey's. It also had Michel Roux on its side, president of Carillon, the US distributors of Bombay (and the folk who had launched Absolut vodka).

Then in 1988, at a time when gin sales were falling, IDV and Garillon launched a new gin – Bombay Sapphire. It was as though they looked at the blue rinse hairstyle of the core British gin consumer and used that as a design cue for their new gin bottle. At the same time they dropped Bombay Dry from their UK portfolio and upset little old ladies throughout the Home Counties who took some convincing that the replacement was not blue gin but merely packaged in a blue bottle.

Love or hate Bombay Sapphire, its launch was daring and inspired. It also marked the turning point for the fortunes of gin. Some three years into its launch, IDV's bright young marketing folk hit the UK drinks industry with another gin-primed bombshell. They reduced the strength of the brand leader Gordon's from 40% to its current 37.5% alcohol by volume. Many other gin brands quickly followed with reductions in their strength, while Beefeater, then ranked UK number two of the international gin brands, stood firm at 40%. We all thought Beefeater would clean up but those clever boys and girls at IDV held Gordon's retail price and invested the excise duty saved in UK marketing with claims that this would help both Gordon's and the whole gin category in general. They were right – Gordon's grew, as did the gin category as a whole.

1980s
THE BRAMBLE COCKTAIL

The gin-based Bramble cocktail was created by Dick Bradsell. To quote the cocktail guru himself (this from *CLASS* in April 2001): "I created this drink whilst working at Fred's Club back in the mid-80s or thereabouts. I wanted to invent a truly British drink for reasons that escape me now. I failed because I could not source an acceptable UK crème de mûre and lemons are not exactly native to our climes." A bramble, by the way, is the bush that blackberries grow on.

Dick continues: "The success of this drink in my opinion is due to its simplicity. It is basically a gin sour with blackberry stuff in. It also conforms to a very common method of blending and balancing flavours that occurs very often in the world of cocktails. Take a spirit: Gin. Sour it with lemon, sweeten it with sugar syrup and flavour it with crème de mûre. Pouring this over crushed ice is another key component because this method adds length to a cocktail that might otherwise veer towards the cloying and sticky."

1990s - A NEW COCKTAIL BOOM BEGINS

Cocktails benefitted from a buoyant economy but in 1989 a major change in Britain's pubs and bars also helped provide the conditions for a cocktail boom. Margaret Thatcher's government introduced a piece of legislation known as the 'Beer Orders' which effectively broke the brewer's stranglehold over Britain's pubs, encouraging entrepreneurs to move in. With them came new ideas, 'gastro pubs' and crucially something occupying the ground between a pub and club, communally dubbed 'style bars'.

One such entrepreneur was Oliver Peyton and in 1994 he restored what was a splendid art deco ballroom near London's Piccadilly Circus and opened the Atlantic Bar & Grill. This very stylish place immediately became London's foremost lounge bar and it was here, in the bar named after him, that cocktail guru Dick Bradsell shook up London's socialites expectations of just what a cocktail was. Thanks to Dick and the many others he inspired, London found itself leading cocktail culture, so

BRAMBLE

Glass: Old-fashioned
Garnish: Blackberries & lemon slice
Method: SHAKE first three ingredients with ice
and strain into glass filled with crushed ice.
Drizzle liqueur over drink to create a 'bleeding'
effect in the glass. Serve with short straws.
2 shots London dry gin
1 shot Freshly squeezed lemon juice
½ shot Sugar syrup (2 sugar to 1 water)
½ shot Blackberry (crème de mûre) liqueur
Origin: Created in the mid-80s by Dick Bradsell
at Fred's Club, Soho, London, England.

MIXOLOGIST
The Journal of the American Cocktail

attracting talented bartenders from around the world like Manchester United attracts footballers.

In August 1997 I played my own small part in building Britain's cocktail culture when I launched **CLASS** magazine with specialist writers, including Dick. Later that same year Jonathan Downey opened the first of his Match Bars, which would go on to greatly influence the standard of bartending in London and beyond.

While Dick was introducing new styles of cocktail such as the fresh fruit 'Martini' in London, Dale DeGroff was working his magic in New York's Rainbow Rooms – both helping drive the popularity of the Cosmopolitan and re-introducing Manhattanites to forgotten vintage cocktails. The back-to-basics, classic cocktail movement developed on both sides of the Atlantic as old cocktails books were dusted off and recipes from the 1930s redis-covered. This movement grew in momentum in the early Noughties leading to events such as The Museum of the American Cocktail displaying its first exhibition in November 2004 at the Riviera Hotel in Las Vegas.

Of course gin features in lots of cocktails – especially vintage ones. Vodka simply did not feature on the shelves of cocktail bartenders before the 1950s – gin was the spirit of choice hence the more modern day bartenders look back, the more they look to gin and now also genever.

1997
IDV & UNITED DISTILLERS MERGER

The merger of two of the world's biggest drink's companies, I.D.V. (Grand Metropolitan) and United Distillers (Guinness), formed what is now called Diageo and sent a shudder through the drinks industry. The combined corporation emerged to be by far the biggest and most powerful spirits company and it fell to the competition authorities in both the UK and USA to cut it down to size. Diageo was forced to shed brands which resulted in the sale of Bombay (Original & Sapphire) to Bacardi along with Dewers Whisky for a combined sum of $1.2 billion – a sum which now looks like a bargain.

This led to successive mergers and acquisitions as its competitors sought to square up to the mighty Diageo, resulting in considerable rationalisation of gin brands and the demise of many members of the gin aristocracy including: Nicholson's, Booths (still made in the USA but a mere show of its former self) and Gilbey's (also available in other markets but not the force it was in the UK).

2000
NEW MILLENNIUM, NEW GINS

Our computers survived the millennium bug and, despite predications to the contrary, there was enough champagne for all to toast the new century. While twelve years earlier the launch of Bombay Sapphire marked gin's turning point, 2000 seemed to kick-start the production of a plethora of new gin brands including Tanqueray No. TEN, Martin Miller's Reformed, Hendrick's and 209 Gin. It was also something of a stimulant for established but previously neglected brands such as Plymouth.

It is uncanny how the rise and fall in the fortunes of gin seem to coincide with that of the cocktail. Both are firmly back and here to stay.

2008
REVIVAL OF OLD TOM

The 'Noughties' saw bartenders increasingly scouring old cocktail books for long-lost recipes and as they did so they discovered many drinks calling for the long defunct 'Old Tom' style of gin. Unsurprisingly this led several distillers to launch their interpretations of what an Old Tom gin was, most notably Hayman's Old Tom Gin with added sugar, and Jensen's London distilled Old Tom gin sweetened using botanicals rather than sugar.

2008
EU GIN DEFINITIONS

On 20th February 2008 a new EU definition recognising and legislating what can be termed a 'gin' passed into EU law as part of the revised EU Spirit Drink Regulations. According to this legislation all gins must be:
1) Made with suitable ethyl alcohol flavoured with juniper berries (juniperus communis) and other flavourings.
2) The ethyl alcohol used must be distilled to the minimum standards stated in the EU Spirit Drink Regulations.
3) The predominant flavour must be juniper.
4) Water may be added to reduce the strength but the gin must have a minimum retail strength of 37.5% abv.
5) Further ethyl alcohol of the same composition used in the distillation may be added after any distillation.

The rules further legislate upon three distinctive definitions of gin: 'Gin', 'Distilled Gin' and 'London Gin'.

GIN
1) The ethyl alcohol does not have to be re-distilled.
2) Flavourings can be either approved natural or artificial flavourings and these can be simply cold compounded (mixed together with the ethyl alcohol).
3) There is no restriction on the addition of other approved colouring or flavouring additives such as sweeteners.

DISTILLED GIN
1) Must be made in a traditional still by redistilling neutral alcohol in the presence of natural flavourings but there is no minimum strength stipulated for the resulting distillate.
2) Additional flavourings, sweeteners and other approved additives may be added after distillation and these can be natural or artificial.
3) Approved colourings may be used to colour distilled gin.

LONDON GIN
1) Must be made in a traditional still by re-distilling ethyl alcohol in the presence of all natural flavourings used.
2) The ethyl alcohol used to distil London Gin must be of a higher quality than the standard laid down for ethyl alcohol. The methanol level in the ethyl alcohol must not exceed a maximum of 5 grams per hectolitre of 100% vol. alcohol.
3) The flavourings used must all be approved natural flavourings and they must impart their flavour during the distillation process.
4) The use of artificial flavourings is not permitted.

5) The resultant distillate must have a minimum strength of 70% abv.

6) No flavourings can be added after distillation.

7) A small amount of sweetening may be added after distillation provided the sugars do not exceed 0.5 grams/litre of finished product (this is a lax part in the new rules which CLASS objects to), apart from water, no other substance may be added.

8) London Gin cannot be coloured.

2008
BOLS GENEVER LAUNCHED

In 2008 Bols launched, or it could be argued relaunched, their Bols Genever in the USA. In doing so they practically single-handedly re-established the export market for genever and even reversed the decline of the category in their own domestic Dutch market. Hurrah.

2008-2012
UK CRAFT GIN DISTILLERS

Two arcane English laws stood in the way of a British craft distilling renaissance following that already underway in the United States. One a law, which dated back to the 1800s, stated that brewers could not also be distillers on the same site. A second stated that the minimum size for a pot still should not be less than 18 hectolitres.

There is probably some truth in the suspicion that law on still size was designed to suit existing large distillers – a law requiring new stills in the UK to be a massive 18 hectolitres effectively prevented small boutique distillers providing unwanted competition.

Two pioneering distillers challenged the 18-hectolitre law: William Chase set up the Chase distillery on his Herefordshire farm in 2008; and Sam Galsworthy and Fairfax Hall, who established the Sipsmith distillery in a residential street in London's Hammersmith in 2009. Sipsmith's copper-pot still, 'Prudence', has a diminutive 300-litre charge capacity.

The other ancient law preventing brewers from distilling had not been challenged because previously no modern-day distiller had apparently dreamt of also selling beer, and conversely, it would appear that no other brewer had passionately wanted to also be a distiller. That was until Jonathan Adnams, Chairman of the Suffolk coast brewers Adnams, decided he wanted to be a distiller as well as a brewer.

In January 2010 Adnams applied to HM Customs & Excise for a distilling licence and to its delight was granted a distiller's licence on 3rd April 2010. By September they had installed German stills with the first vodka coming off of the still at 4pm in the afternoon on the 14th October 2010.

ORE & CO.LD.

ENGINEERS

&

RSMITHS

48

ONDON E3

"I never drink anything stronger than gin before breakfast."

W.C. Fields

Gin Explained

GIN DEFINED

Gin is potable spirit flavoured with juniper and other botanicals either by compounding or distillation. More simply put, all gins start life as neutral spirit (i.e. a high-strength vodka) and are then flavoured with juniper and various seeds, berries, roots, fruits and herbs.

STYLES OF GIN

Although the 'London Dry Gin' style dominates the global marketplace, there are several other styles of juniper spirit.

Genever – The original Dutch juniper spirit which led to the creation of the drink we know today as gin. Genever is also known as geneva, jenever and hollands. Since it retains more of the flavour of the rye, barley and maize on which it is based than gin does, it should arguably be treated as a category in its own right rather than a type of gin. (For more on genever see page 92).

Old Tom Gin – This sweet or 'cordial' style of gin was overwhelmingly popular in the 18th and 19th centuries. At the time, gin was more pungent due to the limited rectification (purification) of the base spirit possible in copper pot stills. The rough-tasting fermentation congeners no doubt present in the gin were masked by flavouring (most commonly with lemon or aniseed) and or sweetening by the addition of sweet botanicals such as liquorice and later, in the 19th century, with sugar. This sweetened style of gin became known as 'Old Tom'.

Old Tom probably started as a general term but it became associated with a particular style of gin. One story has it that a cat fell into a vat of gin at an unnamed distillery, giving the gin a distinctive flavour. However, the creation of this style of gin more likely lies with Thomas Chamberlain, an early gin compounder. (See '1830s – True Origins of 'Old Tom'' in 'Gin History')

In the second half of the 19th century, unsweetened or 'dry' gin grew in popularity, partly led by the then growing fashion for dry champagne. By this time, the quality of the base spirit had improved thanks to the invention of the Coffey still and these dry gins were closer in style to what we know as 'London Dry Gins' today.

During the 20th century, this sweet style of gin, which typically contained between two and six per cent sugar, practically died out, with what little continued to be made in England mainly exported to Finland, Japan and parts of the USA. In 2007, several producers started to once again market Old Tom in Britain and export to markets such as the US.

London Dry Gin – This dry, pure style of gin was originally only made in London and appeared soon after the Coffey continuous still was invented in 1831, enabling production of a nearly pure spirit. The high distillation strength removed the unpleasant flavours found in earlier gins so the new spirits could be sold unsweetened or 'dry'. Despite the name, London Dry can be produced anywhere in the world (See '2008 – EU Gin Definitions' in Gin History)

By Appointment
Gin Distillers
to H.M. King George VI

Gordon's
Special Dry
London Gin.

...w. Gordon & Co. Limited.

...stillery, London, E.C.1.

Plymouth gin – Unlike London gin, Plymouth gin can only be produced in Plymouth using water from Dartmoor. This is determined by an EU Appellation.

Xoriguer gin – This Spanish gin also has its own EU Appellation and can only be made on the island of Menorca.

New Western Dry Gins – This is a loose term championed by the American bartending consultant Ryan Magarian for gins which, some say, border on being legally gins at all due to their relatively low levels of juniper.

To quote Ryan: "This designation seems to have evolved over the past nine years, as a result of efforts from both large brand houses and regional distillers in Europe and in the United States. In taking a good hard look at today's rather loose definition of dry gin, these distillers realized a greater opportunity for artistic "flavor" freedom in this great spirit and are creating gins with a shift away from the usually over-abundant focus on juniper, to the supporting botanicals, allowing them to almost share center stage. And while the juniper must remain dominant in all dry gins these gins are most certainly defined, not by the juniper itself, but by the careful inclusion and balance of the supporting flavors, creating, what many experts believe to be, an entirely new designation of dry gin that deserves individual recognition."

LEGAL GIN DEFINITIONS

Gin is defined in the European Union Spirit Drinks Regulations (Council Regulation EC No. introduced 1989 and updated 2007), the United States Bureau of Alcohol, Tobacco and Firearms (introduced 1991) and by similar regulations in other countries including Canada (introduced 1993) and Australia (introduced 1987). In the EU, genever falls under more general regulations governing flavoured spirits.

The European Union regulations governing gin are the most wide-ranging (see '2008 – EU Gin Definitions' in Gin History).

'Distilled gin' is a legal definition and gins with this term on their label have to be made by redistilling the neutral spirit in the presence of botanicals so that the spirit acquires the flavour of the botanicals.

Gin is usually sold at between 35 and 43% alcohol by volume, with the lower end of this spectrum mainly affected by the prevailing laws in particular markets. Many gin brands also have a higher strength variant aimed at the duty free market, and these typically range from the high 40s to 50% alcohol by volume.

COLD-COMPOUNDED GIN

Cold compounded gins are flavoured with extract of jumpier as an oil and other flavour essences, without distillation. The flavourings are 'compounded' – simply mixed with the neutral spirit. EU and other regulations recognise that cold-compounded gins are inferior to distilled gins.

In a reference to the illicit gins made during Prohibition, cold-compounded gins are often termed 'bathtub gins'. To avoid such gins, only buy gins which state they are distilled on the label.

GIN PRODUCTION

To produce a decent (i.e. distilled) gin requires a two-stage process – first, a base 'neutral spirit' is made and this is then flavoured by re-distillation with seeds, berries, roots, fruits, herbs and spices – collectively known as 'botanicals'.

To make the base spirit, early gin distillers would distil the fermented wash (type of beer) in a traditional pot still. The first distillation using such a still produces a weak, rough spirit known as 'low wines'. Repeated distillation of these low wines (rectification) strengthens and purifies the spirit.

To produce a distilled gin, this base spirit must be redistilled with the chosen botanicals to extract their essential oils and so flavour the base spirit. Lastly, the now gin-flavoured spirit is reduced to bottling strength by the addition of water (hydration).

Different distillers use different distillation methods for redistilling and extracting the flavour of their botanicals, and the botanicals used and their proportions also vary greatly from distiller to distiller.

There are two main distillation methods used for extracting the botanicals flavour:

Steep & Boil Method – This is the most traditional and the most common method for gin distillation. A mix of juniper and other botanicals are steeped in neutral spirit which has been reduced in strength with water (normally to approx. 50% alc./vol.). Some producers leave the botanicals steeping for as long as 48 hours before distillation; others believe that maceration 'stews' the flavours and so distil the mixture immediately. Whichever, as soon as maceration is deemed to be completed, the mixture is distilled in a pot still, producing a spirit full of the aromas and flavours of the botanicals. Water is added to reduce the gin distillate to bottling strength.

Vapour Infusion Method – With this method, the mix of juniper and botanicals do not come into contact with liquid spirit at all. Instead, they are placed in baskets inside modified stills and only encounter the spirit as vapour. The botanical-infused vapour then condenses into a botanical-infused spirit and water is added to reduce to bottling strength.

The two methods above may be combined, with some distillers using a combination of steep & boil and vapour infusion. In this case, some botanicals will be steeped in the boil pot, with the same still also having a chamber to hold the botanicals, through which the botanical infused vapour from the boil pot will pass.

There are also other variables a distiller may employ as follows:

Vacuum Distillation: This is basically the 'steep & boil' method but, as the name suggests, the spirit is redistilled with botanicals under vacuum, so reducing the temperature at which the ethanol alcohol boils. The stronger the vacuum, the lower the boiling temperature.

Proponents of this type of distillation claim a fresher-flavoured gin is produced, as the need to 'cook' the botanicals is negated by the reduced boiling point. The downside to vacuum distillation is the difficulty in scaling up to an industrial rather than lab/small-scale operation.

Individual Botanical Distillation: This variation to the 'steep & boil' method is being increasingly used by new gin makers. Each botanical is steeped and boiled separately and then the numerous resulting single botanical distillates are blended together to create the finished gin. Proponents claim this method allows more control while traditionalists say the interaction between the botanical's essential oils while steeping and boiling inside the still is lost, resulting in a disjointed gin.

One-Shot Verses Multi-Shot: The one-shot method simply means a recipe is followed where a given volume of neutral alcohol is distilled with quantities of each botanical as specified by that gin's recipe.

In contrast, multi-shot gins are made by multiplying the proportion of botanicals to base alcohol during redistillation and then reducing the resulting super-concentrated botanical distillate back to the concentration specified in the original recipe by blending in more neutral alcohol. Thus a two-shot gin will be distilled with twice the amount of botanicals and after distillation thinned back to the proportions stated in the recipe by adding the same volume of alcohol again. Hence, using a two-shot process, each distillation yields twice the volume of gin.

The multi-shot approach has the benefit of saving on still usage, so increasing production capacity and efficiency. Proponents say that multi-shot has the benefit of reducing the influence of inaccurately measured botanicals, as the ratio of inaccuracy is reduced when compared to the same 'miss measurement' in a one-shot gin. Most international brands of gin are multi-shot with one-shot tending to be the preserve of 'craft' or 'boutique' distillers.

RECTIFICATION OF BASE ALCOHOL

Distilling wash (beer) in a pot still produces a liquid with an alcohol content of around 21% alc./vol.. Subsequent pot still distillations can be used to increase the strength of the distillate to 70% alc./vol. and this is exactly how Scotch malt whisky is made to this day. Originally, this is also how the base alcohol used to make gin was distilled. However, 70% alc/vol. means there are 30% 'impurities' present and, while that is acceptable – even desirable – in a spirit that will later be mellowed by aging in oak casks, such a base alcohol would produce a pretty rough gin.

Modern fractional distillation in a column still can produce alcohol up to 96.3% alc./vol. And, in an age where gins are praised for their 'cleanness', so column stills of one type or another are usually employed in the production of the neutral alcohol on which gins are based.

SPIRIT !

In early gin production, prior to the invention of the column still, it was common to mask the hash quality of the base alcohol with strongly flavoured botanicals and the addition of sugar. Today, this style of gin is known as Old Tom.

Grain (particularly wheat and occasionally barley) is most commonly used to make the base neutral spirit for gin production. Thanks to distillers stating 'made with quality grain alcohol' or similar on their labelling, the use of grain neutral spirit is regarded as a premium over molasses neutral spirit, even though some distillers privately say they think it makes better gin. However, gin can be made with alcohol made from any agricultural base and gins made from alcohols including potatoes and grapes are also fashionable.

TRADITIONAL POT STILL DISTILLATION

The rectified neutral spirit at around 96% alc./vol. (often supplied by a third-party supplier), is diluted back to around 50% alc./vol. using purified or spring water. If the 'steep & boil' method is to be employed, the botanicals are added and, as discussed above, often left to steep in the spirit for a period before distillation is commenced.

If the 'vapour infusion' method is to be used then the botanicals will be loaded into a basket or bag and placed inside a chamber in the still's lyne arm, so forcing the vapour through the botanicals on its journey towards the condenser.

The essential oils and other aromatic compounds found in the botanicals used to flavour gin are absorbed by the neutral spirit in which the botanicals are steeped, or by the vapour as it passes through them in the case of vapour-infused gin, and are carried through the distillation process as a part of the vapour.

The stillman exercises considerable control over the distillation – the art is knowing when to 'make the cut'. Different flavouring agents evaporate at different temperatures, and he has to find the right balance. He (and it almost always is a he) will use only the 'middle cut' of the spirit flow for the new spirit. He will assess the standard of the run by taking samples and by measuring the temperature and strength of the distillate as it runs from the condenser.

The first runnings, known as heads (or foreshots), and the last, known as tails (or feints), are either discarded or set aside to be added to the wash of the next distillation. The heart of the run will be collected to become gin.

Because the spirit being distilled is very pure neutral alcohol there will be very little in the way of heads, as methanol and other harmful volatile alcohols, will have already been removed when the spirit was rectified. Hence, in gin distillation there are not really 'heads' as such but a quantity of the initial run will be discarded to ensure any deposits from the last distillation which might remain in the still have been flushed out.

Once the initial 'heads' have been discarded, the distiller will start collecting the 'heart', the spirit which will end up being bottled as gin. The oils from some botanicals will vaporise before that of others so the flavour of the distillate will change with citrus tending to come off first. The distiller will know from experience roughly when bad flavours will start to emerge as unwanted oils and other 'heavier' substances start to emerge. At this stage, he will start regularly sampling to decide when to switch from hearts and start discarding what are called tails due to their emerging at the tail end of the run.

Redistilling an already very pure distillate in a copper pot still helps produce a softer, some say 'smoother' distillate. The copper the stills are made from plays a part in this process. Chemically, copper acts as a catalyst to promote the formation of esters which impart desirable fruity notes to the spirit. Copper also removes unwanted sulphur compounds which smell of struck matches, drains, rotten eggs, farts and cabbage – none of which make for an appealing gin. Copper helps turn these nasty smelling sulphur compounds into easily removed Copper Sulphate (U.S. Copper Sulfate) or copper salt ($CuSO4 \cdot 5H2O$). However, while copper may have these beneficial properties, the fact that such purified neutral alcohol is being used means that sulphur is not typically an issue, allowing many gin distillers to use cheaper stainless steel pot stills.

GIN RECIPES

Every gin has a different recipe, but all gins are flavoured with botanicals – seeds, berries, roots, fruits, peel, spices or herbs – and all must contain juniper. After juniper, coriander and angelica are the most popular botanicals and these three are the main flavours in a London Dry Gin.

More than a hundred different botanicals are commonly used to flavour gin, and individual brands can contain anything from seven to twenty botanicals. It is the balance of these different ingredients and the varying distillation methods that give different brands their distinctive styles.

To keep a gin brand consistent in the light of what are complex recipes and naturally variable ingredients is a real challenge. The master distiller must buy batches of botanicals which best suit a particular gin's style and store these for production over the next year or so. To do this, he or she must sample a number of specimens from every crop as botanicals, even from a single crop, can vary dramatically.

GIN BOTANICALS EXPLAINED

All gins are basically neutral spirit flavoured, either by compounding or distillation, with juniper and various other seeds, berries, roots, fruits and herbs. These are known as botanicals. In distilled gins the aromatic compounds (usually oils) found in the botanicals are absorbed by the neutral grain spirit in which the botanicals are steeped, or by the vapour as it passes through, so flavouring the distillate. There are hundreds of botanicals used to flavour gin but the following are the most commonly used:

Juniper berries (Juniperus communis)

The main flavouring in all gins, juniper is a member of the cypress family and the berries used in gin production usually come from Italy, Serbia, Macedonia and India. The best juniper berries are generally considered to be from mountain slopes in Tuscany and Macedonia. The European berries tend to be darker than the cheaper and much larger Asian ones.

These bluish berries are hand-picked from October to February, but the main flavour comes from the essential oils (Alpine Pinere & camphor) within the three seeds inside each berry. Distillers buy juniper by weight. It is not uncommon for distillers to store juniper berries for two years before using them and during this time the berries lose some of their moisture but the oil content remains constant.

Juniper berries are fragrant and spicy with a bittersweet taste and overtones of pine, lavender, camphor and overripe banana topped by a peppery finish: Hugh Williams (former master distiller of Gordon's) once described juniper to me as having an "oily flavour with a sweet back taste". In short, juniper is pine-like but fruitier.

Coriander seeds
The second most-important flavouring in most gins, Coriander seeds usually come from Morocco, Romania, Moldavia, Bulgaria and Russia. They vary tremendously by region: for example Bulgarian seeds are much more pungent than those from Morocco.

The essential oil in coriander is linalool and this is mellow, spicy, fragrant and aromatic with a candied ginger, lemon and sage taste. Joanne Simcock, the master distiller at J&G Greenall, says the smell of coriander always reminds her of naan bread. It provides a complex citrus top note to gin, although some distillers accuse their counter-parts of using citrus peel as a cheap alternative to coriander.

Angelica root
Angelica is a key ingredient as it holds the volatile flavours of other botanicals and marries them together giving length and substance to gin. Angelica has a musky, nutty,

damp woody/rooty (forest floor), sweet flavour with a piney, dry edge and I find it generally reminiscent of mushrooms. Most distillers think the smoothest and mellowest angelica comes from Saxony in Germany and prefer this to the more pungent angelica from Flanders in Belgium.

Angelica seed
Not nearly as widely used as angelica root, angelica seeds impart hop-like/celery-like fragrant, slightly floral notes to a gin.

Lemon peel
Lemon peel is used to flavour gin instead of the flesh because the skin contains a high proportion of the fruit's flavoursome oils. Most distillers source their lemons from Andalucia in Southern Spain where fruit is still hand-peeled and hung out to dry in the sun. Lemon peel adds fresh, citrusy, juicy, lemony flavours.

Orange peel
Orange peel tends to come from Spain, often Seville, where it is harvested in March. As with lemons, the peel rather than the flesh of oranges is used, and this is usually cut off in one continuous strip by hand.

Different distillers choose different types of orange, some preferring bitter and others sweet. Orange peel adds fresh, citrus, juicy orange flavours to a gin.

Orris Root
The bulb of the iris plant, orris root has a very perfumed character and, like angelica root, can help fix aromas and

flavours within a gin. Three-to-four-year-old plants are harvested then stored for two-to-three years before use to allow the flavour to develop: the finished botanical is very hard and requires grinding into a powder before use. Mainly sourced from Florence in Italy, orris root is very bitter and tastes of Parma Violets, earth and cold, stewed tea, and to my mind has an earthy smell reminiscent of clean stables or a hamster cage. Distillers praise orris for its ability to hold and fix other botanical flavours and adding perfumed floral notes to gin.

Cassia
A member of the cinnamon family, cassia is sometimes referred to as Chinese cinnamon. It is the bark of a tree which grows in Vietnam, China and Madagascar, removed from the trunk and rolled into quills. Cassia adds a taste similar to chewing gum (Dentine) and cinnamon to a gin – somewhat reminiscent to mulled wine.

Cinnamon
From Sri Lanka, cinnamon is commonly used to give a spicy edge to gin. Like cassia, it is tree bark rolled into quills.

Almond
The almond tree is closely related to the peach tree and native to south-west Asia. Two types of almond – sweet and bitter, are used in gin – both are hard and must be ground before use. Almonds have a high essential oil content and give gin an almond/marzipan, nutty, soapy and spicy flavour. Almond also adds to the overall mouth feel of gin. Almond contains trace amounts of arsenic, which along with nut protein does not come over during distillation so gin is not hazardous for people with nut allergies.

Cardamom
These pods come from an aromatic plant which grows in the Malabar region of south-western India and contains numerous tiny black seeds. Of the two varieties, green and black, the green are most widely used as they are considered more delicate. Cardamom adds a spicy, citrusy, almost eucalyptus flavour to gin.

Cubeb Berries
A member of the pepper family, these small, red-brown berries are grown in Java, Indonesia. They add a spicy, peppery, lemony, pine/eucalyptus flavour to the gin. I liken their flavour to a spicy alpine mint.

Grains of Paradise
These dark brown berries are also related to the pepper family and add a hot, spicy, peppery flavour plus hints of lavender, elderflower and menthol.

Ginger
The aromatic rhizome (underground stem) of a plant from south-east Asia. Ginger's distinctive scent and hot flavour means it must be used sparingly in gin.

Liquorice
Liquorice comes from Indo-China and the hard fibrous root of the liquorice plant is ground into a powder for

gin distilling. It gives gin an obvious liquorice flavour but also a light, fresh, bittersweet, woody-earthy taste. It adds base and length as well as sweetening, softening and 'rounding-off' a gin. Liquorice is unusual in that its flavour is carried by glyciric acid rather than essential oils of which it is low in content.

Nutmeg
The nutmeg tree is native to Indonesia but widely cultivated in tropical Asia and America. Its light-brown, oval, rounded seeds are ground to add a warming, aromatic, sweet spice to gin.

AGING GIN
Hardly any of today's gins are aged, although there are signs of a revival of this historic practice. Unlike 'rough' spirits such as whiskey and brandy, gin does not require long periods of aging and if left for much more than six months will quickly become over-woody and dry. To age gin, well-seasoned casks are essential and a mere two to three months maturation is usually plenty long enough.

GENEVER & JUNIPER SCHNAPPS
Also known as jenever, jeneva, geneva and hollands, genever is a juniper-flavoured spirit from Holland and Belgium. Helpfully, the van Dale dictionary, Holland's equivalent to the Oxford English Dictionary, lists the first published use of the word 'genever' in 1672. At that time it was spelt with a 'g' so we have chosen to use that spelling as the generic in this book. The various different spellings stem from the French word for juniper being 'genièvre' while the Dutch word is 'jineverbes'. (It is worth affirming that there is absolutely no connection with the Swiss city of Geneva.)

The juniper flavouring means that genever is technically a gin, and it was the forerunner of the London gin styles which dominate today's market. However, genever is a very distinctive style of juniper spirit. Unlike most gins, it is a blend of two very different spirits – botanical-infused neutral spirit and malt-wine, a kind of un-aged whiskey. Due to this, it retains more of the flavour of some of its base ingredients – rye, malted barley and maize – than most common gin styles, which are based on neutral spirit alone.

Some might describe genever as a cross between a whiskey, a vodka and a gin. In its homeland, it is often sold with fruit flavouring, such as orange or lemon.

GENEVER PRODUCTION
Dutch genever production traditionally centres on the town of Schiedam, near Rotterdam. In Belgium, it is produced mainly around the towns of Hasselt and Ghent.

As stated above, genever is a blend of two different spirits. The first spirit, moutwijn (malt-wine), is what gives genever its distinctive flavour. This is a kind of unaged whiskey made by triple and sometimes quadruple pot-distilling a mixture of cereals, typically rye, corn and wheat with malted barley less commonly used. After the final distillation, the malt-wine leaves the pot still at around 47% alc./vol., a relatively low distillation strength which yields a spirit that retains more of the malty flavours of its base ingredients. The first distil-

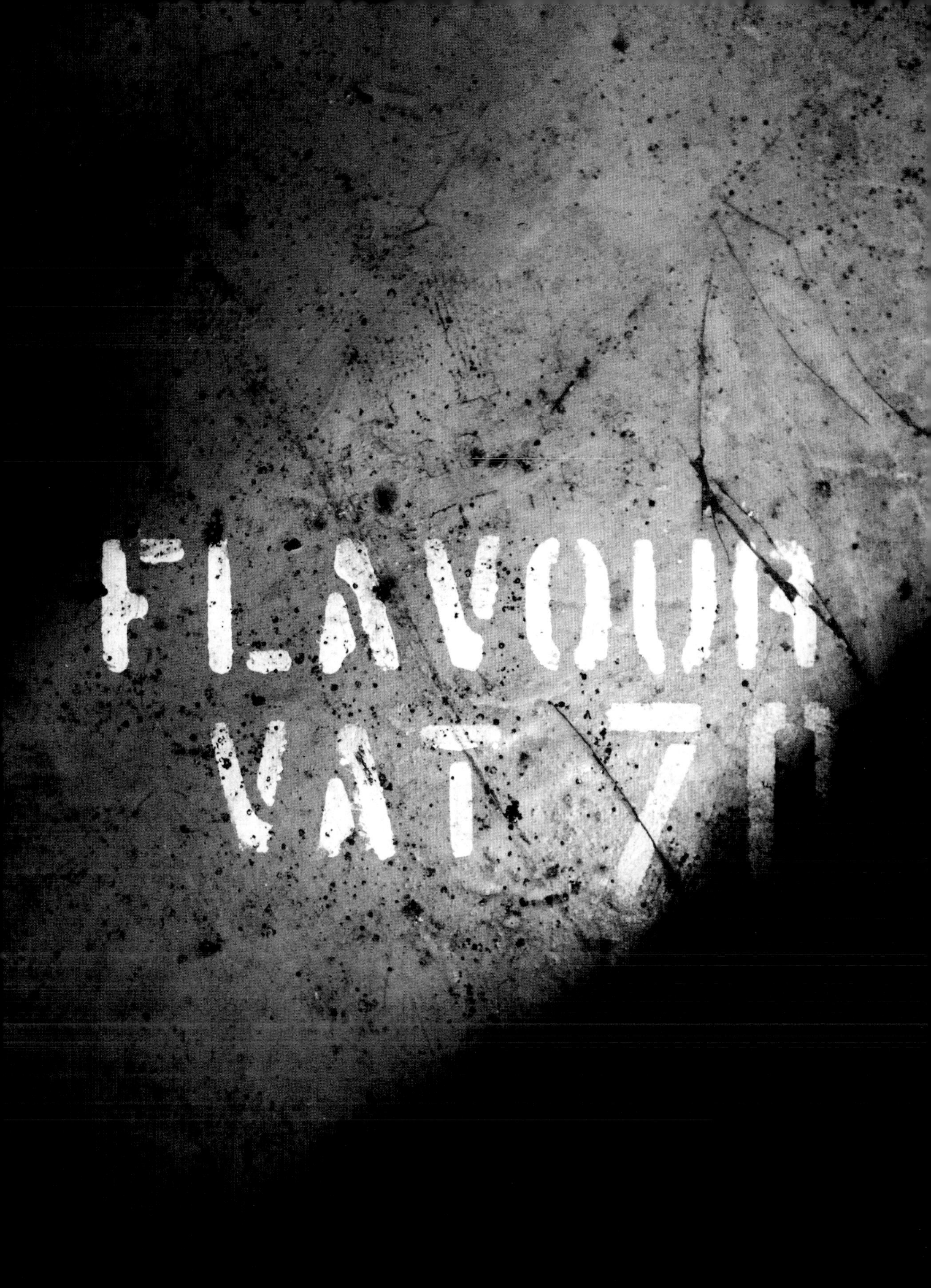
FLAVOUR
VAT 7

lation is called 'ruwnat', the second 'enkelnat', the third 'bestnat' (actually malt wine) and the optional fourth distillation 'korenwijn'.

The second is produced in a very similar way to most London Dry gins. Neutral spirit (very high strength vodka) is redistilled with a recipe of botanical flavourings, most typically including juniper, coriander, caraway, orris, angelica. The result, while the flavour profile can be very different from most London Dry gins, is essentially a gin. Genever must contain juniper, but it does not have to be the predominant flavour, or indeed even be noticeable in the finished genever.

Finally, the two spirits are blended together. The percentage of malt wine used varies according to the style of genever being made. Originally, and until the end of the 1800s, genever was malt wine. The addition of the flavoured spirit to 'stretch' the malt-wine only came about after the invention of the continuous still led to the production of good quality, clean neutral spirits.

If the genever is to benefit from aging in oak then the malt wine and flavoured natural spirits may be aged separately and blended prior to bottling.

GENEVER STYLES

There are four basic styles of genever: 'oude' (literally, 'old'), 'jonge' ('young'), 'korenwijn' ('corn wine') and fruit genevers. They differ in their use of botanicals and the percentage of malt-wine contained: each must contain at least a certain percentage of malt-wine, and this is specified by law.

Jonge Genever

Jonge Genever is so named because it is a modern, young style. It was first developed in the 1950s in response to consumer demand for a lighter flavoured, more mixable genever. Jonge genevers contain a lower percentage of malt-wine than either oude or korenwijn styles, typically only about 5 per cent, and generally have fewer botanicals as well. In some brands, the juniper is barely detectable.

Jonge genever must:
Contain no more than 15 per cent malt wine.
Be at least 35% alcohol by volume.
Contain a maximum of 10 grams of sugar per litre.
If the label states 'graanjenever' or 'grain genever' then the neutral spirits used must be 100 per cent grain-based.

Oude Genevers

Despite the name, Oude Genevers do not have to be aged. They are so-called because they are a more traditional, older-style genever, as opposed to jonge genevers, which are modern. They are usually produced using more botanicals than jonge styles. Proportions and recipes vary from one brand to another, and different brands have very different characters, but aromatic botanicals like aloe and myrrh are often used to flavour oude jenevers.

Oude genevers must:
Contain at least 15 per cent malt-wine.
Be at least 35% alcohol by volume.
Contain a maximum of 20 grams of sugar per litre.

If the label states 'graanjenever' or 'grain genever' then the neutral spirits used must be 100 per cent grain based. Oude genevers do not have to be aged but if a label mentions aging, then the genever must have been aged for at least one year in a barrel of 700 litres or less.

Korenwijn' (corn wine)
The third category of jenever is 'korenwijn' (which Bols spells 'corenwyn').

Korenwijn genevers must:
Contain at least 51 per cent malt-wine.
Be at least 38% alcohol by volume.
Contain a maximum of 20 grams of sugar per litre.
Korenwijn does not have to be aged but like Oude genever if it is it must be aged for at least one year in a barrel of 700 litres or less.

Other terms
The initials ZO stand for the Dutch 'Zeer Oude', or 'very old'. They have no precise implication but suggest that the genever is straw-coloured and slightly sweeter than jonge. Likewise 'Extra Oude' has no legal classification but is often used to emphasise that a genever has been aged.

Fruit genevers
As the term suggests, these are fruit-flavoured genevers. They are a modern phenomenon gaining in popularity since WWII. Fruit genevers tend to emphasise the fruit with little malt wine or botanical character discernible.

SERVING GENEVER
The Dutch and Belgians drink their genever neat, in ice-cold glasses. The traditional Dutch method is known as Kopstoot (pronounced 'Cop-Stout') and literally translates as 'a blow for your head': simply drink a shot of ice-cold genever from a small, tulip-shaped glass, then follow with a sip of beer.

Jonge genever may be mixed with tonic, soda or cola in a similar fashion to vodka. The proportion of juniper in some brands is so low that even those who do not enjoy the taste of London Dry Gin may savour a jonge genever and tonic.

Some people mix genever with bitters. Splash a few drops of bitters in an old-fashioned glass, rotate the glass to coat, then top up with cold genever and ice.
This yields a drink not dissimilar in style to the British Pink Gin.

Distilleries

Some big, some small; some new, some old; gin distillation in the early 21st century bridges tradition with technology in this most dynamic of spirit categories

"It is no exaggeration to say Desmond Payne of Beefeater is the world's most experienced master gin distiller, heir to nearly 200 years of gin-making heritage."

Beefeater London Dry Gin
Kennington, London, England

There are a mere handful of gin distillers left in London and, of those, the Beefeater Distillery at the Oval is the most central and best known.

Founder James Burrough was born in Ottery St. Mary, Devon in 1835 and trained as a pharmacist in Exeter before setting off to seek his fortune in Canada. In 1855, a year after leaving England, he entered into partnership with a Mr Bentley to open a chemist shop in Toronto. He stayed there for a further five years before returning home.

Back in Blighty and as ambitious as ever, in 1863 James paid £400 to purchase John Taylor & Son, a firm that specialised in the rectification of gin and liqueurs. Originally established in 1820, the company's premises were at 56 Cale Street in London's Chelsea. The firm, which he renamed 'James Burrough, Distiller and Importer of Foreign Liqueurs', had a good reputation and its customers included the likes of Fortnum & Mason.

James used his chemist's training to help perfect gin and liqueur recipes and the company still has his early recipe books, including one from 1849 which predates his purchase of the distillery, listing a recipe for blackcurrant gin. His studious efforts paid off and by 1871 he had expanded to such an extent that his family home behind the distillery in Marlborough Square was used to house the company's offices.

By 1876 the company's portfolio of liqueurs and imported spirits also included more gin brands and it was in this year that company papers first record the existence of Beefeater gin, alongside other brands such as James Burrough London Dry and Ye Old Chelsea gin. In 1897 James Burrough died and his sons took over the running of the business. They continued to prosper and in 1906, with only two years left on the Cale Street lease, the Burrough family purchased a premises across the river at 26 Hutton Road, Lambeth. They took the two years they had before needing to vacate the old distillery to equip their new premises with the latest stills from J Dore & Sons (successors to Aeneas Coffey). They named the new site Cale Distillery in memory of their old premises.

In 1911, Beefeater Gin was awarded the prestigious Gold Medal at the Festival of Empire Exhibition at Crystal Palace and six years later Eric Burrough began exporting to the United States. By 1958 the business had outgrown the Lambeth site and moved to its current home in Montford Place near the Oval Cricket Ground, a site which had been vacated by Haywood's Military Pickles due to war damage.

The building's 1950s architecture still overshadows the surrounding Victorian terraced houses. It was expanded in the mid-sixties with a second still hall that more than doubled its capacity and today lines of Carterhead stills which were originally required to purify the base spirit stand idle. However, the distillery's five impressive pot stills, three with a fill capacity of 3,200 litres and another two at twice that size, are all employed in the distillation of Beefeater with only the smaller ones used for Beefeater 24 and special limited edition runs.

The Burrough family sold the company to Whitbread in 1987 and Beefeater is in turn now part of the French Pernod-Ricard Group. Since this acquisition in 2005 Pernod-Ricard has invested heavily in the brand and saved the previously uncertain future of one of London's only remaining large-scale gin distillery.

BEEFEATER LONDON DRY GIN

40% alc./vol. (47% alc./vol. in USA)

As well as juniper from Tuscany, Beefeater is flavoured with coriander seeds, liquorice, orris root, Seville orange peel, Spanish lemon peel, Spanish bitter almonds, angelica root and seeds. These are steeped in wheat neutral grain spirit for a minimum of 24 hours, before steam heat is gently applied to the base of the pot still to start a distillation process that takes over seven hours.

Beefeater is named after the Yeoman Warders who have guarded the Tower of London since appointed as his personal bodyguards by King Henry VIII in 1485, they remain the Queens's official bodyguards at state occasions when they wear their distinctive scarlet and gold state uniforms. The Yeoman Warders also act as visitor guides at the Tower of London where they can be seen in their red and blue 'day' tunics. Beefeater gin keeps close to its namesakes and the Warders are invited to a Christmas lunch at the distillery each year and presented with a bottle of Beefeater gin on their birthday.

In the early 1990s the brand leader and other competitor gins lowered their strength in the UK to the then newly permissible level of 37.5% alc./vol.. Beefeater defiantly held its strength at 40% alc./vol. and, to its credit, retains that strength to this day (47% alc./vol. in USA).

Appearance: Crystal clear. **Aroma:** Clean pine fresh juniper with a subtle lemon and orange zest.
Taste: More orange notes emerge on the palate as do more subtle hints of Parma Violet and coriander. **Aftertaste:** Orange notes re-emerge the peppery, coriander finish.
diffordsguide rating: ★★★★⯪

BEEFEATER 24

45% alc./vol. (45% alc./vol. in USA)

Desmond Payne has been distilling gin for over 40 years, first at the now lost Seager Distillery in London's Deptford, then at Plymouth distillery and since 1995 as master distiller at Beefeater. It is no exaggeration to say he is the world's most experienced master gin distiller but had never been given the opportunity to create his own gin. So when news leaked out in 2008 that he had finally been given free range to formulate his own gin there was great anticipation by all in the gin world, even his competitors.

The inspiration for a radical botanical to use in his new gin came from previous visits to Korea and Japan where Desmond had discovered that due to restrictions on the use of quinine, the locally made tonic water was not a patch on what he was used to drinking with Beefeater back home. As a result their G&Ts lacked bite so he had been forced to look for alternative mixers. He enjoyed drinking the ubiquitous local canned iced teas so tried mixing this with his gin. The result was very acceptable and so 'Beefeater and iced tea' became his default drink in Asia.

Remembering this and the fact that tea is traded like a botanical it seemed logical to Desmond to experiment with tea in his new gin. Initially he simply took leaf tea and distilled it in alcohol using his 2-litre laboratory still. As a result he discovered that both Assam and Darjeeling teas were far too tannic but green tea had the required fragrance and aroma, in particular Chinese green tea.

INGREDIENTS STORE
NO ADMITTANCE WITHOUT
A DIRECTOR'S PERMISSION.

Having already decided on tea based solely on the suitability of its flavour profile in gin, research later revealed that James Burrough's father, William, had been a tea merchant by Royal Appointment to Queen Victoria as part of his grocery business in Ottery St. Mary in Devon.

Beefeater Crown Jewel, the super-premium gin he was set to replace, was known for its use of grapefruit so it seemed logical to combine this with botanicals from the original Beefeater recipe and the Chinese green tea. He knew from experience that all these botanicals would combine well but the challenge was to balance the flavours. Angelica's musky, nutty notes were the nearest to the green tea in the Beefeater's original recipe so Desmond cut this back slightly. He also reduced the amount orange and lemon peel to counterbalance the addition of the grapefruit.

The result of his experimentations was a prototype with the working title 'Big Ben' and this was blind tested by panels in London and New York against six leading gin brands, both neat, in G&Ts, Dry Martinis and Collinses. The feedback was very positive but when the test groups had been told the new gin contained tea, the prototype was so well balanced that they were unable to detect it. It was decided that the tea influence should be increased.

Now tutored in the art of tea tasting, Desmond went back to his tea merchant and tried Japanese Sencha Tea, harvested from the slopes of Mount Fuji. Unusually this rare and expensive tea is steamed to prevent the oxidisation that occurs with other teas and packed in 200 gram foil bags to keep it fresh – even when ordering in the quantities required for distilling. This added an extra fragrant grassy dimension to the gin.

Believing he had now found the perfect recipe using twelve botanicals, Desmond worked to perfect the steeping and distillation process. He had worried that the full 24-hour steeping process used for Beefeater Original might stew the tea but instead found it beneficial. He did, however, find that the tannins from the tea came over towards the end of the distillation so his 'cut' into the tail of the run for Beefeater 24 is much earlier than is usual. This limits the quantity of gin produced in each run but retains the gin's fresh notes of grapefruit and leaf teas. Desmond believes this to be the earliest cut used in the gin industry and it results in close to a third of each distillation being discarded as feints.

Full-scale distillations proved successful and the now production-ready gin was named Beefeater 24 after Beefeater's overnight steeping process. The Royal Doulton factory next door to the old Lambeth distillery proved inspiration for the new gin's bottle design. The ceramics factory was one of the champions of the Arts and Crafts movement and naturally, being neighbours, the Burroughs commissioned Royal Doulton decanters in which to bottle some of their liqueurs. Although these were not directly copied, their design style is very apparent in the bottle.

Appearance: Crystal clear.**Aroma:** Delicate pine, lavender, tea and grapefruit zest.**Taste:** Soft, slightly

- The distinctive blue-black colour is inspired by both the Yeoman Warders day uniform and the colour of the ravens - continuing the link to the Tower of London.

- Yeoman Warder in ceremonial dress.

- Name '24' a reference to overnight steeping of botanicals and the 24 hour London lifestyle.

- Embossed details on bottle influenced by Royal Dalton's Arts and Crafts designs found on a ceramic cask at the distillery.

- Silhouette of Tower of London with the wheel of the London Eye adding a contemporary London landmark.

- Red punt in the base is not only the Beefeater colour but is also a reference to the famous Black Prince Balas ruby in the State Crown amongst the Queen's Jewels on display at the Tower.

- At the base of the embellishments on either side of the bottle is a citrus fruit referencing key botanicals.

- Raven holding the symbolic key to the Tower of London printed on the inside of the back label and visible through a window in the embossed design.

sweet palate. Piny juniper leads with grapefruit, tea, liquorice and violet notes following. Top note of sweetened lemon zest and white pepper. **Aftertaste:** Tannins from the tea are evident in the long, pine-ey juniper fresh finish. All in all brilliantly rounded and balanced.

diffordsguide rating: ★ ★ ★ ★ ★

BEEFEATER BURROUGH'S RESERVE GIN

43% alc./vol.

Launched June 2012, Burrough's Reserve is distilled in a small 19th Century copper pot still and then rested in Jean de Lillet oak casks for a period prior to bottling. It is presented in an embossed bottle that has been individually labelled carrying its batch and bottle number.

Made according to James Burrough's original 1860s Beefeater nine botanical recipe, Burrough's Reserve is distilled using James Burrough's original copper 'Still Number 12' from Cale Street, Chelsea. With a capacity of just 268 litres, this still is dwarfed by the larger stills at Beefeater's Kennington Distillery and was previously unused in recent decades. The use of this small differently shaped retort still and its increased copper surface area to spirit ratio produces small batches of distillate with a different character to the standard Beefeater produced by the larger stills. Burrough's Reserve is also a one shot gin whereas Beefeater is usually a multi-shot gin.

After distillation, the gin is aged in Jean de Lillet Oak barrels in the cellars beneath Beefeater's Distillery for varying periods of time, "weeks rather than years" according to Master Distiller Desmond Payne who created Burrough's Reserve. During this maturation period the gin takes on subtle characteristics of the oak and residual Jean de Lillet in the cask giving the spirit golden hue.

Desmond explained that due to its links with the Dry Martini, Lillet casks were the natural choice over virgin oak or even ex-bourbon casks. Jean de Lillet is an aperitif only produced in exceptional vintage years and each cask will have a slightly different influence on the gin so Burrough's Reserve will vary slightly from batch to batch.

Appearance: Light straw yellow. **Aroma**: Oak aging appears to amplify the juniper with pungent pine, cedar wood, and eucalyptus with green herbal notes (sage and thyme), lemon oil, white pepper and subtle floral notes. **Taste**: Powerful dry spicy and slightly buttery oak with subtle herbal notes. Beefeater's signature citrus notes add freshness but are subdued by the dominant oak. **Aftertaste**: Long dry pine finish with slight smokiness. Personally I'd have taken out of oak a tad earlier but I bow to Desmond Payne's experience.

diffordsguide rating: ★ ★ ★ ★ ★

Producer: Beefeater Distillers (Pernod-Ricard), 20 Montford Place, Kennington, London, England. **www**.beefeatergin.com

"Bols has practically single-handedly re-established the export market for genever, particularly to the USA."

Bols Distillery

Zoetermeer, Netherlands

Boasting a 437-year heritage, Lucas Bols is the world's oldest distilled spirits company, making liqueurs and genever by combining centuries-old recipes, natural ingredients and traditional flavour-extraction methods. For 379 of those years, Lucas Bols has been run by three successive families. It has since been through a series of mergers and acquisitions, finally re-emerging as an independent company, once again in Dutch hands.

Bols was established in 1575, when the Bulsius family set up a distillery in Amsterdam, in the process also shortening their name to the more Dutch-sounding Bols. It is believed they ended up in Amsterdam after first fleeing Antwerp as religious refugees to Cologne where Protestants were welcome. They then settled in Amsterdam, which was independent from the rule of the Catholic Spanish king and a haven for religious refugees.

They may well have settled in Amsterdam slightly earlier but even the 1575 date makes Bols the world's oldest distilled brand. The evidence of the 1575 date is found in a 1763 family document where the writer talks about his great-grandfather starting the family distillery in 1575.

At the time, distillation was not permitted in the centre of Amsterdam, due to the fire risks associated with operating a still amongst Amsterdam's predominantly wooden buildings, so Bols set up its still on the outskirts of the city on the bank of a stream, where the abundant cold water could be used for cooling the condensing column. The still sat under a simple roof with a small wooden building for storing botanicals. The distillery was known as 't Lootsje', which translates as 'the little shed'.

There is much conjecture as to who first made 'genever' with malt wine and juniper distillate. This is thought to date from the 1400s but the first written evidence of "genièvre" is found in a 1551 book. Bols is believed to have started producing juniper-flavoured spirits as well as liqueurs soon after arriving in Amsterdam in 1575, and was certainly the first to establish a genever 'brand'. However, few records survive and the first written proof that Bols distilled juniper is a 1664 record of the purchase of juniper berries.

Bols developed a close relationship with the Vereenigde Oost-indisch Compagnie (VOC), the Dutch East India trading Company. The VOC was established in 1602, when the States-General of the Netherlands granted it a 21-year monopoly to carry out colonial activities in Asia. Europe's first stock exchange opened that same year and the VOC is considered the world's first multinational corporation and the first to issue stock. Bols became a major shareholder in the VOC and their relationship gave them preferential access to exotic herbs and spices shipped to Amsterdam by the VOC, from which Bols created over 200 different liqueur recipes. In return, Bols supplied its spirits and liqueurs to other major shareholders in the VOC and to the sailors of the VOC, which kick-started the international distribution of Bols liqueurs as we know them today in over 100 countries.

The Bols family expanded the distillery into several houses on the Rozengracht, and it was here that the man that the modern Lucas Bols Company is named after was born in 1652. Lucas Bols took over the management of his family's business during the Dutch Golden Age.

Lucas turned Bols into an international brand and

expanded the range of liqueurs to more than 200 recipes, many designed specifically for important customers. After his death in 1719, his two sons, Hermannus and Peter, took over the business. As the generations passed, the Bols family started to neglect the company. By the time the last Bols descendant died in 1816, the Napoleonic War and the British naval blockade of harbours had dramatically affected the company's fortunes.

In 1818, a financier from Rotterdam, Gabriël Theodorus van 't Wout, acquired the Bols Company with the contract of sale including a condition that the company could continue to use the Bols family name in perpetuity. Theodorus had no previous distilling knowledge and he had taken over a neglected business which was in trouble. He became a hands-on, self-taught distiller who also learnt from the employees he had inherited. He turned a loss-making company into profit within the first year.

In 1823, Theodorus exported the first shipment of liqueurs and genevers to the United States. He was an astute business man and also became an accomplished distiller. Fortunately, the accountant in him compelled him to make detailed notes and, in 1830, he embarked on a seven-year undertaking to compile four volumes entitled 'Distillateurs- en Liqueurbereiders Handboek door een oude patroon van't Lootsje' ('Distillers and Liqueur makers Handbook by an old patron of The Little Shed'). The beautifully written books detail recipes, the origin and specifications for botanicals and production methods. Bols still refers to these journals when it wants to revive a long-forgotten recipe and one of the four volumes is on display at The House of Bols Cocktail &

Genever Experience in Amsterdam.

In 1868 the firm was acquired by the Moltzer family who continued to expand the company with their strong marketing skills and a focus on making Bols an acclaimed international brand.

The 1850s saw Bols participate in leading international exhibitions, where its products won numerous medals. In 1954, the last member of the Moltzer family left the board and Bols Distilleries became a public company listed on the Dutch stock exchange. It was also in this decade (1957) that KLM started to give its passengers Delft Blue miniature houses containing Bols liqueur. The practice continues to this day, with a new house design released each year. Since 1986, these Delft houses have been filled with Bols Genever rather than liqueurs.

After two short-lasting joint ventures with first Heineken and later Wessanen – and then a buyout by CVC Capital Partners – Bols was taken over in 2000 by Rémy Cointreau.

In 2006, Bols returned to Dutch hands after another management buyout, led by Huub van Doorne and supported by AAC Capital Partners. A former member of the Board of Directors of Rémy Cointreau, Huub is now the CEO of Lucas Bols. He set about moving Bols' headquarters back to Amsterdam and, in 2007, the acclaimed Bols Bartending Academy opened, as well as the successful House of Bols Cocktail & Genever Experience.

BOLS GENEVERS
Bols Genevers, like all genevers/jenevers, are a blend of 'moutwijn' (malt-wine), a distillate of a secret mix of botanicals including juniper, and neutral grain spirit. In

the 19th century, genevers were one of the four key ingredients in classic cocktails, such as the Tom Collins and the Holland House.

Malt wine is distilled from equal parts fermented wheat, rye and corn with a small amount of malted barley added to provide enzymes to aid conversion of starch to fermentable sugars. The temperatures used in the mashing process where the sugars are converted, and the steps at which those temperatures are dropped, from 90˚C to 30˚C, along with the fermentation process and yeast, are crucial to malt wine's flavour. The fermented liquid (wash) is first distilled using a stripping column before being twice distilled in a copper pot still. After the final distillation, the malt-wine leaves the pot still at around 47% alc./vol.. This relatively low distillation strength produces a highly flavoured spirit, retaining the malty flavours of the grains from which it is distilled. It is this malt-wine that gives Bols genever its distinct flavour.

The second component is a botanical distillate made by redistilling grain neutral alcohol with a recipe of botanical flavourings including coriander, caraway and aniseed.

The third component is juniper distilled separately from the other botanicals in malt wine instead of neutral grain spirit.

Lastly, a secret ingredient is added which the Bols master distiller, Piet van Leijenhorst, has rediscovered from ancient Bols recipes and which gives Bols Genever a distinctive after-taste. If an aged genever is being made then the malt wine and botanical distillate blend will be aged in oak casks, usually a combination of new and used French Limousin oak and, only for the Corenwyn aged six years, also American oak.

BOLS GENEVER

42% alc./vol.

Flavoured with a whisky-like triple grain distillate made of corn, wheat and rye, which the Dutch call malt-wine. This flavour-rich distillate is blended with a juniper-berry distillate. The recipe contains over 50 per cent malt-wine.

Launched in 2008, Bols Genever has practically single-handedly re-established the export market for genever, particularly to the USA.

Appearance: Crystal clear. **Aroma:** Pine forest juniper odours over a nutty malty/bready new make spirit base (malt whisky prior to aging) with delicate floral jasmine tea aromas. **Taste:** Resinous pine and eucalyptus juniper with complex zingy spice, rounded by nutty bready flavours. **Aftertaste:** Slightly bitter, bready, burnt nutty toast. **diffordsguide rating:** ★ ★ ★ ★ ☆

BOLS BARREL AGED GENEVER

42% alc./vol.

Made according to a 19th century recipe, a base of 50 per cent malt-wine, triple-distilled in a pot still from rye, wheat and corn is blended with traditional genever botanicals including juniper, hops, cloves, anise, liquorice and ginger. The blend is then aged for 18 months in Limousin oak casks.

Launched 1st September 2011, this Barrel Aged Genever was originally developed for the U.S. market and is presented in one-litre clay bottles. This is said to be

a re-launch of Bols' first Barrel Aged Genever originally released in 1883.

Appearance: Clear, pale golden. **Aroma:** Pungent wholemeal bready juniper with nutty cream of soda and tinned peach slices. **Taste:** Peach stones, macadamia nuts and rye bread with warm clove, mace and subtle juniper. **Aftertaste:** Toasty, assertive finish with lingering oily tropical fruitiness.

diffordsguide rating: ★ ★ ★ ★ ★

BOLS CORENWYN

Bols Corenwyn is special type of genever with more than 51 per cent malt-wine and is specific to Bols which owns the brand name of Corenwyn, registered in 1962. Like all genevers, it is a blend of malt-wine and botanical distillates, but Corenwyn is differentiated by the high percentage of malt-wine, the botanicals used and the period of aging after the three ingredients are blended together. The three separately made ingredients and the production process are as follows.

1/. Malt-wine is made from equal parts wheat, rye and corn with a small amount of malted barley added to provide enzymes to aid conversion of starch to fermentable sugars. The temperatures used in the mashing process where those sugars are converted, and the steps at which those temperatures are dropped, from 90°C to 30°C, along with the fermentation process and yeast, are crucial to malt-wine's final flavour profile. The fermented liquid (wash) is first distilled using a stripping column before being twice distilled in a copper pot still. After this triple distillation, the 47% abv distillate

produced is then aged in new and used Limousin oak casks, for between two and ten years to produce the various aged Bols Corenwyn variants, which are each unique blends created by the Lucas Bols Master Distiller and his blending team.

2/. To make the juniper distillate for Corenwyn, carefully selected juniper berries are steeped in malt-wine and then distilled in a copper pot still.

3/. A botanical distillate is made in a similar process to the juniper distillate. A botanical recipe specific to Bols Corenwyn including aniseed, root ginger, hops, angelica and liquorice is steeped in neutral grain alcohol and then distilled in a copper pot still.

4/. The malt-wine, juniper distillate and botanical distillate are blended and aged in a combination of new and used French Limousin oak casks. Bols Corenwyn is then bottled into the traditional clay bottle.

Each hand-made clay bottle has the Bols name stamped into the wet clay. Their first use dates back to the 16th century when clay jars from the German Westerwald region were used to hold mineral water and were sold to the rich in Amsterdam. The empty clay water jars were then re-used to hold genever.

BOLS CORENWYN 2 JAAR

38% alc./vol.

Bols Corenwyn is aged for two years and packaged in an individually numbered, brick-orange coloured clay

bottle finished with a white and red ribbon.
Appearance: (Bottle No. 030010) Clear, pale golden yellow. **Aroma:** Malty sweet corn with new leather, macadamia nut and linseed oil. **Taste:** Dry, malty, spicy palate with pine juniper and faint woody tannins. **Aftertaste:** Long, malty, grainy finish with lingering pine spice.
diffordsguide rating: ★ ★ ★ ★ ☆

BOLS CORENWYN 4 JAAR
40% alc./vol.
Bols Corenwyn '4 Jaar Gelagerd', meaning 'aged for four years' is presented in an individually numbered gun-metal-grey coloured clay bottle with a beige and black ribbon.
Appearance: (Bottle No. 009309) Clear, buttery yellow with a hint of green. **Aroma:** Linseed oil, new wood shavings, straw hay bales, cashew nuts and just snuffed candle smoke. **Taste:** Smoothed by vanilla and woody oiliness but with enlivening pine spice **Aftertaste:** Lightly spicy oaky finish with lingering pine fresh juniper.
diffordsguide rating: ★ ★ ★ ★ ☆

CORENWYN 6 JAAR GELAGERD
40% alc./vol.
Corenwyn '6 Jaar Gelagerde', meaning 'aged for six years'. Its maturation takes place in two types of oak casks (French and American). Corenwyn 6 Jaar is presented in an individually numbered, gun-metal-grey coloured clay bottle with a brown and black ribbon. Launched in 2009 as a limited edition.
Appearance: (Bottle No. 035099) Clear, buttery yellow with a hint of green. **Aroma:** Sweet herbal nose with

vanilla, tree bark, ground coriander and thyme.
Taste: Silky, slight oily mouth feel, yet dry, spicy and herbal with juniper and light woodiness.
Aftertaste: Angelica, ground coriander and nutty balsawood finish with lingering pine flavours.
diffordsguide rating: ★ ★ ★ ★ ★ +

CORENWYN 10 JAAR GELAGERD
40% alc./vol.
Corenwyn '10 Jaar Gelagerde', meaning 'aged for ten years' is made in very limited quantities due to its requiring ten years maturation. Even at Bols where large stocks of aged malt-wine are held, stock of such old malt-wine is very limited.

Launched in 2009 as a limited edition, Bols Corenwyn '10' is presented in an individually numbered, gun-metal-grey coloured clay bottle with a brown and beige ribbon.
Appearance: (Bottle No. 000416) Clear, dark golden amber with bright golden highlights.
Aroma: Madeira, cigar, lanolin and vanilla with a drop of linseed oil. **Taste:** Starts sweet with nut oils and faint juniper. Cracked black pepper spice quickly emerges with pine, eucalyptus, vanilla and faint liquorice.
Aftertaste: Long delicately spiced woody juniper.
diffordsguide rating: ★ ★ ★ ★ ★

Producer: Lucas Bols, 61-63 Wattstraat, Zoetermeer, Netherlands.
www.bols.com

"When Bombay Sapphire was launched in 1987 it marked a turning point for the fortunes of gin."

Bombay London Dry Gin

Warrington, Cheshire, England

Bombay Sapphire embodies the idea of a modern gin, indeed it was only launched in 1987. However, both Sapphire and Bombay Dry, its mother brand, can trace their origins and recipes back to the 1760s.

The history of Bombay Gin stretches back to 1760, just after the repeal of the Corn Laws, when a 24-year-old Thomas Dakin built a distillery on Bridge Street in Warrington, north-west England. Due to a poor harvest that year he did not actually start distilling his 'Warrington Dry Gin' until 1761. That year-long delay may have given him the opportunity to perfect his recipe, as it proved not only to be very successful, but nearly 200 years later was chosen to become Bombay Gin and 27 years after that provided the essential DNA to which two botanicals would be added to create Bombay Sapphire.

In 1831 Mary Dakin (Thomas Dakin's daughter-in-law) purchased one of a new breed of steam-jacketed stills, to help reduce burning of the spirit and the consequential production of Furfural and other unwanted compounds, so making cleaner alcohol. The new still was fitted with a then state-of-the-art rectifying head designed by a man named Corty. This column served to purify the spirit.

In 1836 a second still was installed with an even more advanced kind of head built by a coppersmith called Carter who had worked for the famous still engineer John Dore, designing and installing stills on behalf of Aeneas Coffey. His 'Carter head' was a significant advance on the Corty head, constituting a closed column mounted on top of the copper pot.

Both the Carter and Corty heads rectified the spirit to

such a degree that the botanical flavours must have been introduced after this rectification. If botanicals were simply added to the pot beneath these columns the essential oils carrying their flavour would have been stripped out by the heads. The purified spirit produced by the columns could have been redistilled with the botanicals in a standard pot still without a rectifying column, but this would have been costly and time consuming. Instead, at some point – and it's not known when – somebody had the bright idea of introducing vapour infusion baskets, so eliminating the need for a further botanical distillation.

In this method of gin distillation, the spirit vapour travels up the rectifying column to emerge at the top, where it passes along the swan's neck (or lyne arm) and into a small tank where perforated copper baskets hold the botanicals. The vapour passes through these botanicals, so extracting their essential aromatic oils without cooking or denaturing them.

The first written reference to this process is found in the 1855 French book 'Traité des Liqueurs et de la Distillation des Alcools' by Pierre Duplais, but there are much earlier references to such a vapour chamber being used to hold baskets of charcoal for filtering spirit after pot still distillation. Once a rectifying column such as the Corty or Carter Heads had been installed there would no longer have been a need for charcoal filtration so it appears likely that this is when the Dakins cleverly adapted this otherwise redundant apparatus to hold the botanicals, thereby obviating the need for a second botanical distillation. Thus it can be surmised that the vapour infusion of botanicals at the Warrington distillery

started in 1831 after the installation of the Corty Head.

The 1831 Corty still and the 1836 Carter stills remained in operation until 1961 when, as part of a move to a larger site at Loushers Lane on the outskirts of Warrington, the best working parts of each were amalgamated to make one still (using the pot from the Corty and the column from the 1836 Carterhead still). A year later, the John Dore Company built two more Carterhead stills which were exact replicas of the amalgamated still. In 1957 the John Dore Company had also built another Carterhead still for Greenall's with a slightly different shaped pot.

Despite the many changes in ownership and developments in distilling technology, the G&J Greenall continued to make Greenall's gin to Thomas Dakin's 1761 recipe – as indeed it still does to this day. However, the period immediately prior to, during, and after the move to Loushers lane coincided with the development of a new gin brand, one that would go on to become one of the best known in the world.

THE BOMBAY SPIRITS COMPANY

In 1957, a New York-based lawyer who had learnt about the drinks industry whilst working for Seagram's decided there was an opportunity for a new gin brand in America. Allan Subin lived on Madison Avenue and socialised with successful 'Mad Men', bankers, lawyers and entrepreneurs. He was married to an Englishwoman so was also enamoured with all things British. With these influences and his peers' tastes in mind, he sought to create a gin brand that embodied 1920s elegance.

After further research in he concluded that Greenall's were the people to make his gin and that its 1761 recipe and vapour infusion process was just what he was looking for, but with the stipulation that grain spirit was used as per the original recipe, not molasses spirit as used by Greenall's at the time.

Bombay and the days of the Raj proved the inspiration for his gin's name with Queen Victoria, the epitome of Englishness, as the new brand's icon. Interestingly, the use of a British monarch for branding purposes had been prohibited in 1934 but as Subin's gin was aimed at the American market the rule did not apply.

Subin launched his Bombay Dry Gin in 1960, achieving annual sales of 10,000 cases by its third year and 100,000 cases by the turn of the decade. By 1975 the demand for Bombay Dry Gin was such that production demands on the vapour infusion stills forced Greenall's to start also using their pot stills and a steeping process to produce their own Greenall's gin. This freed the botanical basket apparatus for the sole production of Bombay.

In the 1980s, the company then known as I.D.V. (and now Diageo) bought the Bombay brand but continued to contract G&J Greenall to produce it on its behalf. It was not long after this that another American marketing visionary, like Subin before him, looked to the 1761 recipe as inspiration for a new game-changing gin.

Michel Roux of Carillon Importers was famed for masterminding the creation of the Absolut vodka brand and he saw an opportunity to do for gin what he had done for vodka, foreseeing a luxury gin that be believed would revitalise the entire category.

Ian Hamilton, Greenall's head distiller at the time, was tasked with creating a super-premium version of

Bombay Dry Gin. His brief was to remain true to Bombay's original 1761 recipe, but develop it by further adding new botanicals. He experimented with a host of botanicals, test distilling each to access their effect on the recipe. Eventually he settled on two exotic varieties of pepper: Grains of Paradise and Cubeb Berries. Their addition to the 1761 recipe produced a gin with greater liveliness, adding floral pepper and spice notes.

Contrary to popular belief, Ian did not reduce the amount of juniper in the original recipe, or indeed change the ratios of any of the other ingredients used in the 1761 recipe. He merely added the two extra botanicals and it was their interaction with the other botanicals, during distillation and as a flavour in the finished bottle that set the new gin, Bombay Sapphire apart from original Bombay.

The name Sapphire was inspired by the famous Star of Bombay, a stunning violet-blue sapphire stone discovered in Sri Lanka and given to silent movie star and legendary cocktail enthusiast Mary Pickford by her husband Douglas Fairbanks. The gem's colour inspired the square translucent blue bottle, a design so simple and yet revolutionary that it cemented the luxury positioning of the brand and made Bombay Sapphire a design icon.

The combination of Hamilton's liquid, the iconic bottle and the marketing vision of Roux proved an instant hit. When Bombay Sapphire was launched in 1987 it marked a turning point for the fortunes of gin. Sapphire invigorated the gin category and paved the way for the surge of new brands that we see on the market today. Back in the UK a new breed of bartender was emerging and a young Dick Bradsell was inspired to create his now famous Bramble cocktail whilst working at Fred's Club using the new gin.

By 1997 a cocktail resurgence was well underway in London, leading to establishment of *CLASS* magazine in August that year. It also proved to be a significant year for the future of Bombay and indeed the spirits industry as a whole. The merger of two of the world's biggest drink's companies, I.D.V. (Grand Metropolitan), then owners of Bombay Gin, and United Distillers (Guinness), formed the conglomerate now called Diageo and sent a shudder through the drinks industry. The combined corporation emerged to be by far the biggest and most powerful spirits company and it fell to the competition authorities in both the UK and USA to cut it down to size. Diageo was forced to shed brands which resulted in the sale of the Bombay Spirits Company to Bacardi.

Bacardi put renewed vigour into the marketing of Sapphire, commissioning artists and designers to create spectacular sapphire-coloured glassware and properly engaging with bartenders to help drive the cocktail boom.

Despite the changes in ownership, production of both Bombay gins remained in the safe hands of Ian Hamilton at G&J Greenall. In 2005, when a fire at the Lousher's Lane Distillery totally destroyed the bottling hall, the still house and the precious Carterhead stills with their infusion baskets were saved and distilling of Bombay resumed just a week later.

The precious stills which has been so under threat may have been in the G&J Greenall distillery but they were owned by Bacardi. The folk at Bacardi must have felt somewhat helpless as reports of the fire came in, then even more frustrated when supplies of Bombay gins were threatened immediately after the fire. This near catastrophe may have been the catalyst for Bacardi to start thinking about moving their Carterhead stills to their own distillery where they had total control of production,

but Bacardi's eventual announcement that they were in the process of building their own distillery came amid a wider industry move for gin brands to come from their own dedicated distilleries, somewhat like malt whisky.

A derelict mill in Hampshire, England was chosen as the site for the state-of-the-art gin distillery and visitor centre. Renovation and building work started in 2012, overseen by Master Distiller Nik Fordham with completion in summer 2013. Formally at Beefeater and one of the most technically qualified distillers in the world, Nik is the man responsible for the quality assurance of Bombay Sapphire gin.

The new distillery, Laverstoke Mill, sits in a rural idyll astride the River Test. The site was previously used to produce high quality paper for the bank notes of India and the British Empire for over 200 years. The design vision behind the renovation of the derelict mill and its transformation into a state-of-the-art gin distillery and visitor centre was headed by acclaimed London designer Thomas Heatherwick and his team at Heatherwick Studio.

Two dramatic glasshouses form the centrepiece of the distillery and allow visitors to experience the ten botanicals used to flavour Bombay Sapphire gin in environments akin to their Mediterranean and tropical origins. The fact that this is the first distillery and refurbishment to be awarded an 'Outstanding' BREEAM (Building Research Establishment's Environmental Assessment Method) accreditation is a testament to its design and sustainability.

The location may have changed, and in keeping with Bombay's image become more 'designer', but the production process remains the same. Bombay gins continue to be made using the vapour infusion distillation process in Carterhead stills, one being one of the original stills purchased by the

Dakin family in 1831. It's also worth remembering that Bacardi's Master of Botanicals, Ivan Tonutti, has been responsible for the botanicals used to make Bombay gins since 1998 when Bacardi purchased the gin brand from Diageo. The stills have moved to a better looking distillery with more technically advanced laboratory and other equipment but they are operated in the same way with the same botanicals.

PRODUCTION

Bombay Dry and Bombay Sapphire gins are unusual in that they are distilled using the vapour infusion method: unlike most gins their botanicals are not steeped in spirit. Specially adapted Cartherhead stills have a kettle base shaped like a pot still with a bulbous feints chamber on top. A tall rectifying column above leads to a lyne arm, which directs the vapour through a copper infusion basket whose seven sections contain the botanicals. After collecting their essential oils, the vapour then condenses to produce a spirit infused with flavours from the botanicals.

The quality of the base spirit used nowadays is such that the Carterhead rectifying columns are no longer necessary, so in order to increase capacity two McMillan copper pot stills have also been adapted to also feed rectified spirit vapour through the copper baskets.

The botanicals are placed in the seven sections of the perforated copper baskets by hand, first the larger ones: juniper, angelica, lemon peels, coriander seeds, cubeb berries* and grains of paradise*; then powdered botanicals are added on top of these so that they don't fall through the perforations: orris, cassia, almond and liquorice. (*Cubeb berries and grains of paradise are used to make Bombay Sapphire but not Bombay Dry.)

The heads are allowed to run for considerably longer than would be normal for most steep-and-boil gins. This is to ensure the botanicals become properly moist before switching to hearts. Then the still is run quite slowly to allow the vapour to gently strip the volatile essential oils from the botanicals.

The infusion baskets influence the flavour of the finished gin and the folk at Bombay say that vapour infusion extracts a fresher expression of the botanicals, likening the result to being more akin to maceration than steeping and boiling. Vapour infusion does not cook and break down the botanicals in the way that steeping and boiling does, so resulting in fewer cooked and caramelised notes.

Apparently, vapour infusion has the greatest effect on juniper and the way the juniper oils influence the interaction of the other botanicals. Bombay attests that "the fresher juniper note does not suppress or cloak the other botanicals, but allows them a more coherent expression in the finished gin".

Unlike many gins where the botanicals used are a closely guarded secret, those used in Bombay Gins are well-known, to the extent that the ten botanicals which give it its unique flavour are etched onto the sides of Bombay Sapphire bottles.

One of the benefits that came with Bacardi-Martini's takeover of Bombay is the company's botanical expertise courtesy of the Martini side of the business. Ivan Tonutti is a fifth generation professional descendant of Luigi Rossi, schooled through his apprenticeship at the Martini-Rossi company under Giovanni Brezza. Ivan is responsible for the botanicals used in all of Bacardi's products, including Martini, Noilly Prat and Bombay gins. His role is to nurture close relationships built over many years with trusted suppliers and growers and to ensure the quality and consistency of the botanicals used. The botanicals he buys are not the result of vast industrial processes, but are hand reared by artisanal growers.

Every year he selects the best quality botanicals from each supplier, assessing their colour, aroma, freshness and oil content. Excess botanicals are purchased to ensure that if a bad harvest is rejected from one supplier there is still enough of each botanical of a suitable quality held. The botanicals are received at the storage house in England where different batches from each supplier are combined and then combined again with part of the batch from the previous year. This ensures year-on-year consistency. Before a batch of botanicals is sent to the distillery a further ten stringent tests must be passed to ensure the botanicals' suitability.

Juniper from Tuscany, Italy

The main flavouring in all gins, juniper, is a member of the cypress family and its berries contribute a dry, fragrant, herbal aroma with notes of pine and lavender. Ivan believes that the best quality berries come from the hills in Tuscany, Italy. He believes the wild berries grown under the Tuscan sun ripen more fully than the berries available from other producing countries such as Serbia, Macedonia or India. There are two suppliers with whom he has been working with for many years, one of whom harvests exclusively for Bombay.

Every year Ivan selects juniper berries from up to 25 different batches from the two suppliers. In some cases he can tell the quality of the botanical based on the colour alone. The berries should be a dark plum colour, whereas lighter or green colours indicate a bad harvest. The main flavour comes from the essential oils (Alpine Pinere & camphor) within the three seeds inside each berry and this oil content is analysed before selecting the batches that will be shipped to England for distillation.

Lemon Peels from Murcia, Spain

Lemon peel brings a strong citrus character to Bombay gins and also lifts the other botanicals. The lemons come from the Murcia region of Spain, a basin between the mountains and the sea that is renowned for its citrus fruit. The Mediterranean sun and the microclimate in Murcia's valleys allows the citrus fruits to ripen in winter as the temperature never goes below -4°C due to the convections of hot air that are constantly present, so producing sweeter, juicier lemons.

Growing citrus fruits is a tradition in Murcia, and nearly every family grows lemons, oranges and other fruit. They are cultivated as naturally as possible with minimal use of fertilisers and pesticides. The lemon trees bloom with small pink-white flowers, each flower producing one fruit, so it is essential to prune the flowers to avoid excessive quantities of lemons causing branches to droop or even break with the heavy fruit.

The trees bear fruit when they are aged between 3 and 30 years old, and are planted close together to maximise production in the small family-owned groves and gardens, so ruling out the possibility of machine harvesting. Generations of each family hand-pick the lemons to ensure that the trees and fruit are not damaged. The lemons naturally vary greatly in size and colour, ranging from golf ball- to almost football-sized and these are sorted with the 'standard' size we are all familiar with

separated for sale to supermarkets. The over- and under-sized, but still sweet and juicy, lemons are perfect for gin production.

Two types of lemons are used for Bombay gins: Fino (representing 30 per cent of cultivation) and Verna (70 per cent). Fino lemons are harvested during the winter months, albeit in smaller quantities, with their harvest between January and April. Verna lemons are from the summer harvest between July and September.

The main difference between the two types is the thickness of their skin. Fino lemons have a much thicker skin with more oils, but even the Verna has a thick skin compared to other varieties of lemon. This is key to gin production as the zest of the lemons holds essential oils which add a vibrant citrus flavour and a delicate, bitter sweetness. The left-over fruit pulp and flesh is not required for distillation and is juiced for commercial use or sold as additive to animal feed.

The lemons are laboriously hand-peeled in one continuous long winding piece of peel, according to the traditional cut used for generations in Murcia. This labour intensive process avoids the flesh of the lemon and ensures that the whole skin is used. Thinner skinned lemons increase the risk of some of the fruit flesh being left on the skins after peeling, which in turn can rot and ferment causing damage to an entire harvest of dried peels if left unchecked.

Ivan's supplier drives from home to home collecting the dried peels from each family. There are over 4,000 families harvesting and peeling small quantities of lemons in Murcia and also co-operative lemon groves where each family has owned several trees for generations.

Once selected, the lemon peels are broken by hand into smaller pieces, placed in large hessian sacks and shipped to England. Before being sent on to the distillery, the quality of each batch of peels is checked again.

Ivan considers these expensive lemons to be the best choice for Bombay gins. Even when the price of Spanish lemons almost doubled in 2008 he continued to source these variants.

Coriander Seed from Morocco

Along with juniper and lemon peel, coriander seeds add bright, fresh high notes to Bombay Gins. The essential oil in coriander seeds is linalool and this is mellow, spicy, fragrant and aromatic with candied ginger, lemon and pungent sage notes. Most of the world's coriander is produced in Eastern Europe and Russia, however the larger Moroccan seeds contain more oils so are chosen by Ivan for their superior aroma and flavour.

The seeds are harvested in August and September, always in the morning to avoid more of the ripening fruits from falling. They are dried in a circulation of warm air at 30°C.

Orris from Tuscany, Italy

Orris root is the rhizome (bulb) of the iris plant and has a very perfumed character. Like angelica root, it helps fix aromas and flavours within Bombay gins. Mainly sourced from Florence in Italy, orris root contributes light perfumed notes to Bombay akin to Parma Violet sweets and fresh hay.

The orris used in Bombay gins is grown in Tuscany in central Italy where hundreds of terraced flowerbeds house thousands of iris flowers. Three- to four-year-old plants are harvested then stored for two to three years to allow the flavours to develop: the finished botanical is very hard and requires grinding into a powder before use.

Angelica Root from Saxony, Germany

Angelica is a key ingredient as it balances the bright, fresh high notes of juniper, lemon peel and coriander seeds while also fixing and marrying the volatile flavours of other botanicals, giving length and substance to Bombay gins.

Ivan sources angelica root from Saxony, where the multi-headed flowers grow amongst the woodlands in the region surrounding Dresden. When the plants are two-years-old, a special tool is used to pull the root from the soil in one piece.

Bitter Almonds from Spain

Bombay's recipe calls for Spanish bitter almonds, which have a high essential oil content and give Bombay gins an almond/marzipan, nutty, soapy and spicy flavour – much more than if comparatively faint sweet almonds were used.

Almonds contain trace amounts of arsenic, which along with nut protein are removed during distillation, so luckily Bombay is not hazardous for people with nut allergies.

Liquorice from China

Sourced from China's grassy plains, the dried hard fibrous root of the liquorice plant is ground into a powder. Liquorice adds warmth, sweetness and a faint anise aroma to Bombay gins, although liquorice itself does not stand out as a prominent flavour, instead acting as a harmonising agent for the other flavours and aromas.

Liquorice is unusual in that during vapour infusion its flavour is carried by glyciric acid rather than essential oils, of which it is low in content.

Cassia Bark from Indonesia

A member of the cinnamon family, cassia is sometimes referred to as Chinese cinnamon. It is the bark of a tall evergreen tree grown in Indonesia and is removed from the trunk by hand. As the bark dries it naturally curls into quills which are ground into a powder.

Cassia adds light warmth, sweetness and a delicate spice to Bombay gins. As with the other mid-palate flavours of almond and liquorice, its contribution is to help balance the overall aroma and taste rather than as a primary flavour.

Cubeb Berries from Java

Along with Grains of Paradise, cubeb berries are one of the two additional botanicals that distinguish Bombay Sapphire from Bombay Dry.

A member of the pepper family, these small, red-brown berries come from cubeb plants grown in the shade of coffee trees in plantations in Java, Indonesia. The strong smelling berries are gathered before they ripen and then dried in the sun.

Not far removed from black pepper but with a more floral aroma, cubeb berries add delicate notes of lavender, geranium and rose. They also provide a dry, slightly hot flavour which results in the lively peppery characteristics Bombay Sapphire is notorious for.

Grains of Paradise from West Africa

Alongside cubeb berries, Grains of Paradise from the moist coastal areas of West Africa also contribute to the peppery finish of Bombay Sapphire, distinguishing the recipe from that of Bombay Dry.

The 'grains' are actually seeds from large purple flowers that grow from tall bamboo-like stems with long pointed leaves, actually a relative of ginger. They are harvested in June or July at the time of heavy rains.

The dark brown seeds add a hot, spicy, peppery flavour plus hints of lavender, chocolate, citrus and elderflower to Bombay Sapphire. They highlight and accentuate the citrus in Bombay Sapphire and lengthen the finish.

BOMBAY ORIGINAL LONDON DRY GIN
43% alc./vol.

As the name would suggest, this is the original Bombay gin, redating the now better-known Bombay Sapphire. It was conceived by American entrepreneur Allan Subin, who was inspired by one of the oldest known English dry gin recipes, created by Thomas Dakin in 1761. It launched in the USA in 1960.

Appearance: Crystal clear. **Aroma**: Coriander, juniper and citrus with hints of Olbas oil tablets. **Taste**: Juniper, citrus and coriander flavours predominate with liquorice, parma violet and an underlying rootiness. Superbly structured. **Aftertaste**: Lingering juniper freshness with liquorice and parma violets.

diffordsguide rating: ★ ★ ★ ★ ★ ✦

BOMBAY SAPPHIRE LONDON DRY GIN
40% alc./vol.

Flavoured with ten botanicals: juniper berries from Tuscany, coriander seeds, angelica root, liquorice, Italian orris, cassia bark, Spanish almonds and lemon peel, Cubeb berries from Java and West African Grains of Paradise. Unusually, Bombay Sapphire is distilled using the vapour infusion method.

Appearance: Crystal clear. **Aroma:** Fresh, complex nose with juniper, lemon zest and lemon meringue pie filling with pepper and Indian spice. **Taste:** Initially delicate, light and slightly sweet palate with juniper, lemon zest and coriander opens to reveal yet more lemon zest and strong peppery spiced notes. **Aftertaste:** Delicate lavender notes from the pine-ey juniper put up a valiant fight against a mixed pepper assault and a touch of chilli heat.

diffordsguide rating: ★ ★ ★ ★ ☆

BOMBAY SAPPHIRE EAST GIN
42% alc./vol.

Launched in September 2011, Bombay Sapphire East is the first Bombay Sapphire extension since the brand was launched 25 years earlier. This 'eastern' variant is distinctive due to the use of Thai lemongrass and Vietnamese black peppercorns and was created by Master of Botanicals, Ivano Tonutti.

These two Asian botanicals are used with the ten other botanicals shared with the original Bombay Sapphire gin: Italian juniper berries, West African grains of paradise, Spanish lemon peel, cubeb berries from Java, Moroccan coriander seeds, Cassia Bark from Indo-China, angelica root from Saxony, Spanish almonds, Italian orris root and Chinese liquorice. Like the original Bombay Sapphire gin, East is made using the vapour infusion method of distillation.

The first new botanical, Thai lemongrass, has a sweet citrus smell that adds depth to the gin, whilst the Vietnamese black peppercorns imparts a spicy heat.

Appearance: Crystal clear. **Aroma:** Coriander, juniper and citrus with hints of Olbas oil tablets. **Taste:** Juniper, citrus and coriander flavours predominate with liquorice, parma violet and an underlying rootiness. Superbly structured. **Aftertaste:** Lingering juniper freshness with liquorice and parma violets.

diffordsguide rating: ★ ★ ★ ★ ★ ✦

Producer: The Bombay Spirits Company (Bacardi), Laverstoke Mill, London Road, Laverstoke, England
www.bombaysapphire.com

"The 22 native Islay botanicals used in The Botanist are all hand-picked from the island's hills, peat bogs and coastal shores."

The Botanist Islay Dry Gin

Argyll, Scotland

Botanist Dry Gin is distilled on Islay by Bruichladdich, the noted single malt whisky distillers, with nine traditional classic gin botanicals and 22 hand-picked native Islay botanicals in a copper pot-still nicknamed 'ugly betty'.

Pronounced 'Brew-Ick-Laddie' and meaning 'shore bank' in Gaelic, the Bruichladdich distillery was built in 1881 by the Harvey brothers on the western shore of Loch Indaal, making it the most westerly working distillery in Scotland.

Nicknamed the 'Laddie' distillery, it was mothballed in 1994, but Murray McDavid, an independent whisky bottler led by Mark Reynier and backed by local investors took it over Bruichladdich in 2001. Mark persuaded Jim McEwan, the respected distiller, native islander and raconteur to leave his position as distillery manager at Bowmore, the Islay distillery where he started work in 1963 as a cooper, to become production director at Bruichladdich. Since then, Jim has overseen whisky, and more recently also gin production at Bruichladdich.

BOTANIST GIN PRODUCTION

Bruichladdich's managing director, Mark Reynier, had the idea to produce an Islay gin, and in January 2010 repairs to Scotland's oldest wash still (built 1881) necessitated its temporary removal, requiring a large hole to be knocked into the still house wall (this is now a large window). At the same time space in the still room was freed up by the removal of the pot ale vat, intermediate spirits receiver and feints charger, presenting the opportunity for the installation of a gin still.

Initially resistant to the idea of distilling a gin, Jim McEwan rapidly became the most enthusiastic exponent, tasting other gins on the market and looking to his native home for the new gin's signature botanicals. He also enthusiastically set about looking for a suitable still. When Mark and the other investors set about re-instating Bruichladdich, due to limited funds they did so with existing and acquired second-hand equipment. Perhaps, with this in mind, when the gin project was being developed at no time was buying a new custom-made still even considered. Enter 'Ugly Betty'.

The 11,600 litre Lomond pot-still used to distil The Botanist was rescued from the old Inverleven Distillery and is so-called due to its unshapely appearance. She is the last known surviving example of an experimental cross between a Coffey still and a pot still developed after the Second World War by chemical engineer Alistair Cunningham and draftsman Arthur Warren at Hiram Walker.

The Lomond still was designed so that it could imitate the style of distillate produced by numerous other stills by adding or removing sections of its thick, column-like neck, so replicating the effect of different still "neck" lengths. One section housed three fin-like baffles which could be could be opened in varying degrees from horizontal to vertical, so also varying the amount of reflux by moving the internal fins.

Built by Ramsden of London, Betty was the first Lomond still to be built and was originally installed in

1959 at Inverleven, the single malt distillery within the grounds of the huge Dumbarton grain distillery complex, just outside Glasgow. Inverleven single malt itself was made in a pair of regular pot stills while Betty was used to make a single malt named after the nearby Loch Lomond – hence Betty and the other similar stills which followed her, became known as Lomond stills. Incidentally, a Lomond still remains in use at Scapa distillery in Orkney but the internal baffles have long since been removed due to their constantly needing cleaning, involving taking the still to pieces.

Betty is the last Lomond still operating with its internal baffle plates still operational but Jim McEwan has had other modifications made to Betty's top two neck sections. Above the section which houses the Lomond baffle fins he has had another section added which houses 80 copper tubes arranged in a honeycomb pattern. Referred by some to as "Jim's Gatling Gun", this slows the rate at which the vapour rises through Betty's wide neck and also introduces the vapour to a large surface area of copper which removes any sulphates. Many believe that this additional copper contact also softens the spirit. The top section of the still is a water box, cooled by cold water continually being piped through the section so causing reflux and slowing down the passage of vapour to the lyne arm.

Jim not only modified the still itself, he also added a botanical chamber to the middle of the lyne arm. This is used to hold a bag of the more delicate botanicals, particularly the leaves and petals which are hand-picked on the island. The vapour must pass through these botanicals, so extracting their flavour. A return leg pipe in the base of the botanical chamber allows some further reflux back into the still's neck.

Nine traditional botanicals (wild Islay juniper berries, cassia bark, angelica root, coriander seed, cinnamon bark, lemon and orange peel, liquorice root and oris root) form the Botanist's base flavour, augmented with 22 native Islay botanicals.

The 22 native Islay botanicals used are all hand-picked by retired husband and wife botanists, Richard and Mavis Gulliver. They forage the islands hills, peat bogs and coastal shores to collect the botanicals and then prepare them for use in distillation, filling the bags used in the stills botanical basket. The botanicals are used dried or fresh, dependent on their availability – obviously more fresh leaves are available year round than flowers.

BOTANIST'S ISLAY BOTANICALS

The other, more traditional botanicals (barks, seeds and peels) are steeped in the pot still itself in the traditional manner. Betty is charged with 12,000 litres of wheat neutral spirit reduced in strength to around 50% alc./vol. using water from the nearby James Brown Spring at Octomore. Named after the farmer who owns the land where the spring emerges, the water is carried the two miles to the distillery in tanks several times a week.

In the evening prior to a gin distillation, Jim starts the still to raise Betty's temperature just to the point when she can barely be touched. He then starts loading the botanicals into the still, carefully floating

ENGLISH NAME	SCIENTIFIC NAME	BOTANICAL CHARACTERISTICS
1. **Apple Mint**	Mentha x villosa	Sweet, delicate, menthol and apple
2. **Birch leaves**	Betula pubescens	Spring woodlands
3. **Sweet Chamomile/Roman Chamomile**	Chamaemelum nobile/Anthemis nobilis	Sweet, ripe apple
4. **Creeping Thistle flowers**	Cirsium arvense	Honey
5. **Elderflowers**	Sambucus nigra	Pungent, earthy, hint of musk
6. **Whin Gorse flowers**	Ulex europaeus	Coconut
7. **Heather flowers**	Calluna vulgaris	Honey
8. **Hawthorn flowers**	Crataegus monogyna	Heady, sweet, sharp, aniseed undertones
9. **Lady's Bedstraw flowers**	Galium verum	Sweet new mown hay
10. **Lemon Balm**	Mellissa officinalis	Fresh, sweet, lemon, green tea
11. **Meadow Sweet**	Filipendula ulmaria	Heady, sweet, summer meadows
12. **Peppermint leaves**	Mentha x piperita	Strong menthol
13. **Mugwort leaves**	Artemissia vulgaris	Oily musk tones
14. **Red Clover flowers**	Trifolium pratense	Sweet honey, brown sugar, machair scent
15. **Sweet Cicely**	Myrrhis odorata	Aniseed, myrrh, faint camphor
16. **Sweet Gale/Bog Myrtle leaves**	Myrica gale	Warm, sweet, summery
17. **Tansy**	Tanacetum vulgare	Strongly aromatic, pungent
18. **Thyme leaves**	Thymus valgaris	Strong, sweet, piquant, aromatic
19. **Water Mint leaves**	Mentha aquatica	Aromatic, menthol, refreshing
20. **White Clover**	Trifolium repens	Honey, hint of vinegar, machair scent
21. **Wood Sage leaves**	Teucrium scorodonium	Camphor, sage
22. **Spearmint/Garden mint**	Mentha spicata	Strong menthol

them on the surface of the hot spirit. Using juniper berries and coriander which readily float first, Jim builds a botanical raft. The heat gradually causes the berries to pop and the botanicals sink. The steam is turned off and the still and its contents left to steep overnight. Distillation starts the next morning.

Betty has a disproportionately large number of steam heating pipes running across her base, allowing very precise delivery of heat. Jim runs Betty at a low, constant pressure for the slow simmer 17-hour distillation, so gently coaxing complex aromatics from the botanicals.

The final gin distillate is reduced to bottling strength using the same locally sourced spring water as is used in distillation. No sugar or other additives are added and filtration is simply a pad filter at ambient temperature to remove any particles – no chill filtration is used.

Unusually, in common with Bruichladdich's single malts, bottling takes place at the distillery's own onsite bottling hall which was completed in May 2003 and is named after the Harvey Brothers who originally built the distillery in 1881. On site bottling necessitates the bottles (made by France's Saver Glass), capsules, boxes and labels being brought onto the island by ferry for filling, labelling and packing, before being shipped back to the mainland for distribution. This obviously adds significantly to the cost of bottling but the folk at Bruichladdich passionately believe in the use of local water for hydration at the bottling stage and want to keep their products estate-produced as far as possible. This led me to question why they don't distil their own wheat spirit – watch this space.

THE BOTANIST ISLAY DRY GIN

Appearance: Crystal clear.
Aroma: Incredibly pungent, resiny pine, juniper and eucalyptus-led with subtle Parma Violets, heather, candied ginger and sage.
Taste: Dry, juniper with sappy pine dominating but with an integrated herbal complexity and faint liquorice sweetness.
Aftertaste: Junipery pine dominance continues in the clean finish with faint lingering Parma Violets and liquorice. A robust gin.
diffordsguide rating: ★ ★ ★ ★ ★ ✦

Producer: Bruichladdich Distillery Company Ltd, Bruichladdich, Isle of Islay, Argyll, Scotland.
www.bruichladdich.com

"As well as drawing on Celtic heritage, Caorunn takes advantage of Scotland's reputation for whisky distilling."

Caorunn Scottish Gin
Balmenach Distillery, Moray, Scotland

Caorunn, pronounced 'ka-roon', is the Gaelic word for rowan berry which, along with dandelion, bog myrtle, heather and Coul Blush apple, comprise the five Celtic botanicals out of 11 total botanicals used to flavour this proudly Scottish gin.

As well as drawing on Celtic heritage, Caorunn takes advantage of something else uniquely Scottish: the country's reputation for whisky distilling. Caorunn draws upon these skills and is, in fact, made by a whisky distiller, Simon Buley at the Balmenach (single malt whisky) distillery in the Scottish Highlands.

THE BALMENACH DISTILLERY

The Balmenach distillery lies in the Speyside whisky region within the Cairngorm National Park at the foot of the Haughs of Cromdale. The distillery is situated on a road which runs through the nearby village of Cromdale towards one of the oldest crossing points of the River Spey. Ruins of an old castle stand on the hill of Tom Lethendry behind the distillery, where in 1690 Jacobite soldiers took refuge after the battle of the Haughs of Cromdale.

In the early 1800s, three brothers, the McGregors from Tomintoul, set up a farm on the land with one of the brothers, James, operating an illicit still. In 1823 the Excise Act, which sanctioned the distilling of whisky in return for a licence fee and payment of duty per gallon, was enacted. The following year, in 1824, James obtained one of the new licences, so formally establishing his distillery under the name Balminoch, making it one of the oldest distilleries in the Speyside region.

The present-day Balmenach name was introduced in 1897 when the distillery was incorporated as the Balmenach Glenlivet Distillery Company. The distillery remained in the hands of the McGregor family until 1922 when it was acquired by a consortium which in turn went onto become part of Distillers Company Limited (DCL), which we know today as Diageo.

Balmenach was mothballed in 1993 and lay silent until 1998 when its present owners, Inver House Distillers, acquired the distillery and resumed Scotch whisky production in March of the same year.

CAOUNN'S BOTANICAL RECIPE

When Inver House Distillers decided to start making gin, Simon Buley, one of the malt whisky distillers at the Balmenach Distillery, and something of a gin aficionado, was tasked with creating the new gin. He lives near the distillery and it was to the hills of the National Park in which the distillery sits that he looked for both inspiration and ingredients.

Consequently, while Caorunn's recipe includes six traditional gin botanicals: juniper, coriander, lemon peel, orange peel, angelica root and cassia bark, its character comes from five Celtic botanicals, all of which grow profusely in the countryside surrounding the distillery. These are rowan berries, Coul Blush apple, heather, bog myrtle and dandelion.

Rowan berries – these are sharp-tasting piquant red berries and in Celtic mythology the rowan is known as the Traveller's Tree because it was believed to prevent travellers from losing their way. Rowan wood's density

made it popular for walking sticks and its branches were often used as dowsing rods. As well as being crucial to Caorunn Gin's flavour it also inspired its name. In Gaelic the word for rowan berry is Rudha-an (literally meaning 'red one' and pronounced similarly to English rowan) or more usually, Caorunn (pronounced 'ka-roon').

Heather – covers the Scottish Highlands and lends subtle perfumed undertones with a nuance of honey to Caorunn.

Bog Myrtle – is a deciduous shrub which commonly grows in the peat bogs of the Highlands and gives Caorunn soft, sweet resinous aromas.

Dandelions – have long been used as a herb and impart just a hint of sharpness to Caorunn.

Coul Blush Apple – Britain's most northerly apple first fruited in Coul, Ross-shire in 1827. It has golden coloured skin and sweet, soft, cream flesh.

CAORUNN GIN PRODUCTION

Caorunn Gin is made in the former cask-filling store which sits alongside the still room of the Balmenach malt whisky distillery. The old oak spirit receiver – the huge wooden vat which used to hold the spirit which flowed from the stills before filling the casks – still dominates the space.

Caorunn is made slightly differently from other London-style gins – it's Scottish, after all – but still qualifies as a London Gin. A vapour infusion method is used instead of steeping, but while some other gins are

also made by vapour infusion, no other uses a 'Copper Berry Chamber'. This piece of equipment was made in the 1920s, and was originally used for the manufacture of perfumes. The chamber is round and contains four large trays on which the botanicals are spread. As the alcohol vapour slowly rises up through the perforated copper trays it picks up the flavours of the botanicals.

The chamber body itself is made from copper and the trays are made from stainless steel. The insulation is also copper. The internal diameter of the chamber is 91cm with a copper frame that holds the four drawer-like perforated horizontal copper trays which present a large surface area of both botanicals and copper. (A much larger surface area than is presented in either the small chambers modern stills incorporate into their lyne arm for vapour infusion, or even the basket at the atop a Carterhead still). The copper helps remove sulphates from the spirit and some say softens the gin.

Simon accurately weighs each of the 11 botanicals using a set of Avery scales and carefully spreads some of each botanical evenly over each of the four trays. Although he is understandably cagey about the proportions of each botanical used, he did tell us that each batch uses just under 20kg of botanicals.

Caorunn is distilled in small batches, each using 1,000 litres of wheat grain neutral spirit which is held in Vat No.2. (The old vats and distilling equipment used have been re-commissioned for use in Caorunn Gin production so consequently are named according to their original plate numbers, rather than the order in which they are used.)

The alcohol runs from Vat No. 2 into Vaporiser No. 2 (nicknamed 'Little Rocket') where it is heated by a steam jacket to produce an alcohol vapour which is piped into the bottom of the berry chamber. Two diffusers ensure the vapours are evenly distributed and directed to rise up through the copper trays spread with botanicals. The now botanical infused vapour leaves the top of the chamber and is piped into the condenser where it cools and returns the alcohol to liquid. This is collected in Vat No. 1. Once the liquid has picked up the flavours and taste of the botanicals the liquid (now Caorunn) is diverted to Vat No. 3.

This process continues until Vat No.2, the first vat which holds the base neutral spirit, is empty. At this point Simon opens and closes valves to direct first runnings of weakly flavoured spirit from Vat No. 1 into Vaporiser No.2 and then back up through the botanicals as vapour a second time. Now with more concentrated botanical flavours, the vapour passes through the condensor and this time into Vat No. 3 as concentrated Caorunn Gin.

The whole process takes around seven hours and the initial 1,000 litres of neural spirit yields around 945 litres of gin spirit which is reduced with purified Scottish water to a bottling strength of 41.8% alcohol by volume.

THE BOTTLE

Caorunn is a proudly Scottish gin so fittingly the bottle designers were inspired by Celtic art and the Scottish Art Nouveau movement. Both the pentagon-shaped bottle and the symbolic asterisk represent the five Celtic botanicals used to flavour Caorunn and this is even reflected in the bottle's base.

Appearance: Crystal clear. **Aroma:** Floral, citrus nose with spicy pine-fresh juniper. **Taste:** Fresh, clean, slightly sweet palate which quickly turns dry with good juniper notes, zesty citrus, delicate spice and floral flavours. **Aftertaste:** Long, cleansing, lightly spiced piney juniper finish which fades with cracked black pepper. **diffordsguide rating:** ★ ★ ★ ★ ★

SIGNATURE SERVE

Like most gins, it is recommended that Caorunn is served as a Gin Martini or Gin & Tonic. However, unusually, its makers recommend serving with a slice of freshly cut red apple to enhance its fresh, clean and crisp taste.

Producer: Balmenach Distillery, Cromdale, Moray, Scotland.
www.caorunngin.com

ALCOHOL FEED TANK
VAT 2
CAPACITY
4,275 LTRS.

"Having made an award-winning vodka, and with a farm on which to grow fresh botanicals, gin seemed an obvious development for Chase."

Chase Elegant Crisp Gin

Little Marcle, Herefordshire, England

A Herefordshire potato farmer of 20 years, William Chase decided he'd had enough of the drudgery of selling a commodity to supermarkets and in 2002 hit upon the idea of turning his potatoes into 'Tyrrells Hand Cooked Potato Chips'. Having successfully made his crisps a household name he then set about turning his crop into what has become an award-winning potato vodka. His apple orchard then proved the inspiration for a gin.

The commercial success of Chase Distillery and its growing portfolio of products is a reflection of how well its field-to-glass formula – the Herefordshire-based farm and distillery grows its own potatoes, which it then ferments, distils and bottles itself – has won favour with discerning drinkers. But more than that, the launch of a premium vodka and gin off the back of the jaw-droppingly successful Tyrells crisps business, itself born out of bankruptcy, is a classic tale of triumph over adversity.

Looking back at what was arguably one of the most stressful times of his life, William Chase sees an almost comic chink of light in the darkness. It's 1992 and William, then aged 30, was another victim of a diminishing agricultural sector that seemed to have put pay to his career as a farmer and seen him declared bankrupt.

Desperate to raise cash to get back on his feet, he was caught in the farcical situation of alternately making his home and farm buildings look attractive to potential investors, and then ugly the next in order to devalue the house as much as he could so he could afford to buy it back from the bank. "One moment I would be trying to make everything pretty when business angels were due round, then the next I'd be letting the grass grow really long and

leaving the rubbish out," he laments. "It all sounds a bit pathetic now, but at the time it felt like life or death."

For William, bankruptcy marked the end of a childhood dream. He had grown up on the farm and always wanted to be a farmer. Unfortunately, the diminishing returns of beef farming, even before the rampage of mad cow disease in the 1990s and the foot and mouth outbreak in the Noughties, meant that the business progressively struggled. "We just weren't making any money out of it. I had a £200,000 loan, was paying 27 per cent interest to the bank and things were getting tighter and tighter." In the days and months that followed, William hid away in his farmhouse, feeling at best inadequate and at worst a "social leper". He lost the 30 acres he had inherited from his mother and was faced with starting life from scratch again.

That he bounced back so quickly is a sign of his entrepreneurial spirit and tenacity – and some good fortune. "Every entrepreneur gets a bit of luck, and for me it was the development of the 'slow food' and organic market. The public suddenly wanted organic food and supermarkets were demanding 'pretty' potatoes." William was happy to oblige, and reinvented himself as a potato trader, sourcing potatoes from around the country and selling them in batches to retailers. At first, the margins were small, but the business model was sound and over the course of the next decade, the business grew. By the late 1990s, less than a decade after his insolvency, he was making £100,000 a year, trading 20,000 tonnes of potatoes annually and employing a handful of people. He'd still get up early, but instead of being out on the tractor, he sourced potatoes using three mobile phones.

But then the sector changed and supermarkets wanted to deal direct with farmers and William was looking for 'plan B'. Initially the 'B' stood for 'baked' – he thought there might be a market for pre-baked potatoes, but William had something of a potato epiphany when McCain rejected a batch of his potatoes in 2001 that were subsequently accepted by gourmet potato chip/crisp-maker Kettle Chips. Happily, he'd built back his farm to 20 acres by now, and saw a new route to market for his own potatoes.

The development of the gourmet crisp market chimed perfectly with the slow food movement, middle class consumers were tired of the standard cheese and onion/prawn cocktail variants but raring to buy hand-fired 'chips' from a new generation of producers in fancy delicatessens. "I looked into the market, saw a 30 per cent net profit, and quickly realised that unlike the other 'gourmet' crisp companies, which didn't have provenance or traceability, if I started making something myself I'd have an instant USP."

If the idea behind the company that would become Tyrells had been born, bringing it into reality was somewhat harder to accomplish. "These days, you'd just Google 'how to make crisps'. But Kettle Chips refused to tell me, so I flew to America and visited another gourmet crisp company, Cape Cod. They only let me look through the windows. I thought I was going to have to come home empty-handed. But then I heard about a brand of crisps made in rural Pennsylvania by an Amish community. They were far more open, showed me the equipment I would need and where to source it, and they taught me how to make chips – how to cut them, fry them and cook

them. What I thought would be a trip of a few days turned into two weeks and on the plane back I was ecstatic."

He worked quickly and, having had the idea in October 2001, by April William's Hereford farm boasted an up-and-running crisp factory, named after Tyrrells Court, the farm he grew up on. He managed to get his crisps listed at various farm shops and large independents, including Harvey Nichols, but his big break came with upscale supermarket Waitrose. Although he was initially rejected by its buyers, the PA to its chief executive said he could leave a sample with her and he left a box of his vegetable crisps. The phone duly rang and William had lucked out, winning a listing at one of the UK's most influential supermarket chains. After that, the phone didn't stop ringing as other retail chains sought to emulate their competitor.

William turned his attention to marketing, deliberately featuring saucy vintage images and Victorian nudes, hoping to spark controversy and a complaint in the conservative press that would give him a name for being eccentric and British. The uproar followed with stories about the nascent crisp maker appearing in the *Daily Mail* and the *Daily Express*, helping Tyrells turn over a cool £500,000 in its first year's trading. A further boost came in 2007 when he was crowned regional winner in the Bank of Scotland's Corporate Entrepreneur Challenge, netting him a £5m interest-free loan which contributed to the purchase of the 400-acre neighbouring Rosemaund Farm.

Shifting focus to his next obsession, the idea for producing a vodka had actually taken root four years prior when, during a holiday in the Caribbean, he got to

talking to an American who had a bottle of Chopin vodka. Historically, William was a gin drinker and had been unimpressed with vodka, but this creamy, rich, potato-based vodka gave him a glimpse of what could be achieved. He realised what a brand story he would have if he used the very potatoes he grew to create his own vodka. (Crucially, he had retained ownership of the farms that supplied the potatoes to Tyrells as well as his newly built distillery).

"I looked at it all and realised no-one in vodka went into the provenance of what they were selling – it was all about cocktails and Elton John. If shops could charge £35 for mass-produced vodka, I thought we could charge a premium for a single-estate vodka. And when I heard that a potato farmer in Jersey had applied for a licence to distil that spurred me into action and I got in touch with Christian Carl, the German still maker."

Almost entirely self-taught in the art of distilling, William would visit distilleries as he marketed Tyrells – in France, Hong Kong, America. He enlisted Jamie Baxter, his resident biochemist, technician and all-round boffin, to start looking into still designs and the technical challenges of turning their potatoes into vodka. Jamie's background was in food technology and, specifically, cereals: together, they were on a steep learning curve, about which sort of potatoes worked best, which enzymes they would need for fermentation and when to make the cuts.

Rosemaund Farm was previously a government-owned experimental hop farm and the building which now houses the distillery is a 1950s converted hop kiln barn lying derelict before William converted it into a modern distillery. William remembers when the distillery equipment arrived in 2007. He, Jamie and some farm hands unpacked and put the still together. "We spent about 12 months just creating mashbills, using different varieties and combinations of potatoes."

In 2008 William sold 75 per cent of Tyrrells to Langholm Capital, a private equity firm, netting him a whopping £40m. He retained ownership of the farms that supplied the potatoes to the crisp business as well as his newly built distillery, which remained outside of the deal. The first batch of what is still England's only potato vodka followed soon after in April 2008. "The biggest shock was when we put the first load through the still. I thought about the massive pile of potatoes we had started with, looked at the ten litres of spirit that came out, and realised that inefficiency was probably why no one used potatoes. For the next year I wondered what on earth I had done."

Incidentally, while the vodka was in development, there was never any question that it would share the Tyrells brand name. However, it quickly became clear that snack food branding was not appropriate for the sophisticated and glamorous world of international vodka, and his new vodka was quickly renamed, taking on his surname. Just as he'd done with Tyrell's, William now embarked on a marketing mission to get his vodka listed in retailers. By now, he was rich enough to have employed people to do that for him, but he says he "didn't want reps in shiny suits pushing something in people's faces" and preferred to convince discerning buyers of the merits of Chase vodka through his own passion.

The first willing recipients were small farm shops and

some larger independents such as Fortnum & Mason and Selfridge's. William would turn up in a 1952 Land Rover that had originally been bought for the farm, with the intention that they could run it using the vodka in some way. (He had bought a convertible Rolls-Royce after his £40m windfall, and briefly considered using this as a branded marketing tool, but rejected the idea as too flashy early on).

Persuading retailers to listen could be challenging but the on-trade proved another beast. William quickly realised that getting a product on a back-bar was one thing, whereas getting bartender buy-in required a bit more of a sell-in, to hammer home how Chase was, and remains, the UK's only distiller that grows, ferments, distils and bottles its own product. Reaching these opinion formers resulted in a suitably quirky two-day Rock Da Farm music festival attracting some 2,500 individuals, the majority bartenders.

Despite being well-received, sales were relatively slow at first, as William doggedly stuck to personal face-to-face sell-ins, but the still house now puts out an impressive 10,000 bottles a week, with a 70:30 domestic/export market split, though William wants to reverse this bias.

William's son Harry is equally passionate about the family's farming operations – of which he is now in charge – and when visiting the distillery and driving around Rosemaund Farm it becomes clear that it is not only potatoes which the Chase family farm here. Sure, there are rolling fields of potatoes but there are also apple orchards, cereal crops and grazing Herefordshire cattle.

Part of the reason for this is due to the effect growing potatoes has on the soil, meaning you can only cultivate potatoes in a field every one year in five. This is great news for James, William's other son, who is key to marketing the vodka in the all-important high-end bars, as the diversity of produce from the farm has already led to the production of a range of liqueurs – and a very successful cider-based gin.

Having made an award winning vodka, and with a farm on which to grow his own fresh botanical ingredients, making a gin seemed an all-too obvious development for Chase. However, a gin made from a potato vodka did not have quite the right ring to it. Most people would simply have followed convention and used grain – most likely wheat – and the Chase family already grew cereal crops on their farm. However, William being William decided to experiment. He looked elsewhere on the farm and decided to distil from fermented apples – cider, that is.

Chase uses its own organically grown cider apples, ferments them into cider, then distils vodka using the same stripping still and rectification column used to make potato vodka. At this stage the rectified apple spirit is diluted with the farm's own well-purified water and bottled as Naked Chase Vodka.

Chase Elegant Crisp Gin is finished in a 450-litre purpose made Carl steam jacket-heated copper pot still, topped with a single bubble plate and small reflux condenser. A vapour botanical chamber sits in the Lyne arm forcing the vapours to pass through a pillowcase loaded with the botanicals within the chamber on their way to the condenser.

The still is charged with rectified cider spirit at 96%

alc./vol. diluted back to 45% alc./vol. with well-purified water before the eleven botanicals are added. Heads, of around ten litres, are discarded before a heart of around 200 litres can be collected at an average of 72% alc./vol.. Chase cuts to tails at around 65% alc./vol.. Chase is what some would refer to as a 'two-shot' gin as the botanical flavoured distillate is cut 50/50 with neutral cider distillate before being hydrated to bottling strength with well-purified water.

Eleven botanicals are used: juniper, coriander seeds, angelica seeds, angelica root, liquorice root, orris root, orange and lemon peel, hops, dried elderflower and fresh Bramley apples cut into eighths. The small amount of hops used not only balance the palate but are a fitting reminder of the distillery building's heritage as a hop kiln barn.

The already decorated screen-printed bottles are filled and hand-sealed by literally bashing each cork stopper in with a mallet and the capsule applied by hand over the top. Each bottle is then hand-packed. At present, the hand-bottling operation takes place in the still hall itself but an adjoining newly built space 'clean-room' stands ready to house the small bottling line which is quickly becoming essential for Chase to keep up with demand. William is adamant that Chase will remain estate-grown, estate-distilled and estate-bottled – a truly field-to-glass operation.

All in all, William is pleased to have changed from crisps to spirits. "We're not just chopping up and cooking potatoes anymore," he says. "Distilling is more of a science, and we've gone from making people fat to making people happy."

CHASE ELEGANT CRISP GIN
48% alc./vol.

Appearance: Crystal clear. **Aroma:** Clean, subtle nose with good piny juniper aromas and zesty citrus notes. **Taste:** (reduced to approx 43%) Leads with spicy hop and piney juniper with more subtle floral elderflower and spiced apple. Spicy and barky in style rather than being light and zingy but very full flavoured and strong enough to stand up to tonic. **Aftertaste:** Spicy finish with bursts of dry liquorice and a pleasingly spicyness.
diffordsguide rating: 4/5

Producer: Chase Distillery Ltd, Laddin Farm, Little Marcle, Herefordshire, England.
www.chasedistillery.co.uk

"15kg of olives are used in each distillation batch of Gin Mare, along with hand-picked juniper from the Giró Ribot family's estate."

Gin Mare Mediterranean Gin

Barcelona, Spain

Pronounced 'mar-ray', this Mediterranean gin is made in a 19th-century chapel on the outskirts of Barcelona, Spain and flavoured with botanicals from the region.

Gin Mare is made in the small Spanish fishing town of Vilanova i la Geltrú on the Costa Dourada (literally 'golden coast') in a former chapel which sits in the grounds of the family-owned Destilerias MG. What, I hear you ask, is a chapel doing in the grounds of a distillery? Well, the property was originally a monk's retreat, which the Giró Ribot family bought in the 1950s to house its growing drinks business.

The chapel which now houses Gin Mare's pot still used to stand on the town's beach and is where local fishermen would pray for a good catch and a safe return before they set out to sea. In the 18th century the monks moved the chapel from the beach, brick-by-brick, after the town's mayor decided the chapel was detrimental to the beach, the town's major asset.

Barcelona is only 50 kilometres away but the bustling city is a world away from the relaxed way of life of the town of Vilanova i la Geltrú on the Catalonian coast, between Cunit and the mouth of the Ebro River. As Barcelona grew, so the small fishing town became popular as a weekend retreat for Barcelona city dwellers, attracted by the town's splendid sandy beach, hence the mayor's insistence that the chapel was moved as the beach, rather than the fishing industry, started to drive the town's economy.

The Giró Ribot family have been making aromatic cordials and dealing in wine since 1835 – after all, this is the Penedés wine region. By the early 1900s, they had also become distillers of brandy and whisky. During the Spanish civil war, Manuel Giró Sr was hiding in the local mountains when he noticed an abundance of juniper bushes growing there. So began the family's connection with gin, and in 1940 it launched the highly successful Gin MG brand which is now one of the best-selling gins in Spain.

Brothers Marc and Manuel Giró Jr, the grandsons of Manuel Giró Sr, represent the fourth generation of the distilling dynasty. They were raised to enter the family business and, in the shadow of the family's successful MG Gin, understandably wanted to assert their own contribution to the family business. They sought to create a new, truly-Mediterranean gin inspired by the area in which they grew up, using locally sourced botanicals.

The brothers realised that while they had the production skills necessary to produce a great gin they lacked marketing skills and a route to market. Hence, the brothers entered a strategic alliance with Global Premium Brands to develop Gin Mare, with the brand owned fifty-fifty by the Giró Ribot family and Global Premium Brands, with Global responsible for packaging, marketing and distribution of the brand.

In 2007, development of the new gin commenced with the family's highly experienced distillers using a mini pot still to test 45 different botanicals, each separately distilled and the resulting distillate assessed. The abundance of locally available botanicals made choosing which ones to use all the more difficult. Indeed, when forced to flee France during the

Right: Mark with some of
the 15kg of olives used in
each distillation.

revolution, the Monks of Chartreuse chose to establish
their abbey in nearby Tarragona, where they produced
the now collectable and very rare Tarragona Chartreuse
liqueur, using Catalonian botanicals in place of those
from their home in the French Alps.

The local Catalonian region is famous for its
Arbequina olives and, of the 45 botanicals the brothers
tried, these proved key to the creation of a genuinely
unique gin worthy of the region. Cultivation of the
prized Arbequina olive trees has remained organic and
the olives are harvested by hand so as not to bruise the
fruits, which are mainly pressed for extra virgin olive oil
production. Due to this variety's relatively small size and
low juice yield, Arbequina is one of the most expensive
olive oils available. To make Gin Mare, 15 kilos of olives
are used in each distillation batch. These are broken
with an electric crusher prior to maceration in the still.

Along with the Arbequina olives, Gin Mare uses
rosemary, basil and thyme from the Mediterranean
along with more traditional gin botanicals: coriander,
cardamom, citrus and, of course, juniper berries, which
are hand-picked from the Giró Ribot family's own estate
in Teruel. The variety of juniper which grows
abundantly on the family's land produces a berry with a
very soft skin. The family says these wild juniper berries
are vital to the flavour of its gins, and only these hand-
picked berries are used to make Gin Mare.

The citrus (cítricos) maceration also has
Mediterranean origins and is a blend of sweet oranges
from Seville, bitter oranges from Valencia and lemons
from Lleida. The fruits come to the distillery whole and
are hand-peeled to produce long zests which are
macerated in French-made barley neutral spirit for a
year in stainless steel flagons. Each maceration has 14kg
of peel macerating in 40 litres of neutral spirit reduced
from 96% alc./vol. to around 50% alc./vol. Presently, a
year's production calls for 200kg of orange peels and
80kg of lemon peels. To put that in perspective, even
when expertly peeled, it requires 8 to 9kg of fruit to yield
just one 1kg of peel.

Of the other botanicals, the thyme (tomillo)
comes from Turkey, basil (albahaca) from Italy,
rosemary (romero) from Greece, coriander seeds
(coriandro) from Morocco and cardamon
(cardamomo) from Sri Lanka. While the trio of citrus
zests are macerated together, most of the other
botanicals are macerated separately for more than 36
hours and then individually distilled.

The custom-made Florentine still used has a 250-
litre capacity and this is filled with 200 litres of botanical
maceration, or in the case of the olives, fresh olives and
neutral alcohol reduced from 96% alc./vol. to 50%
alc./vol. The still takes around one-and-a-half hours to
reach the 80°C necessary for distillation to start.
Roughly the first five litres of the run are discarded
before the heart starts to run and around 105 litres is
produced from each batch before switching to the tails,
of which there are approximately 90 litres. Each batch
takes between four to four-and-a-half hours to distil.

The stainless steel jug used to fill the still has a mark
showing 30 litres and is a replica of a jug used at the
distillery for over 30 years. The original literally wore
out over time and until the new replica jug was made
there was a concern that the distillery's recipes would be

corrupted by the use of a different measuring jug. It was not so much concern about the measure being exact as the distillers' 'feeling' they had measured the correct quantity: distillation is an art as much as a science and years of experience mean, like driving a car, much of the distillation process is instinctive.

In all, six different distillations are produced and these are carefully blended with neutral spirit and purified water to make Gin Mare. The mixture is bottled a few hundred metres away from where it is distilled, in the main plant next to the chapel.

A Latin motto runs around the stained glass window above the chapel's door, and also appears on the bottle: "Mundus appellatur caelum, terra et mare". It translates as "the world is called heaven, earth, and the sea". This, and the fact the chapel, which now houses the distillery, used to sit on the town's beach, helps to explain the origins of the name Gin Mare, literally 'Sea Gin'. Although the brand's inspiration was 'Mare Nostrum', the modern usage of which embraces the full diversity of Mediterranean cultures.

Incidentally, that Latin motto is not the only embellishment on the otherwise white walls of the chapel. The domed ceiling above the Gin Mare still – which sits in the area where the altar would have been – is covered with a fresco painted by Joachim Mir in 1928 which represents the convergence of heaven, earth and sea.

The Giro brothers and Global Premium Brands launched Gin Mare in 2008. While the brothers oversee the production of Gin Mare as an annex to their family's main distilling business, it is Global which handles product development, marketing and distribution of Gin Mare. Indeed, while few bartenders around the world will have met either Marc or Manuel, there is surely not a high-end bar in any of the world's major cities that has not received a visit from Gin Mare's enthusiastic Chilean brand ambassador Jorge Balbontin.

When I visited the distillery in April 2012, there was much excitement as the first sample of the slightly tweaked new bottle had just arrived. While a very similar shape to the original Gin Mare bottle, the new design is slightly taller and has a diagonal section sliced from its base. Patience and a steady hand prove it is possible to stand the bottle on the diagonal, so it sits balanced at an angle – surely a new bar game in the making.

GIN MARE

Appearance: Crystal clear. **Aroma:** Spicy nose with herbaceous notes reminiscent of a humid pine forest filled with tomato plants. Subtle rosemary and black olives. **Taste:** Boldly flavoured palate bursts open with juniper and fresh coriander before turning bitter with spicy notes of thyme, rosemary and basil (as promised on the label). **Aftertaste:** Slightly bitter finish has green olive notes with cardamom and basil. A gin offering genuinely different flavours.
diffordsguide rating: ★★★★☆

Producer: Destilerías Miquel Guansé, Vilanova i la Geltrú, Barcelona, Spain.
www.destileriasmg.com

"Thomas Dakin, Greenall's first distiller, started production in 1761, and his botanical recipe is used to this day."

STILL No 5

Steam   Column   Condenser

29/0480
S9786
BERKELEY SQUARE
DRUM
Nº'S 251 — 2?

G&J Greenall Distillery

Warrington, Cheshire, England

At its Warrington distillery, G&J Greenall distils and bottles Bombay Dry and Bombay Sapphire under contract for Bacardi-Martini. It also produces own-label gins for most of the UK's supermarket chains. When it comes to making its own gin, it does so with the benefit of some considerable experience. Indeed, G&J Greenall is England's oldest continuous gin distiller.

Its story begins in 1760, when Thomas Dakin built his distillery on Bridge Street in Warrington, north-western England. The grain harvests of the preceding few years had been so poor that the government prohibited gin manufacture in order to maintain the grain supply for bread making. This had delayed the project and Dakin did not start distilling until 1761.

Back in 18th century Warrington, easy access to both the river Mersey and the canal network meant the town was at the centre of trade routes between London and Liverpool, ideally situated to take full advantage of the Industrial Revolution. This gave Dakin, then a young entrepreneur, a ready supply of the botanicals and other raw ingredients he needed to make a top quality gin. It also gave him easy access to markets where he could sell it.

Warrington's location also helped it become a centre of scientific knowledge and technical expertise with its renowned Warrington Academy, home to notable luminaries including the scientist Joseph Priestley, and Reinhold Forster, Captain James Cook's botanist. No doubt Dakin did not have to look far for the best scientific advice of the day.

Thomas Dakin was one of the first of a new age of gin distillers who set out to distil gins of a much higher quality

than the 'mother's ruin' of his predecessors. The industrial age not only provided better stills and distilling technology, it also brought a more discerning customer base in the newly emerging middle classes. Dakin prospered until his death in the 1790s when the gin recipe passed to his son Edward Dakin, who took over the distillery. The precious recipe and the distillery continued to pass down the generations of the Dakin family.

Meanwhile, a mere twenty miles away in the Lancashire town of St Helens, a brewery which had been established in 1762 by Thomas Greenall was also prospering under the control of Thomas's sons Edward, William and Peter. The two familes' businesses came together in 1860, following the death of William Dakin, the founder's grandson, Edward Greenall leased Dakin's Bridge Street distillery and, in 1870, purchased the enterprise outright.

Incidentally, the 'G' & 'J' of the now familiar G&J Greenall comes from Edward Greenall's younger brothers, Gilbert and John, and in 1894 G&J Greenall became an incorporated company. Dakin's Warrington Gin was renamed Greenall's but continued to be made according to Dakin's original 1761 recipe.

Sadly a fire in 2005 destroyed much of Greenall's distillery, and with it most of the records from both the Dakin and Greenall's eras, so it is not known what stills Thomas Dakin used when he started out, nor what infusion method he used for his gin. However, it is known that the Greenall family followed Thomas Dakin's example and continued to invest in new technology to improve the quality of their gin.

Quite separately the brewing arm of the Greenall's family also experienced rapid growth and the successive

generations that followed Thomas Greenall built the business by acquisition of competing breweries and their tied pub estates to make what became known as Greenall Whitley, one of the largest regional brewers in the country. In 1923 Greenall Whitley's Chairman, Lord Gilbert Greenall (who was given the hereditary title First Baron Daresbury of Walton by King George V in 1927), decided to diversify into the distilling business through the acquisition of Gilbert & John Greenall Limited. Thus the brewing and distilling interests of the two branches of the Greenall's family were united.

By 1961, the company boasted more than 1,200 pubs and what had started as simple roadside inns had grown to become the Compass Hotels division. The distilling business also thrived and in 1961, two centuries after Dakin had established the original distillery, G&J Greenall moved to a larger site at Loushers Lane on the outskirts of Warrington. The new distillery was equipped with new, larger stills, a state-of-the art bottling hall and warehouses that allowed Greenall's to expand into contract distilling.

In the 1980s, the company then known as IDV (and now Diageo) bought the Bombay Gin brand but continued to contract G&J Greenall to produce it on their behalf. Up to that point the Greenall's and Bombay gins were made using the same recipe and, as I understand it, both gins were made using the vapour infusion method, where, unlike most gins, the botanicals are not steeped in spirit, instead specially adapted stills force the spirit vapour through the botanicals on its way to the condenser. I have previously been told that in order to differentiate the two gins, production of Greenall's Original was moved to pot stills and the more usual steeping process while

Bombay continued to be made by the vapour infusion method. However, Bacardi-Martini, the present owners of Bombay Gin, claims the vapour infusion method was developed specifically for Bombay Dry in the 1850s. Whatever the truth in this claim, Dakin's 1761 botanical recipe continued to be shared by the two gin brands (as it does to this day).

G&J Greenall was then contracted by IDV to produce and bottle Bombay Sapphire which was launched in 1988 based on the Bombay Dry recipe, using the same botanicals in much the same proportions but with the addition of cubeb berries and grains of paradise. Incidentally, Bacardi-Martini, who bought Bombay Dry and Bombay Sapphire from Diageo in 1997, continues to contract G&J Greenall to distil and bottle both brands on their behalf.

Then in 1989 the Monopolies and Mergers Commission introduced its 'Beer Orders' regulations effectively banning the 'tied house'. In 1991 this, coupled with overcapacity in Britain's brewing industry, forced Greenall Whitley to close its 230-year-old brewing operation. In turn 770 pubs and 69 budget lodges were sold to Scottish and Newcastle in 1999 for £1.1bn, The Belfry was sold to The Quinn Group in 2005 and the De Vere Hotels were sold to The Alternative Hotels Group, as was G&J Greenall.

In 2005, a fire at the Lousher's Lane Distillery totally destroyed G&J Greenall's bottling hall but fortunately the still house was saved and distilling resumed just a week later. The company took the opportunity to move to a new site in Risley, still in the Warrington area, where they built a brand new bottling hall and two new still houses for their precious 1960s copper stills – so spreading the risk

should there be another disaster in the future.

In 2006 the Greenall family connection was eventually severed when Lord Daresbury (a descendant of founder Edward Greenall) stepped down from the post of non-executive Chairman and much of the family's interest was sold. However, the company continues to proudly use the Greenall's family coat of arms and the motto, "I strive higher".

A WOMAN'S TOUCH

Joanne Simcock started working at G&J Greenall's laboratory whilst still a student and, after passing her degree in biochemistry, immediately started work at the distillery. After working her way from the lab to the still hall she eventually became the master distiller in 2006, the first woman in the gin industry to do so. She was then given the opportunity to create her own gin. As part of this project Joanne developed a gin flavour wheel which illustrates gins various botanicals flavours.

Joanne started with the traditional London Dry Gin core botanicals of juniper, coriander and angelica and says that these three botanicals work harmoniously as "juniper provides treble notes, coriander is the soprano, whilst angelica provides the base notes." To this melodic base Joanne added cubeb berries to give some fresh alpine notes. These four botanicals form the base to her two new gins, Bloom and Berkeley Square.

GREENALL'S ORIGINAL GIN
40% alc./vol.
Greenall's Original is made to Dakin's original 1761 recipe using eight different botanicals – juniper berries, coriander, lemon peel, angelica, orris, liquorice, cassia bark

and bitter almonds. These are macerated in wheat neutral spirit and purified water in a pot still for at least 24 hours prior to distillation. This allows the dried botanicals to rehydrate and start infusing their aromas into the spirit.

Greenall's gin is widely distributed by UK supermarkets and is a major player in Russia where its pre-mixed gin and tonic is a brand leader.

Appearance: Crystal clear. **Aroma:** Clean, coriander, juniper and angelica roots nutty, forest floor notes. Subdued citrus notes. **Taste:** Very classic London dry clean palate with surprisingly creamy mouthfeel. Juniper leads with liquorice, parma violet and cracked black pepper. **Aftertaste:** Nutty, balsa wood notes emerge in the finish where previously subdued citrus also shines. Lingering peppery minty freshness.
Diffordsguide rating: ★ ★ ★ ★ ⯪

GREENALL'S BLOOM GIN
40% alc./vol.
One day whilst sipping camomile tea, Joanne Simcock realised that edible flowers had not yet been used to make a gin and so naturally experimented with camomile flowers which she found added spearmint freshness to her base of juniper, coriander, angelica and cubeb berries. Next came honeysuckle flower stamens and their distinctive stewed floral note. Tests revealed that while these six botanicals worked well together, they needed a citrus note. Rather than using the predictable orange or lemon peel Joanne chose pomelo, a citrus fruit native to Southeast Asia and nicknamed Chinese Grapefruit. This has a very fragrant skin but contains little pulp – perfect for the distiller – and

although a variety of grapefruit, this seventh botanical actually adds an orangey note to the finished gin.

Bloom is made in a traditional copper pot still which is charged with wheat neutral spirit, demineralised fresh spring water and the botanicals, which like Greenall's other gins are left to steep for 24 hours prior to running the distillation. Bloom is a naturally sweet gin, due to the use of honeysuckle and pomelo and bottled without the addition of sugar or glycerol.

With its floral notes, Bloom is unashamedly a lady's gin and the heavily embossed bottle has flowering vines winding up its neck. The bottle also prominently features the 1761 date stamp, a reference to when Thomas Dakin, the company's first distiller started production.

Appearance: Crystal clear **Aroma:** Floral Parma Violet nose. **Taste:** Parma Violet also predominates the palate with honeysuckle and pomelo providing apparent sweetness and possibly contribute to the silky mouth feel. Soft sweet tangerine and chamomile balance delicate piney juniper. **Aftertaste:** Floral, fruity finish – reminiscent of liquorice and Turkish delight, with fresh black pepper and orange pine notes.
diffordsguide rating: ★★★★☆

BERKELEY SQUARE GIN
40% alc./vol.
Starting with a botanical base of juniper, coriander, angelica and cubeb berries, Joanne Simcock was inspired by the English Physic Garden in her quest to add a lightness, green-ness and fresh herbaceousness. Basil, known as 'the king of the herbs', was her first choice and

this adds peppery green tea notes to the gin. Sage came later as she searched for a botanical that would soften and round the high green notes of the basil. French lavender was an obvious choice but added heavy oily notes so she choose Kaffir lime leaves which add a sherbet lime note which cuts through the oiliness of the lavender.

Initial lab distillations of what was known as 'Recipe No.5' produced a fabulous gin so a larger scale test distillation was tried in the company's small 220 litre capacity No.8 Still, known as 'baby'. Much to the amusement of her fellow still workers this produced a green distillate. Not perturbed and learning from this, Joanne then made a further more gentle distillation with the basil, sage and lavender placed in a cotton bag in the style of a bouquet garni. Like other Greenall's gins this was left to steep for 24 hours before starting a much gentler distillation, running the still at a very slow rate to simmer rather than boil. This gentle reflux of the botanicals better allowed the release of the delicate essential oils and resulted in a perfectly clear distillate. The result was a very upmarket tasting gin so the name 'Berkeley Square' seemed appropriate.

Appearance: Crystal clear. **Aroma:** Deliciously aromatic nose with lime cordial, basil, crushed lavender, menthol eucalyptus and piney-freshness. **Taste:** Wonderfully balanced traditionally juniper led palate with a creamy mouthfeel. Obvious basil and sage influence. **Aftertaste:** Alpine-fresh finish with lingering lime, basil and sage.
diffordsguide rating: ★★★★★

Producer: G&J Greenall, Warrington, Cheshire, England. **www**.gjgreenall.co.uk

"Using vine flowers as a gin botanical was a somewhat unorthodox concept – the flowers otherwise go on to become grapes so are typically left untouched."

G'Vine Gin
Merpins, Cognac, France

Oenologist, raconteur and bon vivant – meet Jean-Sébastien Robicquet, the charismatic French wine-maker who successfully became a master distiller. Having turned his attention to gin, Jean-Sébastien, a characteristic nonconformist, looked to his local vineyards to provide an innovative new botanical to flavour his spirit.

Back in the 16th-century, the Robicquet family was heavily involved in the cognac business, and several members of the family were actually mayors of Cognac itself. Over the centuries, the family became less involved in cognac and more involved in viticulture in general, and, in particular, the significance that it exerted on French politics. Jean-Sébastien Robicquet's parents were instrumental in building the Assemblée des Régions Européennes Viticoles (AREV), an organisation of political and trade representatives of wine regions within the EU and Eastern Europe.

"The story of vines and wines was always there," recalls Jean-Sebastian. "I was born and raised in vineyards, forever picking grapes, playing with grapes."

He went on to study biology and oenology at university in Bordeaux, and then became a lawyer, though still focused on wine and spirits. "I did not envision being in a vineyard or producing wines and spirits without understanding what drives the business and the relationships between consumers and wine," he says.

He moved into sales and marketing, working for cognac house Hennessy in Singapore for three years, before returning to France in 1993, continuing to specialise in Asian trading. Staying within Louis Vuitton Moët Hennessy he then moved to fellow cognac house Hine. Suddenly ten years had passed, and he felt a calling back home in Cognac.

"I wanted to be free, to run my own destiny and to create things – even when I was at university I always said I wanted to make my own wine and spirits. I felt it was time to go back, to recreate and refurbish what was now in bits and pieces across Bordeaux and Cognac. It was a question of seeing who owned what, what vineyards and buildings there were and where they were."

Partly, this longing reflected something of a deep-seated feeling of responsibility towards grapes and their role in history and society. "I have a true belief in the virtue of grapes – in education, food, history and culture, grapes are part of building blocks of old Europe," he says. "I wanted to convey their virtue, the beauty of it all and the way they cement Europe. It's inspiring and dates back to the Romans – when soldiers retired they were given vine plants and wheat as gifts to settle in the place they were, hence the spread of the Latin culture in Gaule."

But what to make? Option one was to make cognac. The family had vineyards, buildings in which to distil and was familiar with the cognac fraternity. But this was 1999, cognac was in crisis, and Jean-Sébastien was worried about being a small fish among far more established players.

"I decided cognac wasn't the answer. Travelling the world, I realised white spirits was the fastest-growing area, and knowing that, according to the legal definitions, you can make them from any source of agricultural origin, then there is a huge number of opportunities."

The grapes that surrounded Jean-Sébastien could provide the necessary fermentable sugars to create spirits, including vodka and gin. "I was convinced we could bring 'nobility' to the categories – there's an expression 'grain for people, grapes for the king'. That was the beginning of his journey with grape-based white spirits and Jean-Sébastien was vindicated in his approach when Diageo asked him to make its ultra-premium vodka Cîroc. But that's another story.

It was during one warm evening at the end of May 1999 that Jean-Sébastien realized he should make gin. He'd been sipping cognac on the patio of the family's 16th-century farmhouse, when he had a sort of epiphany. He recalled how gin-makers were increasingly using strange botanicals from far-flung destinations. "I remember wondering why were they going abroad for botanicals, and, looking out over our own vineyards, which were flowering, thinking how we have some unique material here at home. All these other guys are putting exotic flowers in but we have the vines."

Using vine flowers as a gin botanical was a somewhat unconventional concept. It is the flowers that become the grapes themselves, and so they are typically left untouched on the vine. "But when you walk in the vineyards in June they smell so good and bewitch your senses. After all, you get tropical fruit flavours from Ugni Blanc grapes, buttery notes from Chardonnay, and red fruit and berry notes from Merlot – and in the flowers you get the precursor to the aromas you find later in the grape."

In addition to being unorthodox, using vine flowers as a botanical also had logistical challenges – they only bloom for 10-15 days, so are ephemeral by nature. "If you miss them you have to wait until next year."

So began a process of experimentation in 2002 to investigate if extracting the flowers' flavours was both possible and desirable. Jean-Sébastien and a small group including his business partners and his brother visited a newly planted vineyard – while they are young their grapes are not used to make wine – and hand-harvested 50kg of the tiny yellow flowers and their stems.

"I figured we had three options to extract: we could dry the flowers and infuse the spirit like a tea; create an infusion using fresh flowers; or extract the flowers' essential oils." Flower maceration in grape spirit was successful and Jean-Sébastien then re-distilled the mix in a Florentine pot still he had bought, to mix with various third party botanical infusions to create a gin. "It worked," he says. "The 2005 vintage was really good."

Not that his nearest and dearest were immediate converts. "It was just like when I started making vodka with grapes – everyone thought I was crazy. In history no one had done anything with the flowers. No one had ever had the argument. We were breaking the rules essentially, though my brother was enthusiastic."

He had everyone involved sign non-disclosure agreements during the distillation experiment and only a handful involved knew the full reasons the flowers were being used.

Luckily one thing worked in Jean-Sébastien's favour. During the Asian financial crisis in 1990-95 that dramatically impacted cognac sales, the region's grape growers wanted to diversify. They felt cognac was no longer enough and began to cultivate Merlot and Cabernet Sauvignon to make table wine. "But then that too collapsed and those growers had no market for their grapes. If they simply replanted to make cognac then they would still have to wait three years until they could use their grapes to make eau-de-vie."

Jean-Sébastien suddenly became these growers' fairy godfather – by renting him the land, so he could access the flowers from their vines, they could actually yield revenue per hectare. "I found one or two growers who embraced the idea. With others I didn't disclose what I was doing straight away. But I was basically a light at the end of the tunnel for a lot of them."

From that first successful distillate in 2005, by the end of 2006 he had a network of growers covering 50 hectares, all now devoted to cultivating vine flowers, and enabling Jean-Sébastien to build stocks of vine flower distillate. "The secret is that if you have a deal, you keep the deal. Good year, bad year, you have to take the flower."

Most of the intervening years have been largely kind. But the harvest in 2012 was bad. "We had a lot of rain, really chaotic weather, and while the flowers in each vineyard usually come in phases, blooming for 15 days or so, this year everything came at the same time." His 150-strong team of harvesters had to work double-time to ensure they got to all the flowers in time.

With his gin's USP proved, Jean-Sébastien now turned his attention to tweaking the other botanicals to reach his preferred formula. Much of this was, however, already done in his head. "When you're training to become an oenologist you spend weeks sniffing,

identifying defects and the quality of wine, and to identify flavours. I've a very sensitive nose, so you get to know molecules and flavours and you know that by blending this or that you'll reach such a result. So I already had 80 per cent of the formula done in my mind."

The rest of the hard work took place in his office at home. "It's where the chickens used to live. I have lots of drawers where I put everything, but it's really a big mess. Anyway, it was there that I analysed 20-30 gins, tried to identify what was their strengths and weakness and to define a level of spices, writing it all in notebooks and on my computer. Over four months I refined my recipe, while in the daytime we were also experimenting with infusion time, distillation and cuts, blending of the botanical distillates and redistilling them."

Fast forward to today, G'Vine has some 10 full-time staff and Jean-Sébastien has begun turning his attention to some new 'fun' products, including bottled cocktails (a Hanky Panky was released in 2011), an award-winning tequila, and a ground-breaking vermouth expected to be released in 2013. A limited edition G'Vine, made to one of the first recorded recipes of gin that was found in a London museum and calls for wine distilled on the lees, is also expected in late 2013.

PRODUCTION

Convention has it that gin is based on a neutral grain spirit, and indeed most of the world's gins are wheat neutral spirit based with a few breaking convention to use barley. Therefore G'Vine Gin is distinguished by its being based on grape spirit.

The grapes are harvested during autumn, and vinified before being distilled continuously. The fact that EWG Spirits & Wines distils its own neutral base spirit also sets it apart from most of the world's other gin distillers who invariably buy-in third-party distilled neutral spirit.

The two different expressions of G'Vine – 'Floraison' and 'Nouaison' each embody a different stage in the vine's life cycle. G'Vine Floraison made by macerating fleurs de vigne – the green flowers which blossom on the Ugni Blanc vine. In contrast, G'Vine Nouaison represents a later stage in the vines' development, when the fertilised vine flowers form tiny green berries that eventually ripen to become a juicy grape.

G'Vine Floraison Gin, the original of the two G-Vine expressions, is distinguished by a lime green screw cap, while G'Vine Nouaison is finished with grey detailing. Both are packaged in a stocky, round bottle with square shoulders.

G'VINE FLORAISON GIN
40% alc./vol.

G'Vine Floraison Gin is based on grape neutral spirit which is used to make five separate botanical infused spirits. The first is made by macerating fleurs de vigne – the green flowers of the Ugni Blanc vine; the others are made from more traditional fresh gin botanicals.

The use of vine flowers as a key botanical is the other distinguishing factor in G'Vine's production. The flowers blossom in mid-June and last a little over a week, so presenting an annual challenge of harvesting enough of the aromatic flowers in the short period they are available. If not immediately hand-picked in time

they will mature into grape berries. The delicate petals are put into small fabric bags and these are steeped in Ugni Blanc neutral spirit for several days and allowed to percolate before then being distilled in a small Florentine pot still.

The other fresh, whole-fruit, botanicals are sourced from all over the world and include juniper berries, ginger root, liquorice, cassia bark, green cardamom, coriander, cubeb berries, nutmeg and lime. These are sorted into four groups according to flavour profiles, such as sweet or spicy botanicals, then each group is independently steeped in grape spirit for two to five days before the four infused spirits are separately distilled in small bespoke pot stills.

The grape flower infusion and the infusions of the other botanicals are blended with water and more grape spirit and redistilled together in a copper pot still nicknamed 'Lily Fleur' to produce the final G'Vine Floraison distillate.

Appearance: (bot No. 05X07405) Crystal clear.
Aroma: Floral pot-pourri with zesty lime notes – almost lime cordial – and a hint of cardamom. **Taste:** Hints of rosewater, lime zest, cardamom and liquorice alongside some relatively subdued juniper. **Aftertaste:** Ginger builds and lasts through a long, dry lime zesty finish with liquorice still shouting from the wings.
diffordsguide rating: ★★★★☆

G'VINE NOUAISON
43.9% alc./vol.

Grape spirit is used in the five botanical infusions on which G'Vine Nouaison is based. The first is made by

steeping the tiny green berries formed after the vine flower (known in French as 'Nouaison') has been pollinated. These eventually ripen to become juicy grapes.

The other nine fresh, whole-fruit, botanicals used to flavour G'Vine Nouaison are prepared using the same process used to make its sister gin, Floraison. The botanicals, which include juniper berries, ginger root, liquorice, cassia bark, green cardamom, coriander, cubeb berries, nutmeg and lime are sorted into four groups which are then independently steeped in grape spirit for two to five days before the infused spirits are separately distilled in small bespoke pot stills.

Finally the infusions are blended in a different proportion to that used for G'Vine Floraison to create a more spicy spirit that's stronger in juniper and alcohol. Water and more grape spirit is added the blend and it is redistilled in a copper pot still affectionately nicknamed 'Lily Fleur'. After distillation, it will be hydrated to bottling strength to be sold as G'Vine Nouaison.

Appearance: (bot N0. 08B1460) Crystal clear
Aroma: Floral, mineral nose with aromas of juniper, coriander and lime zest with fainter hints of fresh root ginger and rose water. **Taste:** On the huge palate, piney juniper notes rightly predominate with fresh coriander right up there and lime zest close behind. Spicy notes of nutmeg, ginger and sweet liquorice follow with floral flavours. **Aftertaste:** Nouaison is bigger and spicier than G'Vine's Floraison making it more suited to traditionalist gin drinkers such as myself.
diffordsguide rating: ★ ★ ★ ★ ★

Producer: EWG Spirits & Wine, Villevert – Merpins, Cognac, France. **www.eurowinegate.com**

"The Hayman story starts with James Burrough, a London distiller who, in the 1860s, created Beefeater Gin."

Hayman Distillers
Witham, England

The Hayman family is England's oldest gin distilling dynasty. It is currently headed by Christopher Hayman, one of the world's most experienced 'gin masters' with 40 years of experience, and legatee to great grandfather James Burrough, creator of Beefeater Gin. With his son and daughter, Christopher continues to make classic styles of English gins to family recipes.

The Hayman story starts with James Burrough, a London distiller who, in the 1860s, created Beefeater Gin. Formerly a pharmacist, in 1863 James Burrough paid £400 to purchase John Taylor & Son, a Chelsea-based firm of gin distillers and liqueur makers which had been founded in 1820. He renamed the company 'James Burrough, Distiller and Importer of Foreign Liqueurs' and established a good reputation with a client base that included fancy food shop Fortnum & Mason.

James used his skills as a chemist to perfect the firm's gins and liqueurs. Tellingly, one of his early recipe books listing a recipe for blackcurrant gin is dated 1849, predating his purchase of the distillery by 14 years. The business thrived and by 1876 papers show that the company's large portfolio included gin brands such as James Burrough London Dry, Ye Old Chelsey and Beefeater.

In 1897 James Burrough died and his sons, Frederick, Ernest and Frank, took over the running of the business. They continued to prosper and in 1906 purchased premises across the river at 26 Hutton Road, Lambeth. They equipped the new distillery with the latest stills from J Dore & Sons and named the new site Cale Distillery in

memory of their old premises in Cale Street, Chelsea.

In the early 1900s, the third generation entered the family business and Eric Burrough, who didn't have children and practically lived for the company, drove the company forward with the first shipment of Beefeater to the USA leaving in 1917. He died in 1970, but his cousins Alan and Norman continued to build the business, having moved to a larger premises in Montford Place, Kennington, in 1958. This distillery near the Oval Cricket Ground remains Beefeater Gin's home today but was one of a number of sites owned by James Burrough Ltd, which by this time was selling a huge range of liqueurs. The Fine Alcohols Division which moved from London in the late 1970s to a site in Witham, Essex supplied pure alcohol to the drink, cosmetic and pharmaceutical industries as well as bottling numerous gins and other products.

By the 1960s, the company's shares were held by many extended family members but the board comprised of James Burrough's living grandchildren, Alan Burrough and Norman Burrough, with their sister Marjorie Burrough represented by her husband, Neville Hayman, who happened to be an accountant.

The company remained family-owned, with Norman Burrough as chairman, until October 1987 when the majority of family decided to sell to Whitbread. This was partly driven by the recent threat of grain products, including gin, being banned from import into the USA, their main export market. The Hayman side of the family were against the sale but there were some 150 members of the family who held shares, the vast majority of which were not involved in the running of the business.

Christopher Hayman (the son of Marjorie Burrough and Neville Hayman) had started working for the company in 1969, moving from department to department to experience all aspects of the rapidly growing business. After the Whitbread deal went through, he became operations director of Whitbread Spirits Group, responsible for production at Laphroaig, Ardmore, Tormore and Strathclyde distilleries in Scotland, as well as the Beefeater Distillery in London. Although Christopher liked the challenge of running so many distilleries, he decided that working for a conglomerate was not for him and yearned to return to a family business.

His opportunity came when the results of a management consultancy report commissioned by Whitbread advised it to sell James Burrough Limited's Fine Alcohols Division (F.A.D.). When Christopher heard the Witham plant was going to be sold he, backed by other members of the Hayman Family, negotiated to purchase F.A.D. from Whitbread to maintain his family's involvement with the gin industry. This business made and contract-bottled numerous third-party gins and other products and today is known as Hayman Limited. With Christopher's purchase of F.A.D. on 17th November 1988 came three bottling lines. Subsequently, he also became a major shareholder of Thames Distillers in South London, so maintained his direct involvement in gin distillation.

Christopher, initially created gins for a number of markets such as the USA and Japan. However, in September 2004, now joined by his son James and daughter Miranda launched Hayman's 1820 Gin Liqueur. They expanded the range and set out to create different styles of classic English gins under the Hayman's label, recreating old products from the family's recipe books rather than making new modern gins with unusual botanicals. All Hayman's gins use the same ten

botanicals, it's just the intensity of each botanical which changes between each specific gin recipe. For example, Hayman's Old Tom uses almost twice as much juniper as its London dry. The ten botanicals are:

Juniper Berries from Bulgaria or Macedonia
Coriander seed from Bulgaria
Nutmeg from India
Cinnamon from Madagascar
Orange Peel from Spain
Angelica root from Belgium or France
Orris root from Italy
Cassia bark from China
Liquorice from Sri Lanka
Lemon peel from Spain

With Christopher's interest in Thames Distillers, understandably production of Hayman's gins was undertaken at Thames' Clapham, south London home. However, the Hayman family wanted to bring distilling in-house, back to their Witham site where they bottled Hayman gins. So, fittingly, 150 years after their ancestor James Burrough entered the gin distilling business, on 6th June 2013, the Hayman's family installed a German-made Christian Carl Still.

Named Marjorie after Marjorie Burrough, Christopher Hayman's mother, the 450-litre Carl Still is element-heated, boasts six optional plates and a pre-condenser. The pictures on page 231 of Christopher, James and Miranda Hayman standing proudly by their new still were taken just a few days after it was installed. Christopher talked excitedly about how this modern, all-copper still with optional botanical chamber and rectifying column will allow the family to experiment as well as create both new and old recipes from the family archives.

The new bottles launched in August 2013 complete the family's celebration of 150 years of distilling and mimic a bottle from the family archives dating from 1947, the year that Christopher Hayman was born. The bottle design incorporates the Hayman family crest which includes a cat, a reference to Old Tom gin, the insignia of the school all three members of the family attended, juniper sprigs and droplets, a reference to the family's five generations of gin distilling.

HAYMAN'S LONDON DRY GIN

Launched in 2008 and a classic London Dry gin in style, it is distilled with ten botanicals: juniper berries, coriander seed, nutmeg, cinnamon, angelica root, orris root, cassia bark, liquorice and Spanish orange and lemon peel – which are steeped in the pot still for 24 hours prior to distillation. **Appearance**: Crystal clear. **Aroma**: Crystallised lemon zest and orange peel with aromatic lavender and camphor rich juniper. Delicate rooty earthy notes with freshly cut celery. **Taste**: Piney juniper with dry, slightly bitter orris root and zesty citrus – practically lime zest (although this is not a botanical used in this gin). Complex and bone dry. **Aftertaste**: Slightly bitter rooty notes continue through the rooty juniper finish.
diffordsguide rating: ★ ★ ★ ★ ⟨

HAYMAN'S OLD TOM GIN

Launched in November 2007, Hayman's Old Tom is a modern-day recreation of an original family recipe dating from the 1860s which, interestingly, contains sugar. It is made with the same ten botanicals which feature in other Hayman gins but with more botanical intensity and the addition of the sugar.
Appearance: Crystal clear. **Aroma**: Clean fresh juniper and orange zest nose. **Taste**: Juniper led, clean, slightly sweet palate. Juniper is very much to the fore but backed by citrus notes and subtle spice. **Aftertaste**: Clean, cracked black pepper lingers throughout the long finish.
diffordsguide rating: ★ ★ ★ ★ ☆

HAYMAN'S SLOE GIN

26% alc.vol.
This traditional sloe gin liqueur is made by steeping wild English hand-picked sloe berries, harvested in the Autumn in Hayman's Gin for several months. Launched 2009.
Appearance: Slight haze, rusty red with brown edges. **Aroma**: Good sloe berry nose with underlying gin aromas and almond notes. **Taste**: The bitter-sweet palate has good sloe berry flavours wit balanced syrupy sweetness. Gin notes rise through the fruit and develop towards the finish. **Aftertaste**: Warm, fruity, spicy gin finish.
diffordsguide rating: ★ ★ ★ ★ ⟨

HAYMAN'S 1850 RESERVE GIN

40% alc./vol.
Made to a recipe dating from the 1850s, using the same ten botanicals as other Hayman gins, but with an influence more towards the juniper and coriander rather than the usual citrus-led house style. After pot still distillation, Hayman's 1850 is rested for three to four weeks in ex-Scotch whisky casks. In the 1850s, gin was transported in wooden casks rather than in bottles. During this period it was also sold in

establishments known as Gin Palaces were the gin was also served straight from the barrel. The passing of The Single Bottle Act in 1861 allowed spirits to be sold in bottles.

Launched in 2011, Hayman's 1850 Reserve Gin is distilled in small batches of 5,000 bottles, with each bottle carrying the batch and individual bottle number. **Appearance**: (batch No. 00-001, Bot No. 0855) Crystal clear. No colour from oak ageing. **Aroma**: Clean attractive and aromatic nose with generous pine forest-like juniper and fresh coriander. **Taste**: Reassuringly traditional, pine-fresh juniper and coriander palate with earthy Parma Violet (orris root?), liquorice and gentle dry spice. **Aftertaste**: Cleansing spice continues in the finish with lingering dry oaky bitterness.
diffordsguide rating: ★ ★ ★ ★ ★

ROYAL DOCK
57% alc./vol.
Royal Dock Gin is produced by the Hayman family, previous generations of which from 1863 supplied a gin named 'Senior Service Gin' to the Royal Navy's Royal Dock in South London's Deptford. The term 'Senior Service' was the nickname for the Royal Navy.

The Royal Dock, England's largest naval port, was established in 1513 by Henry VIII and home to the Navy's Victualing Board for 400 years. The Navy stipulated a high strength gin so gunpowder would still light if the barrels containing the gin should leak and wet the gunpowder. Members of the highest ranks of the Navy are said to have appreciated the style of Senior Service Gin.
Appearance: Crystal clear. **Aroma**: Classic pungent London dry nose with piny juniper, candied ginger and

zesty lemon coriander seeds, nutty angelica and faint earthy parma violets. **Taste**: Slightly sweet with amplified jammy citrus straddling piney juniper and sweet parma violets. **Aftertaste**: Parma violets and zesty citrus linger on the longer black peppery juniper finish.
diffordsguide rating: ★ ★ ★ ★ ★

HAYMAN'S 1820 GIN LIQUEUR
40% alc./vol.
Claiming to be the world's first gin liqueur, Hayman's 1820 was created by Christopher and James Hayman, direct descendants of James Burrough, founder of Beefeater Gin. The 1820 statement refers to the date when the distillery James Burrough acquired was first established.

Hayman's use their usual ten botanicals to create a gin but a touch of sugar adds the sweetness associated with a liqueur. Lunched in 2004, Hayman's 1820 is popular in Spain where the extra sweetness is appreciated when mixed with tonic water.
Appearance: Clear, transparent. **Aroma**: Gin-like pine-ey juniper and fresh orange zest with white pepper spice.
Taste: Clean, sweet and easy on the palate. Zesty orange followed by subtle juniper and spice. While obviously a liqueur, Hayman's is not overly sweet. **Aftertaste**: Gin-like finish but with bitter resiny notes subdued by lingering icing sugar flavour.
diffordsguide rating: ★ ★ ★ ★ ★

Producer: Hayman Distillers (Hayman Ltd), Eastways Park, Witham, Essex, England.
www.hayman.co.uk

"The cucumber in Hendrick's is certainly an unusual ingredient in a gin while also making for a very recognisable garnish."

Hendrick's Gin

Girvan, Scotland

Created in Scotland in 1999, Hendrick's was successfully launched in the US in 2000, followed by the UK a few years later in 2003. The story goes that one summer's afternoon a Scottish whisky distiller was visiting Janet Sheed Roberts, a very special lady known to her friends as Aunty Janie who is not just the oldest woman living in Scotland (109 this year) but the granddaughter of William Grant the famous distiller. Well it turns out David was also something of a closet gin lover and while in Aunty Janie's garden he was enjoying a cucumber sandwich washed down with a little gin sat amongst the roses (as you do). Struck by how well the flavours combined, our hero set about distilling a gin with a hint of both rose and cucumber. However, as a Scotch distiller of some repute he was loathed to associate his name with a gin, so he named his new libation for Aunty Janie's gardener, 'Hendrick', the man he had been chatting to at the time of his cucumber epiphany.

While the above is true enough, the actual story behind Hendrick's creation was more of a team effort. David Stewart, a revered whisky distiller, did indeed have the inspiration for a the flavour profile of a new gin while in Aunty Janie's rose garden eating cucumber sandwiches, but he wasn't heavily involved in its development. His idea was brought to life by Lesley Gracie and John Ross who are still charged with the distillation of Hendrick's to this day. They worked with the Scotch Whisky Research Institute, who helped with botanical analysis, to perfect the artisanal dual distillation method and realise David's epiphany by balancing a traditional London dry gin with complex rose and cucumber essences. Janet Roberts was first to endorse David's suggestion that the new gin be named after her gardener.

It's a great name and Hendrick's branding is the envy of many older, more established products. It's short, dumpy bottle, which incidentally is made out of 45% recycled glass, is reminiscent of those once found in Victorian apothecaries and with its paper label and cork stopper this packaging suggests bygone times. Hendrick's is positioned, rather tongue-in-cheekily, as being a tad upper crust with a signature Victorian/Georgian quirkiness. Typical experiential marketing stunts and events feature croquet, Victorian outfits, waxed moustaches and gramophone record players along with those obligatory cucumber sandwiches. The strap line used in its advertising, "A Most Unusual Gin", is often accompanied by quirky little line drawings featuring cucumbers – after all, cucumber is certainly an unusual ingredient for a gin while also making for a very recognisable garnish.

Hendrick's does not come from a bygone-age but from a quiet corner of William Grant & Sons' huge Girvan grain distillery in Ayrshire, Scotland. This former munitions site is also home to the impressive, state-of-the-art Ailsa Bay malt distillery. What is grandly, and maybe a little unjustly, titled 'Hendrick's Gin Palace' is a much smaller affair set apart from the main buildings. Unlike the rest of the distillery Hendrick's two stills are totally manually operated without a computer in site, just the skill and expertise of John and Lesley.

The distillery lies just north of the pretty harbour town of Girvan, close to Turnberry Golf Course (where The Open was played in 2009). Just off-shore, the island

of Ailsa Craig rises some 1,110 feet from the Firth of Clyde – its peak often topped by clouds. At only 2.5 miles around its base this is a very small island but geologically unique, being formed from very hard Ailsa granite - the favoured stone for making the curling stones used in the Winter Olympics sport.

PRODUCTION

This "Most Unusual Gin" may be flavoured with rose and cucumber, but its other eleven botanicals are more classic: juniper berries, angelica root, coriander seeds, cubeb berries, orris root, camomile flowers, caraway seeds, elderflowers, meadowsweet, lemon and orange peel. These are distilled in two different stills, a 1860s Bennett copper pot still and a 1948 John Dore Carter-Head still, both acquired by Charles Gordon at London's Taplow auction in 1966. The process water is sourced from the Penwhapple reservoir, high in the hills beyond the distillery. This water is so pure that when used to charge the stills, it is not purified or treated, merely filtered to remove sand, plant matter and such like.

The Carter-Head was invented by the Carter-Head Brothers who were originally apprentices to Aeneas Coffey, the inventor of the continuous column still. This is basically a steam jacket heated pot still that rises into a feints chamber and then directly into a column still with copper plates layering it like floors in an office block. At the top of the column is a cooling jacket, which can be used to force reflux but with modern high quality neutral spirits this function is superfluous, so not used in Hendrick's production. The Carter-Head still was originally designed to rectify the poor quality base spirit of yesteryear but today this extra distillation and copper contact serves to smooth and round the spirit.

From the top of the column the lyne arm directs the vapour into the botanical chamber, which contains a holed colander-like basket with a three-sectioned outside ring surrounding a central section. It is imperative that the distiller carefully packs the baskets with the biggest particles of the botanicals at the bottom, otherwise there is a risk that the vapour will push the botanicals through the holes in the base of the basket, also the way the vapour passes through these botanicals dramatically affects the extraction of essential oils and so the flavour. From the botanical chamber the now flavoured vapour passes into the condenser directly below where it is liquefied.

The Carter-Head is charged with wheat neutral alcohol hydrated to 55-60% abv using water from the Penwhapple reservoir. The foreshots (high wines/heads) which consist of the first 10 to 15 litres of the run are allowed to pass through the botanicals and serve to wash and prepare the herbs and spices for the clean vapours which quickly follow and will be used in the final gin. The heart of the run or 'cut' is approximately 350 litres at around 80% abv with the rest of the run, being feints (low wines/tails). This method of gin distillation is known as the 'vapour infusion method' and is employed by relatively few gin producers.

Conversely the Bennett still is a fairly standard steam jacket heated pot still (alembic) using the more common steeping method of gin distillation. The Bennett still is charged with wheat neutral alcohol hydrated to 55-60% abv and the botanicals, which are left to infuse in the spirit for between 24 and 36 hours before commencing distillation depending on the ambient temperature (extraction of

the essential oils takes longer in cooler temperatures). It is essential to heat the still slowly to avoid burning the juniper berries and detrimentally affecting flavour.

Both stills have a maximum charge capacity of 1,000 litres but the fill is never quite the same and can be anything from 800 litres. The same botanicals are used in both stills but to slightly different proportions as the flavour extraction of the botanicals between the two stills is so different. The two resulting spirits are then blended together in roughly equal proportions (the exact blend being a closely guarded secret).

Finally, essences of Bulgarian Damascena rose petals and Dutch cucumber are added, in line with the tale of that infamous sandwich. The rose petals are pressed to release the oil, which is then dissolved with alcohol to produce the essence. Cucumbers are mashed up in water and the flavours are extracted at around zero degrees Celsius using a cold distillation process.

HENDRICK'S GIN
UK & rest of world 41.4% alc./vol., USA 44% alc./vol.
Appearance: Crystal clear.
Aroma: Hints of pine, eucalyptus and lime marmalade combine with juniper and spicy floral fragrances in a fresh, complex nose. **Taste:** Slightly sweet and silky smooth, with a burst of juniper and citrus set against fresh green flavours. This is followed by cumin, cracked black pepper and salty liquorice back notes. **Aftertaste:** Long and lingering with floral hints and a quinine and juniper bitterness.
diffordsguide rating: ★★★★☆

Producer: Girvan Distillery (William Grant & Sons), Girvan, Ayrshire, KA26 9PT, Scotland
www.hendricksgin.com

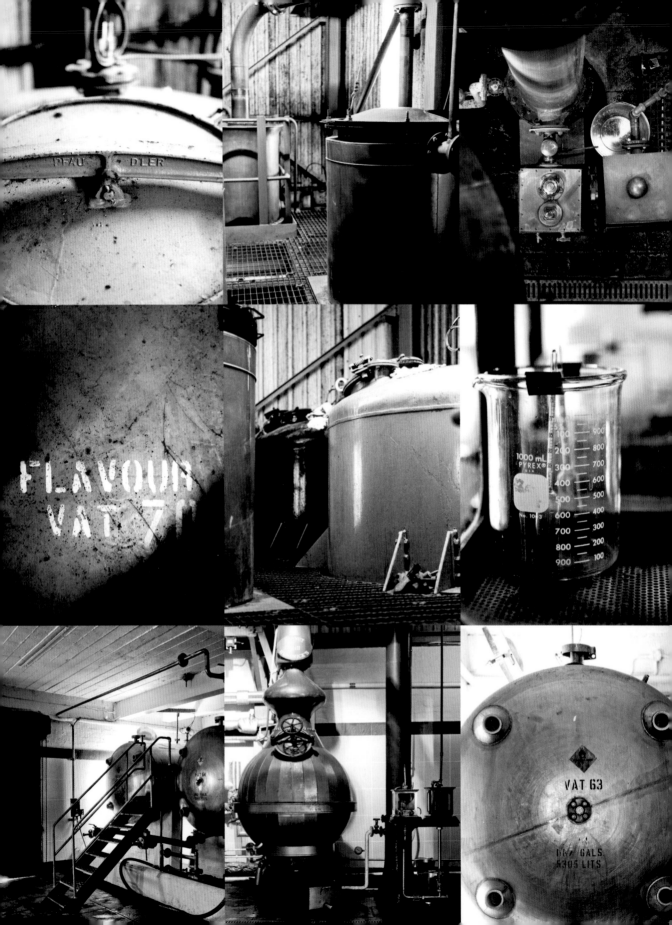

"Jensen's gin was inspired by a long-forgotten gin recipe, and its recreation tells a tale that runs the distance from Tokyo to south London."

Jensen's Bermondsey Gin

Bermondsey, London, England

Almost all of the gins in this book are the result of one man's dream, and Jensen's Bermondsey Gin is no exception: Christian Jensen, the man behind it, was driven by a desire to recreate in England the Dry Martinis he'd become accustomed to while living in Japan.

In 2001, Christian Jensen's job as a banking IT specialist saw him relocate to Tokyo. One evening after a particularly hard day at the bank he stumbled upon one of Tokyo's legendary hidden bars. Set in a high-rise building, this tiny establishment comprised of one small, dimly lit room with an ancient plank that served as the bar. The old man that stood behind it introduced himself as Oda-San, and said: "You look like you could use a drink." He set a crystal tumbler containing a clear liquid, garnished with a lime peel, in front of Christian and explained that it was a "Naked Martini made with pure gin from your city, London, nothing more." The drink buzzed with flavour and over the following months Christian stopped at Oda-San's place almost nightly for the same elixir.

When his Japanese sojourn was at an end, Christian stopped in to say farewell to Oda-San and was handed a gift: a bottle of gin, the label almost completely worn away, to the extent that it read only 'don Gin' with the brand – which Christian had never heard of – barely discernable. "Take this," Oda-San told him. "The last bottle, the soul of London and its gin. No-one makes this anymore, and once it's gone..." he trailed off. Oda-San had once owned two cases of this old gin, but over the months Christian had consumed practically all of it in what were sublime Martinis.

Christian moved back to Europe and his apartment on Bermondsey Street SE1, but over the course of the following year, not a day went by when Christian didn't think about Oda-San and the amazing gin. He had the one remaining bottle, possibly in the world. He mischievously challenged the concierge service he had subscribed to to investigate where he could buy more of it. As Oda-San had told him, the gin had not been made for decades, though he did manage to buy the odd bottle via online auctions.

Just as he was about to accept that he had purchased all the bottles that remained, the concierge service telephoned so say that they had found a public records office which held documents from the distillery which used to make the gin, including recipe books. Christian hurried there and filed his request to view the hundreds of papers and books dating from the mid 1800s to the 1960s by their reference number, five at a time – the maximum allowed. He worked his way through all the dusty books and papers the records office held from the distillery. Amongst these was a recipe book with gin recipes, including one for his beloved gin.

Christian returned to the records office with a camera and photographed recipes from several of the recipe books. His challenge was then to find somebody who could turn the original recipe into a modern-day gin which he could then use to make the Martinis he'd come to enjoy in Tokyo. A series of recommendations led him to master distiller Charles Maxwell at Thames Distillers in Clapham, south London (see page 294). The new gin craze we are presently enjoying had yet to hit and Charles welcomed the opportunity this IT man from the banking world presented. The two men worked with the remnants of the bottle from Japan and the original recipe to recreate the long lost gin. A series of experiments and trial distillations ensued.

"After 10-15 trial distillations we ended up with a gin I really liked, and was faithful to the original," says Christian. Charles produced some 800 cases of the gin and Christian stocked up his apartment and persuaded his local watering holes, Hide bar on Bermondsey Street and Bedales in Borough Market, to buy cases from him. Once again, he could visit his local bar and order his favourite Martini.

Christian's career in the banking industry meant he had no knowledge of, or connections in the drinks world, so his gin was created more for his friends' enjoyment than any thought of creating a new brand. Investigations found that the brand name of the old bottle from Tokyo was owned by a large drinks company: although it had not been used for years, it could still not be used. "Deciding on the name was tricky, but eventually I was guided by wanting it to be both relevant to me and to old London, so the name 'Bermondsey' fitted perfectly." Hence, it was christened Jensen's Bermondsey London Dry Gin.

I also live in Bermondsey and from time-to-time pop into Hide bar. It was on one of these visits when Paul Mathew, the bar's owner, told me about a banker who lived locally and had made his own gin. Paul thought we should meet, and a week or so later Christian came to my own bar clutching a bottle of his gin. I remember asking him why his gin was so special. He replied: "It's the smoothest gin I've ever tried." All I knew was that he was a banker that had made a gin. I had no idea where the recipe had come from or his story, so I was more than sceptical. Christian claimed 'smoothness' so I reached for a bottle of Plymouth Gin to taste comparatively. To my astonishment, he was right, plus it was also very classic in its flavour profile – juniper-led with subtle botanical complexity.

Christian then told me the full story and said that he was sat on hundreds of cases and had no distributor. Less than a week later, my friend Sukhinder from Speciality Brands and The Whisky Exchange called round and asked if I'd come across anything interesting recently. I poured him Jensen's gin and told him about Christian. Predictably, it was not long before Speciality Brands started selling Jensen's gin.

Word of the new gin initially spread slowly, organically, though it was instantly appreciated by gin connoisseurs. A series of well-respected bars began to stock it and as consumer enthusiasm for gin grew Christian saw demand ever-increasing.

One day Christian told me about the other recipes he had taken from the old distillery's archive, including a recipe from a book dating from the late 1840s for something called Old Tom Gin. Excited, I asked to see the recipe. It immediately struck me that it did not call for sugar, just sweet botanicals. Up until then I'd been led to believe that all old tom gins were sweetened with sugar. This recipe dated from a time when sugar was still an expensive commodity, not something that would be viable to use in a gin aimed at the mass market consumer of the period. Naturally I pleaded with Christian to make an Old Tom gin.

I heard nothing more until a few months later when Christian once again turned up with a bottle of Jensen's London-Distilled Old Tom Gin. At the time, there were few such gins available, and those few that did exist were all sweetened with sugar. Like his original London Dry Gin, Jensen's Old Tom Gin was quickly adopted by bars around the UK and Europe. Today, Christian's gins are stocked in Selfridges and Harrods as well as being served in The American Bar at the Savoy hotel, The Connaught Bar at the Connaught Hotel and of course, Hide bar on Bermondsey Street.

Creating Bermondsey Gin would have been impossible without Charles Maxwell and Thames Distillers, but such is its success that Christian has now decided to set up his own distillery. As of 2013, all distillation of Jensen's Bermondsey London Dry Gin and Jensen London-Distilled Old Tom Gin will take place in a small distillery in railway arches near London Bridge on fashionable foodies' market Maltby Street (a trendier version of nearby Borough Market, if far smaller). Stills from John Dore & Co are arriving as this book goes to press, before Christmas 2012, with first spirit expected to come off in January 2013.

Jensen's new home is more about having a face for Bermondsey Gin rather than changing anything about the flagship spirit, though it will also be open to visitors. It also allows Christian to spend more of his own time with all of the elements of gin production, in particular distilling, which was the main reason for the move, and stands as a coming-of-age for his 'baby', now more than a decade old.

"I am looking forward to having a place to welcome guests who want to know more about the brand, the category and me," he says. "Part of becoming a gin geek means I also have a huge collection of gin-related items – from old bottles, labels and cocktail books to distilling-related equipment and books about gin companies – all of which I will move to the distillery."

Yet to come is a range of infused gins. Scouring the market and the surrounding area for local produce, the idea is to make a small production of gin infused with seasonal fruits and spices. Masterclasses and tastings also beckon as 2013 rolls on.

From the first trials with Charles Maxwell it has been something of a slow journey preparing Jensen Gin to stand on its own feet. Now Christian's product is finding its way on to more and more menus and back-bars, and there is even talk of opening a bar near the distillery, so curious customers can see the gin in-the-making before they enjoy its historical flavours. And what about that secret recipe? I'm afraid I've been sworn to secrecy.

JENSEN'S BERMONDSEY LONDON DRY GIN

Bermondsey Gin is made to a very traditional style: it is a true London-distilled dry gin made only using the botanicals found in gins from the 1800s. Bermondsey Gin does not include cucumber, rose, grains of paradise or any other 'contemporary' botanicals.

Appearance: (sample version 1.1) Crystal clear.
Aroma: Clean pine-ey juniper with lavender and parma violet, generous coriander, orange and lemon zest.
Taste: Clean dry palate with pine fresh juniper to the

fore with coriander and strong hints of Parma Violet
from the orris, liquorice and nutty almond notes.
Aftertaste: Liquorice starts sweet and dries throughout
the long piney finish.
diffordsguide rating: ★ ★ ★ ★ ★ +

JENSEN LONDON-DISTILLED OLD TOM GIN

This is a real Old Tom, replicating the style of original
'sweet' gins from the late 18th and early 19th centuries,
not just a bog-standard London dry with added sugar.
Jensen's Old Tom is made to an 1840s recipe, and is
naturally sweetened with larger quantities of sweet
botanicals such as liquorice.

Appearance: (1st bottling) Crystal clear.
Aroma: Eucalyptus and pine-ey juniper with woody
liquorice, parma violet and earthy cold stewed tea with
zesty orange and a soapy hint of almond. **Taste:** Strongly
eucalyptus influenced palate with green vegetal notes
and woody liquorice. This is far from tasting sweet – it's
not that kind of Old Tom – it is in fact dry with the merest
perception of sweetness. **Aftertaste:** Eucalyptus and
pine-ey juniper with lingering vegetal notes.
diffordsguide rating: ★ ★ ★ ★ ⟨

"Although 'cold distillation' is a new technique, Oxley is steeped and distilled with all the botanicals in the kettle at once – just as you'd expect of classic gin methods."

Oxley Classic English Dry Gin
Clapham, London, England

Using a fairly classic London dry gin recipe, Oxley is made with 14 botanicals traditionally steeped in grain neutral alcohol. Unusually, however, it is made at extremely low pressures and sub-zero temperatures using revolutionary distillation methods.

The work to create Oxley started with the exciting prospect of how much fresher a classic London dry gin might taste if it was made using a cold distillation method, so avoiding the 'marmalade' flavours, particularly affecting citrus peel, resulting from traditional distillation. While a few experimental distillers have used basic laboratory equipment to distil at reduced pressure and temperatures of 25°C to 50°C, no one had yet tackled the technical challenges or financial investment to attempt sub-zero vacuum distillation.

Distilling at low temperatures means three-dimensional 'terpenes' (a sort of organic compound), such as limonene, geraniol, pinene, eucalyptol; and 'terpenoids', such as citral or menthol, do not have the opportunity to 'stereoisomerise' into their more 'stewed' versions. This is recognised as the marmalade-like and bitter flavours prevalent in gins traditionally distilled at high temperatures. In layman's terms, traditional distillation can burn botanicals with delicate oils such as orange and lemon peel. Even if they are not burnt, proteins and molecules in the botanicals' essential oils are liable to be distorted by heat.

There are not many large corporations whose shareholders would approve the millions required to develop an experimental 'cold-distilled gin', and not many family-owned companies that can afford to, let alone have the

idea and ambition in the first place. Enter Bacardi and its herbalist, Ivano Tonutti.

Ivano, Martini's eighth 'Master of Botanicals', has been in charge of searching for the best botanical ingredients for Bacardi-Martini since 1994. He sources more than 40 botanicals from counties all around the world, which arrive in their natural form at Bacardi's botanical hub having been slowly dried using traditional techniques to preserve their aromatic character. Responsible for purchasing Bacardi's annual requirement of 250-300 tonnes of dried botanicals, it would be fair to say that the finished quality of the company's products is largely dependent on Ivano's purchases – he's a man with a lot of responsibility. Oxley only uses a minute proportion of Ivano's annual purchases but the gin benefits from the quality attainable with such buying power.

Working from his base at Bacardi's botanical hub at Tradall in Geneva, Switzland, Ivano is also responsible for the laborious and meticulous quality checks. Juniper berries, for example, are tested with samples taken from the top, sides and bottom of every bag within every batch of berries to arrive from Tuscany.

While Oxley's recipe was being developed, tests were carried out to see which botanicals were best suited to cold distillation, the lengthy process involving test distillations of various combinations to find the perfect recipe. During this process it emerged that citrus peels from grapefruit, lemon and orange, normally used in a dried state to make other gins, were best used fresh.

The 14 different botanicals used to make Oxley form a recipe known in Bacardi as 'Vacuum Distiller's Recipe No.38' and the botanicals are weighed and vacuum

HBF Product Number
9216050100

RC 5010 2.366 KG 1 BOX

Batch nr: 0010046895

Net Weight: 2.366 KG

Weighing Date	09.01.2012	
Best Before	29.12.2013	
Gross Weight	0.000	KG
Tare	2.366 —	KG

Delivery Address

TRADALL S.A.

IPC : 9216050100
Formula # RC 5010-001
Batch # 0010252412
Best Before 27 February 2014

Customer : OXLEY

packed into pouches, each with the exact quantity required for one distillation. While some of the 14 botanicals which flavour Oxley are used fresh, others, such as vanilla, which provides the texture (trigeminal) of vanillin, are used in dried form. The pouches of fresh botanicals are frozen and the other botanicals freeze-dried to ensure the flavoursome natural oils are preserved and only released during distillation.

The overly strong pine notes that juniper berries acquire when exposed to prolonged heat do not appear in Oxley, which instead has more of the berry flavour itself. Other botanicals such as meadowsweet were chosen after tests found it particularly well-suited to cold distillation, providing a 'rounded' almond flavour.

Presently Bacardi does not own a distillery in the UK, although it is in the process of building a distillery for its Bombay gins, presently contract-distilled by Greenall in Warrington. Bacardi, wanting Oxley to be a genuine London dry gin distilled in London, approached Thames Distillers in Clapham, south London, to house Oxley's state of the art still. Matthew Pauley, Oxley's distiller, is employed by Thames Distillers as 'Project Distiller', operating the high-tech still owned by Bacardi. A scientist with a biochemistry background, he has been closely involved with the Oxley project since its inception and personally devised some of the methods employed in Oxley's sub-zero distillation.

While Oxley is an innovative, space-aged gin, the operation is squeezed into a corner of Thames Distillers with much of the high-tech cooling equipment housed in little more than a Portacabin. With Matthew's enthusiasm and ingenuity lying behind every drop distilled, as Rich

Hunt, the brand's ambassador says, "there is something of a 'man-in-shed' fervour so common-place in the English psyche."

PRODUCTION

All methods of reduced pressure distillation work on the principle that the lower the pressure the lower the boiling point of liquids, including water and ethanol alcohol. Thus the use of a vacuum pump allows you to reduce pressure and so distil at temperatures barely warmer than a hot summer's day. Use a more powerful vacuum pump and you can distil at sub-zero temperatures. The challenge, then, is to reliably reach and control these extreme temperatures and to custom-design and build a still which will withstand these extremes.

In contrast, and to put things in perspective, Ian Hart of Sacred, the other noted English reduced-pressure distiller, uses apparatus which operates at between 126 and 63 Torr, while Oxley is made using a much stronger vacuum of between 9 and 7 Torr. Ian distils at balmy summer's day temperatures of between 25°C to 50°C, depending on the botanical being distilled, while Oxley's botanicals are steeped at 16 to 24°C and all the botanicals distilled together at a decidedly chilly -5°C. Oxley condenses at a frostbite inducing -120°C around a cold finger probe cooled by nine different refrigerants, including liquid nitrogen and argon.

Many reduced pressure distillers distil each of their botanicals separately, but traditional gin distillers, and the makers of Oxley, believe the interaction between botanicals during distillation is an essential part of the gin-making process, helping to lock flavours together to

create a more rounded gin.

The neutral alcohol and botanicals are held in the boil kettle. Maintaining a steady operational temperature in this boil kettle is one of the main challenges during Oxley's unusual distillation process. The coil within the kettle is used to cool the contents to -5°C but, as the spirit requires energy to convert liquid to vapour, so the element is gradually switched over from to cooling to maintaining the temperature at the target -5°C. However, towards the end of distillation the boiling temperature drops to -11°C, and sometimes even -14°C, as the spirit in the kettle drops below the level of the coil and more energy is needed to vaporise the last of the neutral spirit. The purported benefit of reduced pressure or cold distillation is that the natural botanicals are not 'cooked' during the distillation process, so reputedly giving fresher flavours to the finished gin. As no heat is applied, the structure of the botanical molecules remains unchanged, thus preserving their original intensity. Indeed, the lack of energy needed to vaporise the spirit in Oxley's cold distillation process means the structure of both the essential oils and the alcohol remains unchanged.

Cold distillation not only avoids the introduction of harsh cooked notes, it also means the bad-tasting volatile high alcohols (heads) and particularly the heavy alcohol and oils (tails), which are produced and have to be discarded in traditional gin distillation processes, are not present. The base neutral wheat spirit used for the distillation of Oxley is so highly rectified that no methanol or other unwanted substances are present. To this, only food-safe botanicals are added and because the molecules of these botanicals are preserved by the cold distillation process, all the spirit used ends up in the finished bottled gin.

There is no cut and no heads and tails to discard: 25 litres (measured by mass) go into the still and 23 litres come out, the two missing litres lost by being soaked up by the botanicals and the inevitable inefficiencies in the system, in particular through the vacuum pump as it extracts air from the still.

Throughout the distillation Matthew, the scientist-turned-distiller, dives in out of his 'Matt cave', a cabin housing the high-tech cooling equipment, as he continually tweaks temperatures. As distillation continues, gin condenses and collects in the receiving column which houses the cold-finger probe. The system is closed to maintain the vacuum. To draw the gin off, every half an hour or so Matt switches a valve over and starts a second pump which works against the vacuum to draw off the distillate and fill a stainless steel bucket, the not so high-tech spirit receiver.

Oxley is made using a 'three shot' process, i.e. the distillate is stretched by blending with two parts neutral spirit, thus 46 litres of neutral alcohol are blended with the 23 litres produced in each distillation, so each 23 litre batch of distillate produces 69 litres of gin at an average run strength of 87.7% alc./vol.. This is diluted to bottling strength with water meaning some 120 bottles are produced from each distillation. Five distillations are run every week, producing 600 bottles per week.

Something of a space-age gin, Oxley perhaps doesn't appear to have much classic about its production, but when launched was labelled "Classic English dry gin". Apparently, and rather contentiously, the word 'classic' was used in reference to its use of juniper, coriander, angelica and citrus which are, of course, 'classic' gin flavours. Interestingly, Oxley conforms to all the requirements to be labelled a 'London dry gin' and while cold distillation is a very new technique, Oxley is steeped and batch-distilled with all the botanicals in the kettle at once – as you'd expect of classic gin distillation. So perhaps inevitably, Oxley is now labelled 'Cold Distilled' and 'London Dry Gin', but I think it could also be termed a 'contemporary classic'.

OXLEY CLASSIC ENGLISH DRY GIN

Appearance: (bottle No. B03796) Crystal clear.
Aroma: Superbly clean, fresh nose with very mild piney juniper and generous freshly zested citrus, particularly orange. **Taste:** Bursts alive with sweet zesty orange citrus, moderate juniper and herbal complexity. Pink grapefruit emerges and then dominates. **Aftertaste:** Zesty, pronounced juniper finish with lingering liquorice. Not as rounded as some gins but then they're not as fresh and zesty.
diffordsguide rating: ★★★★⯪

Producer: Thames Distillers, Timbermill Way, Gauden Road, Clapham, London, England.
www.oxleygin.com

"Plymouth is enjoying a well-earned renaissance and is once again popular in America — its journey from Plymouth could be said to be following that of the Pilgrim fathers."

Plymouth Gin

Plymouth, England

Once a Dominican priory and the site where some of the Pilgrim Fathers sheltered before setting sail on the Mayflower for the New World, The Black Friars distillery has been home to Plymouth Gin for more than 150 years.

Located on a cobbled street close to the dockside in the heart of Plymouth, parts of The Black Friars Distillery date back to the early 1400s when the Dominicans or 'Black Friars' built a priory. In 1536 it became a debtors' prison when Henry VIII dissolved England's monasteries and stripped their assets. The building then had numerous occupants, but perhaps most famously, it is purported that in 1620 some of the Pilgrim Fathers spent their final night on British soil in the priory before setting sail on the Mayflower on their voyage to the New World. Later, in 1685, the building became a refuge for Huguenots fleeing persecution in France.

The medieval monks' refectory became the town's main meeting hall and this impressive medieval hall with a hull-shaped timber roof, the most intact part of the original priory, now houses the distillery's bar. Built in 1431, this is one of the oldest buildings in Plymouth and protected as a national monument.

Evidence of distillation dates back to 1697, with records showing that a 'mault-house' existed on the site at this time. The present day Plymouth Gin name was introduced in 1793 when Mr Coates joined the established distilling business of Fox & Williamson and converted the old Black Friars priory. The business soon became known as Coates & Co.

Coates made a gin that was fuller-flavoured with less citrus and more pungent root flavours than its typical London dry counterparts. The Royal Navy purchased large quantities of gin for its officers (by contrast, ratings were issued with rum) and as Plymouth was a naval dockyard much of Coates' business was to the officers' mess. Other naval towns such as Bristol and Liverpool also had distilleries supplying the Navy with the town's particular style of gin, but Plymouth is the only one to survive. Indeed, Plymouth is also the only British gin still made at its original distillery.

Thanks to the busy naval port, Plymouth Gin quickly became the most widely distributed gin in the country and London distillers clearly envied Plymouth's name and reputation. On 13th March 1884, and then again in 10th February 1887, Coates successfully obtained injunctions preventing London distilleries from making 'Plymouth gin'. In 1933, Plymouth also won a court case against Burrough's, the producer of Beefeater Gin which had attempted to produce its own gin labelled 'Plymouth'.

These court cases helped underpin Plymouth Gin's claim that only a gin made in Plymouth should be termed 'Plymouth' gin. As a result, in 1987 Plymouth became the first defined spirit to be granted a PGI – Protected Geographical Indication – thus only gin made in the town of Plymouth can have the name Plymouth on its label. (It's a shame London Dry gin is not equally protected.)

Although Plymouth Gin is still made in the same distillery in which it was created, Coates has been owned by a range of different companies. Seager Evans, based in Deptford, London but controlled by Schanley

12,820
BULK LITRES

PLYMOUTH GIN
MIDDLE CUT

VAT No. EIGHT

of New York, purchased Coates in 1958 and changed the formula to fall more in line with the predominant London Dry style and with American tastes. In 1975 Plymouth was acquired by Whitbread, then an English brewing company with a vast tied pub estate in which to market its own brand of gin.

The brand's heyday was already behind it when the now defunct Allied Domecq took over Plymouth. It had gone from being a premium gin to a brewer's 'house' pour, and to Allied it was a secondary brand, especially when gin sales in the UK started to plummet. Sadly, the response was to lower Plymouth Gin's alcohol strength to 37.5% alcohol by volume. It took a band of entrepreneurial private investors led by John Murphy (of Interbrand and St. Peter's beer fame) and Charles Rolls (now Fever Tree) to recognise how special Plymouth Gin was and to step in and save it.

On 1st May 1996, they bought Plymouth and set about restoring the brand, firstly by ordering that the base neutral spirit be made once again from grain instead of the cheaper sugar beet spirit introduced by Allied. The alcohol strength was upped to a distinctive 41.2% (17 underproof), so firmly returning Plymouth to its premium stature. New packaging was also introduced by its new owners, who copied a vintage bottle they had seen in the distillery's archive. This featured the Mayflower ship on the front label, with a monk printed on the reverse of the back label: once his feet were dry, it was said to indicate it was time to buy another bottle.

On the production side, they returned Plymouth to being a 'direct' or 'one shot' gin, meaning the spirit coming off the still is only reduced to bottling strength with water, rather than being 'stretched' by blending with more neutral alcohol, as is the case with most other gins.

Charles, a keen amateur pilot, regularly persuaded unsuspecting journalists to board his tiny plane so he could fly them to Plymouth airport and show off the quaint old distillery. At this time, the 'super premium' gin category didn't exist, in the UK or anywhere else, and Britain's Asda, the brand's first supermarket presence, soon delisted the gin as they could not sell a gin above a £9.99 price point. The partners then achieved a limited listing for Plymouth at Tesco, with a price reflecting its premium nature. Volumes remained small, however, at less than 5,000 cases per year. It wasn't until 28th January 1997, when TV wine expert Jilly Goolden raved about Plymouth on the BBC's *Food & Drink* show and sales rocketed by 1,000 per cent, prompting Tesco to elevate the spirit to a national listing.

It was during this period of growth, when Plymouth Gin was being rediscovered by bartenders and consumers alike, that I first visited Plymouth and become a convert – it's hard not to. Then, in 2000, I was in a meeting with Nick Blacknell, at that time in charge of the UK marketing of Absolut, when he mentioned that he was looking for a great gin to bring into the Seagram's portfolio. I instantly thought of Plymouth and put Nick in touch with Charles Rolls. It was a beautiful marriage, consummated in 2005 when Vin & Sprit, the Swedish state-owned company which then produced Absolut vodka, purchased Plymouth Gin.

Vin & Sprit, a company famed for its design and marketing of Absolut, unveiled new packaging for Plymouth in April 2006. The sleek modern bottle borrowed Art Deco styling and shocked some loyal followers of the brand (including us) with the radical change from its previous identity. Then in 2008, Plymouth and Absolut were purchased by Pernod Ricard, the present owner of both brands, where incidentally, Nick now heads up Jameson.

Nick's part in this tale cannot be underestimated. He recognised the potential of Plymouth and worked his brand magic with the support of a multinational corporation – originally Seagram and then Vin & Sprit. Pernod Ricard has continued to invest in Plymouth despite also owning and investing in Beefeater. The latest manifestation of this support was the launch of another radically different, but this time 'old-fashioned', rounded-shouldered bottle in January 2012 (to be released January 2013 in the UK). This prominently returned the square-rigged Mayflower to the front label with the monk reinstated, now on a sticker on the back visible through the bottle as a ghost-like image to the bottom right of the oval, inverted horseshoe-like label. With this packaging change came a repositioning of the gin, reflected in its price, as a super-premium brand. These changes have helped drive sales in the USA which is set to become Plymouth's main market in 2013.

Back in 1958, Schanley of New York purchased Plymouth Gin due to its popularity in the USA, something attested by its being named as the gin of choice in numerous early American cocktail books. Indeed, the first-ever printed recipe for a Dry Martini in Stuart's *Fancy Drinks and How to Mix Them*, published in 1896, called for Plymouth Gin.

Plymouth is enjoying a well-earned renaissance and is once again a popular gin amongst aficionados in America – the journey from its Plymouth home could be said to have followed that of the Pilgrim fathers. As I write, in October 2012, production is close to hitting 100,000 cases per year. Plymouth Gin can be considered saved and in rude health.

PRODUCTION

The production of Plymouth Gin is overseen by Master Distiller Sean Harrison. He joined Allied Domecq in November 1994, after responding to an advert in the local paper. He had been a naval officer for the previous nine years – not a traditional background for a gin distiller – but he was chosen by Desmond Payne, the then master distiller who had been with the company since the late 1950s, to come on as assistant distillery manager.

After Brian Martyn, the master distiller at Beefeater, which was also within the Allied group, retired, Desmond began to run both distilleries from Beefeater's London home. A year later, however, Plymouth was sold, the connection between the two gins was severed, and Sean became master distiller. In 18 months he had gone from being a sailor with no knowledge of distilling to being the man in charge of buying botanicals and making the spirit. "I can remember the first time Desmond wasn't here, looking at the still and thinking 'oh shit! I hope this doesn't go wrong'," he recalls. Though it was a steep learning curve, for the first four years Desmond remained involved in Sean's day-to-day duties, making himself available at the end of a phone. Meeting Sean now and

Welcome
to Plymouth
Twinned with Tonic

1793
PLYMOUTH
ENGLISH GIN

DISTILLERY
&
TOUR

BRASSERIE

COCKTAIL LOUNGE

SHOP

www.plymouthgin.com

Caution
Watch your
step
Use
handrail

ency Exit
&
ory Tours
Only

orised access

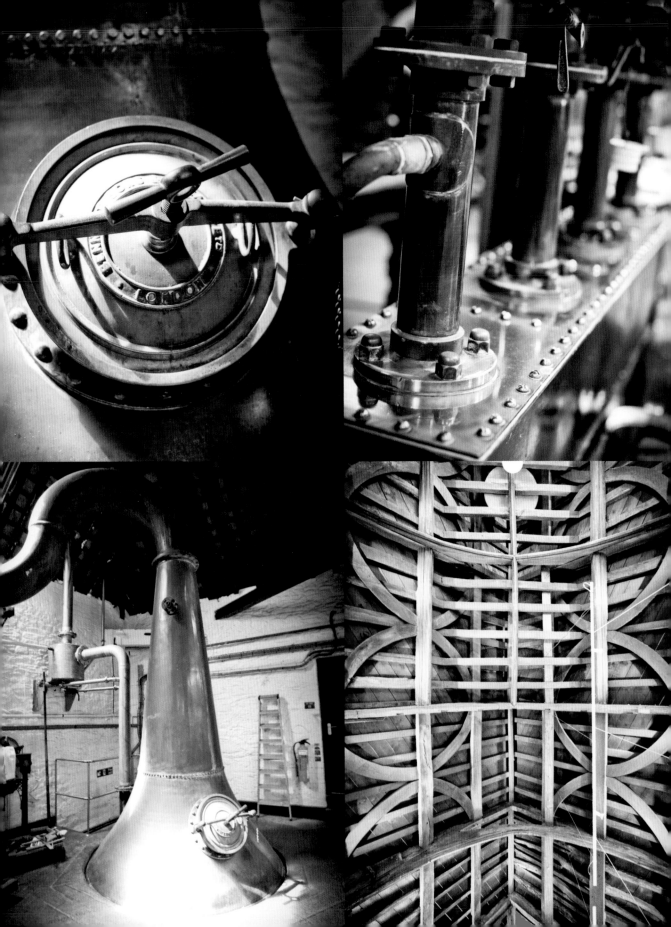

talking to him about distilling, you'll wonder that he was not born into gin making.

Plymouth Gin is flavoured by redistilling wheat neutral alcohol with seven botanicals. In order of dominance these are: juniper berries, coriander, lemon peel, sweet orange peel, sweet angelica, orris root and cardamom. Unusually, no bitter botanicals are used – the orange peel being sweet orange rather than the more commonly used bitter varieties.

When discussing Plymouth's botanical sourcing, Sean notes: 'If you are a decent distiller, you never guarantee to buy from the same place each year, because you don't know what nature is going to do – where it grows, the rain, the soil content, the bedrock and everything else affects the essential oils. Unless you go hunting for perfect botanicals how can you keep your flavour profile the same?'

Plymouth Gin is made in a 7,000 litre copper pot still which was installed in 1855 and has been in regular use since – more than 150 years. It sits in the still room next to a rectifying and carterhead still, fitted by Seager Evans when it closed its distillery in Deptford and moved the stills to Black Friars (two other pot stills were removed to make way for the relocated rectifying and carterhead stills). While old photographs show the original three pot stills in place, their 'footprint' remains on the floor and a dent in the wall marks where they sat.

The rectifying still was originally installed to improve the quality of the base alcohol used in the gin's production but now the quality of modern grain neutral alcohol is such that this is no longer required. However, due to lack of tank space this still is now used to increase

the strength of the feints from about 40% to 90% alcohol by volume or above. This by-product of distillation is then sold to a French company for industrial applications.

The base alcohol used to make Plymouth gin is a wheat neutral spirit, which at the time of writing is sourced from north east France, the spirit bought on a one-year contract with stipulations that it is made from wheat grain and has certain required characteristics: Sean looks for what he calls a 'neutral buttery smelling alcohol' when sourcing this spirit.

The juniper and other botanicals are loaded into the pot still with neutral spirit and water. Some producers leave the botanicals to steep for as long as 48-hours before distillation. Others believe that steeping 'stews' the flavours and so distil the mixture immediately. At Plymouth they choose not to steep the seven botanicals that go into Plymouth, instead, loading them just before firing the still, which takes 1½ hours to reach boiling point. The run lasts up to 7 hours, of which 5½ hours is the desirable gin spirit with feints following for about 1 to 1½ hours after that, these are not heavily oiled. There are no heads as such and the little spirit discarded at the start of the run is really only the result of cleaning out the pipework from the previous run.

Plymouth is made according to the 'one shot' or 'direct gin' method so after distillation the spirit is only reduced to bottling strength with water. (The botanical-infused distillate is not stretched by the addition of more neutral spirits as is typical with most other gins.) Some 90 per cent of all gin produced at Black Friars is approved by Sean Harrison, although the whole process is also

overseen by fellow distillers John Tagent and Nigel Garnham. Once approved, the spirit, which comes off the still at 83% alc./vol., is watered down to 65% alc./vol. and sent by tanker to Hayman's bottling operation in Essex, where Plymouth has been bottled since 1996.

PLYMOUTH GIN
41.2% alc./vol.
Plymouth Gin is the only British gin to be continuously made at the same distillery. Indeed it has been made in the same 7,000 litre copper pot still for over 150 years. It is also one of the few gins to be sold globally at the same alcohol strength and the only seven-botanical recipe.

Appearance: Crystal clear. **Aroma:** Juniper notes of pine, lavender and camphor with lemon zest, sage and eucalyptus. **Taste:** Fresh zingy juniper with zesty lemony bite and orange ripeness; character and interest are enhanced by more subtle rooty notes with fresh coriander and mild white pepper spice.
Aftertaste: Refreshing pine freshness lingers with subtle white pepper and liquorice-like rootyness.
diffordsguide rating: ★ ★ ★ ★ ★

PLYMOUTH GIN NAVY STRENGTH
57% alc./vol.
By 1850, Coates & Co, the makers of Plymouth Gin, were supplying more than 1,000 casks of navy-strength gin to the British Royal Navy each year. Naval officers would mix it with Angostura aromatic bitters and lime juice for 'medicinal' purposes. Its high strength was important as this meant gin could be spilt on gunpowder without

affecting its ability to ignite when needed in battle – a sensible precaution, given casks of gunpowder and gin were stored alongside each other in the ship's hold.

Plymouth Gin's navy strength was reintroduced in 1993 when Desmond Payne, the master distiller at the time, sought to create a gin to celebrate Coates & Co's 200th anniversary.

Appearance: Crystal clear. **Aroma:** The addition of a little water releases a wonderfully floral, citrus nose with strong notes of lavender, camphor and pine.
Taste: Supercharged Plymouth in both flavour and strength. The wonderfully flavoursome palate includes more floral notes with rounded lemon and sage coriander, lemon zest and clean juniper notes.
Aftertaste: Pine freshness dominates with spicy naan bread and lingering citrus zest.
diffordsguide rating: ★ ★ ★ ★ ★ +

Producer: Black Friars Distillery, 60 Southside Street, Plymouth, England.
www.plymouthgin.com

"Portobello Road No. 171 Gin and the Ginstitute above the Portobello Star in Notting Hill are educating hundreds of thirsty consumers about gin, distillation and blending."

Portobello Road No. 171 Gin

London, England

"**M**aking gin started as a hobby, but it could become the tail that wags the dog." For Ged Feltham, owner of Leelex Group and the entrepreneur behind a fleet of bars in Leeds and London, becoming a drinks brand owner was never on the agenda.

But after 15 years of opening and running bars – helping drive a thirst for cocktails in Leeds with Oporto, Jake's Bar, Angel's Share, Neon Cactus and the just-launched Cielo Blanco, then returning to London to open the Portobello Star – his gamble has paid off and Portobello Road No. 171 Gin may prove to be his greatest success yet.

Ged had opened the Portobello Star in 2008, fronted by long-term collaborator Jake Burger, who moved down from Leeds for the job. And after a shaky start – opening on the day that Lehman Brothers imploded was not the most auspicious beginning – by 2010 the business was washing its face and Ged began to think about whether two underused floors above the bar could be put to better use.

After a chance tour of the Beefeater distillery in south London, combined with Jake's idea that they create a miniature gin museum in the space above the bar, Ged, 41, had an epiphany. "I came up with the idea of having our own tiny still on site, making our own single botanical distillates, and combining a gin museum with the chance for people to blend their own gins," he says. "The idea of creating a tourist attraction came before we even conceived of creating a gin."

Jake curated a museum – London's second smallest – acquiring a collection of late 1800s/early 1900s gins and discovering one of Jerry Thomas's business cards on eBay. And on the second floor a 30-litre Portuguese still named Copper-Nicus – the smallest licensed copper pot still in

London – was installed alongside a school lab-style blending room. Like boys with toys, late night experiments saw Ged and Jake create single botanical distillates using everything from conventional gin botanicals through to hops, tropical fruit, Yorkshire Tea and even Worcestershire Sauce, then playing with blending the resulting liquids.

They were in essence doing the groundwork for what would become Portobello Road No. 171 Gin, which quickly took shape as they refined a classic gin recipe using juniper berries, lemon peel, bitter orange peel, coriander seeds, orris root, angelica, cassia bark and liquorice, with the unique addition of nutmeg to bring a warm, aromatic, sweet spice.

Ged realised this might have commercial possibilities, but admits he didn't yet regard it as a compelling business proposition. "I did all the costings and took the formula we'd developed to Charles Maxwell of Thames Distillers, but figured we could simply use it in-house at all our bars if it didn't take off commercially. Charles said to give him a couple of weeks, and came back with a scaled-up version of what we'd made in Copper-Nicus."

Thames delivered the first batch in September 2011 – Number #1 now has pride of place in the Ginstitute's museum, as it had been named – and Ged recalls his first visits to wholesalers to try and convince them to distribute the product. He was proud of the cork-sealed, cognac-style bottle, with its Victoriana-inspired label, each hand-labelled, signed and stamped, but well-aware he was just the latest in a line of new gin-makers.

"I could tell they were thinking 'not another gin', you could see it in their eyes – particularly because many new

gins don't taste as good as they sound like they should, and because we didn't have any quirky botanicals and were so classic in style. But they'd reluctantly agree to take a couple cases. Then we got a lucky break with Selfridges, which took it straight away, and thedrinkshop.com too, and suddenly we were getting repeat orders."

Released just in time for Christmas 2011, buyers snapped up the first consignment of the gin, and Ged hasn't looked back. Fast forward to mid-2013 and Portobello Road No. 171 Gin is selling up to 700 cases per month, distributed in the UK – where it's also just been listed by high-end supermarket Waitrose – Norway, Sweden and Italy and soon to enter Spain, Australia and Singapore. And nearly 2,000 people have paid £100 each to participate in the Ginstitute's blending sessions, leaving with one bottle of Portobello Road No. 171 Gin – and one bottle of their own blend.

Next for the nascent brand are some small batch, limited edition gins made in Copper-Nicus, due out for Christmas 2013, while a makeover of the Portobello Star will see its gin list grow and the bar become more obviously linked with the Ginstitute upstairs.

"The success of the gin has taken us completely by surprise," says Ged. "We're still pinching ourselves. And there's no sign of the gin craze slowing down – there are a huge amount of vodka drinkers to convert and few people really have a clue about distillation, so there's plenty more room for growth for the Ginstitute and the gin itself."

PRODUCTION
Portobello Road No. 171 Gin was first conceived at No. 171 Portobello Road, Notting Hill, west London, but it is made at Thames Distillers in Clapham, south London. First, a botanical distillate is created, by combining the botanicals – juniper berries, lemon peel, bitter orange peel, coriander seeds, orris root, angelica, cassia bark, liquorice and nutmeg – with neutral alcohol and water and distilling the mixture in a small stainless steel pot still called Tom Thumb. (The still, built in March 1984, was the last to be made by John Dore & Co. in London before the company moved outside of the capital.) More neutral alcohol and water is then added to create a larger batch for bottling, which is also conducted at Thames Distillers.

PORTOBELLO ROAD NO. 171 GIN
Appearance: (bottle No. 358) Crystal clear.
Aroma: Elegant, floral nose with junipery lavender and camphor. Generous use of orris root imparts its characteristic parma violet and clean hamster cage while citrus aromas are subdued.
Taste: Juniper is centre stage but not screaming, while citrus is way down the billing. As London gins go, Portobello is on the spicy side, but it's a 'warm interest adding', rather than a 'hot pepper' spice, with nutmeg and cinnamon (from cassia bark) with savoury celery-like notes (angelica root).
Aftertaste: Lingering liquorice and nutmeg finish.
diffordsguide rating: ★ ★ ★ ★ ☆

Producer: Thames Distillers, Timberhill Way, Gauden Road, Clapham, London, England.
www.portobellostarbar.co.uk/portobelloroadgin

"Sipsmith's journey so far has been a short one, but nonetheless epic in terms of the role it has played and its inspiration to others."

Sipsmith Gin

Hammersmith, London, England

When the first batch of gin poured from a still named Prudence on 14th May 2009, Sipsmith became the first copper pot distillery to open in London in nearly 200 years, arguably marking the start of the modern craft distilling movement in the UK but also a poignant return for the capital to its cottage distilling heritage.

"We really didn't know anything about distilling when we started talking about opening a distillery," recalls Fairfax Hall. At the time, he and Sam Galsworthy, Sipsmith's co-founders and life-long childhood friends, were working separately in America and were unconnected to the world of spirits production. But as they caught up over a G&T in a cafe in Philadelphia, the conversation between Fairfax, then an MBA student and Sam, working for Fuller's brewery, happened to turn to the emergence of the craft distilling movement in the US.

"Tuttlehilltown had kicked off, Hangar One and Philadelphia Distilling had just got going, and they were all getting a great reception," remembers Fairfax. "I think we were drinking Junipero – it was certainly a big, strong gin and that was essentially when the seeds of an idea were sown. It was probably Sam who actually suggested opening a distillery, but I was just as keen."

This was in 2002, and over the next few years the two friends would return to the topic again and again, becoming more earnest with each conversation. Fairfax joined Diageo – a strategic decision to learn more about the world of spirits – but it wasn't until five years later that they agreed they had reached tipping point. They could either go on talking about it, or get off their butts and do

something. In January 2007 the two jumped ship.

"It was a gamble, and the storm clouds were gathering around the economy, but our confidence was really high because there wasn't anyone else in the UK doing what we were proposing," says Fairfax. "But it started to feel real when we both sold our houses and took the equity to invest in Sipsmith."

One of their first steps was to commission a still from German firm Christian Carl. Incidentally, Prudence's name is a cheeky reference to the straitened economic times in which Sipsmith launched – the concept of 'prudence' seemingly the then-prime minister Gordon Brown's favourite topic. Sam and Fairfax had nowhere to actually site Prudence yet, but managed to find the property that now houses Sipsmith in a serendipitous twist of seemingly random events that now look like fate.

First, Fairfax remembers being at a wedding, chatting to another guest who turned out to be a sculptor. Separately, a few days later he was looking on the internet for property and came across a studio/garage space in a residential street – he and Sam were keen they should be part of a community and not relegated to an out-of-town industrial park. Next, Fairfax paid a visit to the property at 27 Nasmyth Street, Hammersmith W6 and, looking through the window, spied a huge collection of dusty spirit bottles. If that were not a good omen in itself, it turned out the space had previously been rented by the late drinks writer Michael Jackson (27 March 1942-30 August 2007).

And in another twist of fate, the owner of the building proved to be that very same sculptor who Fairfax had met at the wedding. Spooky. Finally, they discovered that the

building previously housed a micro-brewery, supplying ale to a pub on the street behind. (The Rising Sun which from 1890 to the 1960s was at 20 Cardross Street.) It was practically meant to be.

Unfortunately, starting up the site as a distillery was, they found, easier said than done and it took nearly two more calendar years to get a licence. This being the earliest days of the craft distilling movement, Her Majesty's Revenue & Customs officers were unused to the idea of a small commercial still in a neighbourhood environment and quickly decided that what the budding distillers were proposing was, well, illegal. Technically, they cited anachronistic laws that prevented the location of a still close to retail operations (to prevent black-market sales).

Fairfax and Sam appealed – after all, many Scottish distilleries already had visitor centres and bars – and their case was referred up to Glasgow. Having started this quest for a licence in January 2007 – the time they had quit their jobs – it wasn't until December 2008 that they were ultimately rewarded with a licence, now proudly displayed in a frame in the still house.

By this time, the economy had really tanked and bars were going out of business left, right and centre. Sam and Fairfax had not been earning money for nearly two years, and they'd also persuaded their friends and family to invest in the business too, so the pressure was mounting. "That was definitely the most nervous that we've been," says Fairfax.

The next challenge was addressing the technicalities of distilling – as much as they had read around the subject and sought advice from gin distillers, including Beefeater's Desmond Payne, none of that gave them the expertise to deal with the nuance of making a consistent spirit, the effects of different still designs, and the logistics of operating and maintaining a still day-after-day. The question of whether they could actually make a decent gin was answered at a Negroni Club party at the Beefeater distillery, where gin writer Geraldine Coates introduced them to Jared Brown and Anistatia Miller, the drinks writers and historians. Sam and Fairfax were thrilled to learn Jared and 'Stash' had been involved in the early days of a tiny little distillery and bar in Idaho called Bardenay. In another serendipitous twist, they were now living in Ealing, west London, close by to Hammersmith, having recently relocated from the US.

"When Jared and Anistatia learned Sam still had friends at Fuller's, they asked to go on a brewery tour, and it was on that that I remember being incredibly impressed about the depth of their knowledge," says Fairfax. "You can't fail to be blown away with how much they know, and we gently sounded them out, discussing the still design and the gin recipe." It wasn't long before Jared joined the duo as master distiller.

In fact, it was the very next day, as Jared recalls: "I realised they shared my belief that the best possible gin is one that reflects the mastery of previous generations of distillers. Reinventing the wheel, coming up with new and different botanicals simply didn't appeal. They shared my passion for tradition and so I started working with them first thing the morning after we met."

Work began on the recipe, though, as Jared admits, most of the hard work had been done by generations of long-dead distillers. "For us, the major task was fine-

tuning the formula to our palates, and also to Prudence. Imagine a world where no two cookers performed in the same way: recipe books would be rough guidelines at best. That's distilling."

If they expected their first run through Prudence to be a walk in the park, they were in for a nasty surprise. "We'd spent ages designing the recipe and we naively thought it was a question of extrapolating the recipe, wacking it in, turning it on and turning it down if it boils too much," says Fairfax. "But what came over was so disappointing – it was a car crash of different flavours. We learned that the still had its own personality and it was Jared that said we had to slow everything down so each of the botanicals could shine through. It was astounding to see how his palate could detect how each of the botanicals emerged at different points."

That first batch came through in mid-January 2009, but it was another two months before the first production batch came off on 14th March 2009. "It was the same day as my daughter was born," says Fairfax. "I came from the hospital to the distillery to see my second baby born."

The next chapter in the Sipsmith story was getting their product into bars. Sam, proud owner of a Yamaha moped, would load up with a few bottles of gin, and buzz around town hitting the bars. His first stop was The Bar at the Dorchester Hotel on Park Lane – an admirably courageous philosophy of 'aim high'.

"We'd all written down the types of bars we wanted to be seen in and I knew the guy at the Dorchester's name was Giuliano Morandin," says Sam. "I didn't give him the 'hard sell' – in all honesty this was unfamiliar territory. I told him I'd love to have a meeting and he couldn't believe what we'd done. He asked me how many venues were we in and was quite flattered that we weren't actually listed anywhere. When I returned to meet with the Dorchester's F&B director, they said they didn't want another supplier, but Giuliano was quite insistent and placed an order for a case. We've still got the photos of that first case – I delivered it to the loading bay where they were more used to dealing with pallets. And then we told everyone we knew to go in and order Sipsmith gin drinks."

With the Dorchester as their first client, the nearby bar at the Metropolitan followed suit, then the Martini Mecca of Dukes Hotel, and it waterfalled. After eight months of moped-ing around in the wind and the rain, Sipsmith boasted more than 50 accounts. They shifted 40 cases the first month, doubled it in the second, then they got a shock when demand seemed to stagnate at 85 cases. "We thought 'whoops'," says Fairfax, "but then we were into October and it started picking up again."

By this time, the moped was blatantly insufficient to their needs. "I'd have two cases between my legs, two on the seat, and then another two in a pizza box on the back," says Sam. "I wasn't stupid but we had a few near misses: two cases fell off on the way to Gerry's once. I had to explain what the dents were in the box. I remember those days so fondly partly because we got to know all those guys in the loading bays. I think they enjoyed the ridiculousness of it all." The tipping point came in Spring 2010. With a presence on the back-bars of some of the best venues in town, and listings in Majestic, Waitrose and Ocado, they switched to a distributor.

Today, Sipsmith produces 80,000 bottles a year, with Prudence practically running every day, making 300

bottles in each batch. Jared or assistant distiller Chris Garden taste every batch: "There will always be slight variations as the still is too small to produce exactly identical gin every time," says Jared, "but that's what I love about it. I haven't hit even a slightly dodgy batch since the first few months we were operating."

In addition to the core vodka and gin, Sipsmith has taken on the might of Pimm's with its Summer Cup ("sales have gone bonkers," says Sam), and now there's sloe gin and damson vodka too. Jared, who cultivates his own gin botanicals, such as iris, angelica and coriander – and sloes and damsons for that matter – in his garden in the Cotswolds (for play, rather than production purposes), constantly experiments with potential new variants that may or may not make it on to back-bars and supermarket shelves. "I do a lot of new product R&D and testing these days. Some, like the Summer Cup, work out. Others, like the English Mustard Gin, aren't sufficiently shelf-stable to bring to market."

"We're still young in our brand life cycle," adds Sam, "but we're never going to be a performing monkey adding more and more lines: we're all about two core brands and a handful of seasonal extensions."

Volumes continue to head north, which puts Prudence's capacity in the spotlight – as well as whether the brand can still call itself a craft operation – and headcount is now at seven people.

"There's definitely Prudence No. 2 on the cards," says Fairfax, "but I would categorically say we'll always be a hand-crafted operation, making small batches by just a few hands. When we expand and get another still it will be more batches and more hands but we won't compromise what we set out to do."

Sipsmith's journey so far has been a short one, but nonetheless epic in terms of the role it has played and its inspiration to others – a move which is seeing more and more cottage distillers entering the fray, not quite on the scale of the US craft movement but certainly with similar intent.

"We've heard of a number of other business plans for gins that reference what we've done, but that doesn't worry me," says Fairfax. "I've always been firmly in the camp that the more small batch craft distillers producing quality products the better. I would definitely like to think we come to be seen as leading the craft movement in the UK."

PRODUCTION

Sipsmith's copper pot still, 'Prudence' was built by Germany's oldest distillery fabricator, Christian Carl. Sam and Fairfax opted for an all-copper still as they believe the metal contributes to mouth-feel and texture, even though there is little sulphate in the high quality neutral spirit they use to charge the still.

Prudence has a 300-litre charge capacity and is designed with a narrow neck and boil ball to generate maximum reflux. It is heated by six independently controlled heating elements in its base. Unusually, the design allows the optional use of a botanical vapour chamber and also a five plate column. Each of the five plates in the column can be opened or closed, or the whole column can be completely bypassed. Prudence is a very flexible lady.

Incidentally, the Sipsmith name comes from a comment by Fairfax's father who is a silversmith. He suggested that a distiller was also a specialist craftsman and so a '-smith' suffix was equally appropriate.

VODKA PRODUCTION

To make Sipsmith vodka (also the base spirit for its gin), Sipsmith charges Prudence with English barley neutral spirit hydrated from 96% alc./vol. to 60-65% alc./vol. using tap water. At the start of vodka production, a feedback loop (reflux pipe) from the foot of the column returning vapour to the pot is opened to prevent the vapour rising up though the fractional distillation column. The vapour is sent around to be redistilled in the pot for the first two hours before the feedback loop is closed and vapour allowed to rise up the column which initially has all its five plates closed. These are then steadily opened and adjusted until an equilibrium is reached.

The first five litres of distillate to emerge from the still are discarded (around 2 per cent of the run), with hearts starting to coming over at around 91% alc./vol. These run for about two hours before the cut to tails at around 85% alc./vol.. The decision on when to switch to tails is purely made on smell and taste, although they know within a window of around 15 minutes when this will need to be made.

Demand for Sipsmith Gin far exceeds that for its vodka, so some vodka distillations are only carried out to produce the base spirit used to make their gin. However, if the distillate is destined to be bottled as Sipsmith Vodka then the first 40 per cent of the heart is separated and the second part of heart is kept for re-distillation to make gin. The 'vodka' distillation produces a distillate at around 89% alc./vol. (average) across the run. The spirit is then reduced to bottling strength with Lydwell Spring water.

SIPSMITH GIN PRODUCTION

Sipsmith Gin is distilled using Sipsmith vodka as its base – namely English barley neutral spirit which has been redistilled in Prudence, a 300-litre copper pot still. The spirit is diluted to 60% alc./vol. with purified Lydwell Spring water before the botanicals are added. The Lydwell Spring is one of the sources of the River Thames and amazingly the chaps at Sipsmith simply drive from London to the source and fill a tank in the back of their van and drive it back to London. Thankfully they don't require much of the precious water as their batches are genuinely small - just around 300 bottles a time.

Ten tradition London dry gin botanicals are used: Macedonian juniper, Bulgarian coriander seeds, French angelica root, Spanish liquorice root, Italian orris root, Spanish ground almond, Chinese cassia bark, Madagascan cinnamon, Seville orange and Spanish lemon peel. The spirit and botanicals are heated to 60-65°C for 15 minutes before being left to stand for 12 hours to allow the botanicals to steep prior to distillation.

When making Sipsmith Gin the fractional distillation column on Sipsmith's Prudence's still (used when making vodka) is bypassed so the swan neck goes straight to the condenser. The gin comes over at around 84% alc./vol. and is reduced to bottling strength using more Lydwell Spring water.

Sipsmith is a genuine London distilled, one-shot gin - something of a rarity (two-shot gins are distilled with twice the botanical recipe and then stretched after distillation by the addition of neutral spirit. The doubling-up saves still time).

DISTILLERY TOUR

The chaps at Sipsmith are rightly proud of opening the first new distillery in London for two centuries and like to show it off. Aside from the majority of the drinks industry seemingly always casually popping in, they run official

distillery tours on Wednesday evenings every week.

The term 'distillery tour' conjures up images of tour guides, visitor centres and sampling rooms, culminating with the obligatory visit to the gift shop. Well, there are no branded key rings, caps or T-shirts at Sipsmith, nor a tour guide. This is a one-room operation in a space little larger than a double-size garage and your guide will be the owners and distillers themselves. Naturally, you'll be greeted with a drink and talked through a tasting of their products. Pre-booking is essential. £12 per person.

SIPSMITH GIN
41.6% alc./vol.
Based on English barley neutral spirit and distilled in a small copper pot still in London's Hammersmith using ten tradition London dry gin botanicals: juniper, coriander seeds, angelica root, liquorice root, orris root, ground almond, cassia bark, cinnamon, Seville orange peel and lemon peel.

Appearance: (batch LDG/215) Crystal clear.
Aroma: Clean, assertive fresh, pine forest juniper with perfumed, floral lilac, pine and lemon meringue.
Taste: Clean with juniper and coriander rightly leading with zesty citrus and spice. **Aftertaste:** Rich old-fashioned liquorice becomes evident and coats the tongue to the end of the finish.
diffordsguide rating: ★ ★ ★ ★ ★

SIPSMITH SUMMER CUP
29 alc./vol.
Based on Sipsmith Gin with added fruits, herb and spices, including Earl Grey tea, fresh Lemon Verbena and cucumber,

this summer cup is bottled at 29% abv, a bottling strength selected to mimic the original Pimm's bottling.

The label recommends serving Sipsmith Summer Cup with three parts lemonade over ice with summer fruits.

Appearance: Clear, brick red. **Aroma:** Wonderfully aromatic nose like walking into a gin distillery's botanical store with pronounced juniper oils and herbal aromas, peppery spice and cassia with zesty citrus.
Taste: Enlivening spicy, herbal, fruity palate with strong piney juniper, invigorating cracked black pepper and clove spice. The Lemon Verbena and tannic Earl Grey tea are easily detectable. **Aftertaste:** Far more powerful in its flavour and drier than Pimm's. Long spicy finish with lingering cracked pepper corn heat.
diffordsguide rating: ★ ★ ★ ★ ★ +

SIPSMITH SLOE GIN
Launched in September 2010, Sipsmith sloe gin liqueur is produced as a limited edition each year and is based on Sipsmith's Gin. Each bottle is individually numbered.

Appearance: (2010 vintage) Clear, ruby red.
Aroma: Ripe red fruits with a greeny woodyness (freshly cut hedge). **Taste:** Sweet yet tart sloe berries, cherry and black currant with cleansing cracked black pepper. **Aftertaste:** Fades with green sloe berries and cracked black pepper.
diffordsguide rating: ★ ★ ★ ★ ☆

Producer: Sipsmith, 27 Nasmyth Street, Hammersmith, London, England.
www.sipsmith.com

"*The vintage copper stills used to make Tanqueray are beautiful examples of hand craftsmanship, and it is easy to forget you are in one of the largest distilleries in Europe.*"

Tanqueray London Dry Gin
Argyll, Scotland

Tanqueray is one of the oldest and most respected brands of gin and is seen by many as the gold standard to which all other gins should be compared. It is made at Diageo's Cameronbridge Distillery near Edinburgh which houses the famous Old Tom pot still.

The Tanqueray family were originally silversmiths and left France for England early in the 18th century, where three successive Tanquerays became rectors in Bedfordshire. In 1830 Charles Tanqueray, then aged just twenty, broke with family tradition and rather than become a clergyman, established his Vine Street Distillery in London's Bloomsbury, then an area noted for its spa water.

He experimented with many ingredients, testing botanicals from around the world but the balance of flavours in the Tanqueray recipe is so good that Tom Nichol, Tanqueray's present master distiller, suspects that he was aided by an already experienced distiller. However he managed it, in 1832 Charles Tanqueray started making his eponymous gin using a perfectly balanced recipe with a rich, full flavour.

Charles died in 1868 aged 58 years and his son Charles Waugh Tanqueray took over the business at the age of twenty, the same age at which his father had begun distilling. Waugh quickly built on his father's success, particularly in export markets where he promoted the brand through a network of international agents.

Waugh was an innovator who continually looked for ways to grow his business and towards the end of 1897 he began talks with Reginald C W Currie, the head of

Gordon & Company. The next year the two companies merged to form Tanqueray Gordon & Company. After the merger all production was transferred from the Vine Street Distillery to Gordon's Goswell Road site, in Clerkenwell, which as the name suggests was also an area noted for its water. From that period onwards Tanqueray was promoted in America and this remains the brand's largest market to this day. Charles Henry Drought (also known as Harry Tanqueray), was the first Secretary of the newly formed Tanqueray Gordon & Company. In 1922 Tanqueray Gordon & Company joined the Distillers Company, an organisation formed in 1877 when six Scotch whisky distilleries had joined forces. This proved to be an advantageous and very successful alliance. Fast forward some 60 years and the 1986 acquisition of the Distillers Company by Guinness would form United Distillers, which would go on to become Diageo, the world's leading premium drinks business.

During World War II a 1941 air raid almost completely destroyed the Tanqueray Distillery and only one of the stills, now lovingly known as 'Old Tom' survived. Repairs were made and although production was seriously affected it was not long before Old Tom was back in action.

Up until 1948 when the now familiar bottle was redesigned, Tanqueray was sold in numerous different shaped bottles. The design we recognise today was inspired by a 1920s range of Gordons pre-mixed cocktails that were sold in bottles designed to resemble a cocktail shaker - not a fire hydrant as some mistakenly believe. This new bottle celebrated the brand's link to

All over the world at cocktail time they call for **TANQUERAY'S**

Tanqueray's Special Dry is imported for men and women who appreciate the subtle

The Tanqueray Black Pearl.
Tanqueray Gin on the rocks with a new twist, a black olive.
A singular experience. Imported from England.

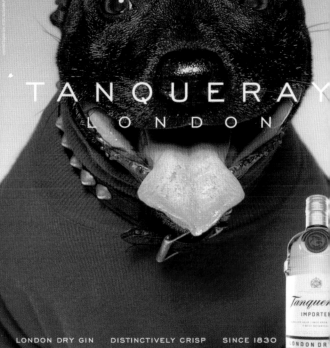

TANQUERAY
LONDON

LONDON DRY GIN   DISTINCTIVELY CRISP   SINCE 1830

If this were an ordinary gin, we would have put it in an ordinary gin bottle.
Charles Tanqueray

Read my lips.

Tanqueray. A singular experience.

There's nothing as perfect as an iced cold **"T&T."**

IMPORTED
Tanqueray

Imitation is the sincerest form of flattery.

Tanqueray. A singular experience.

"The Tanqueray people said they needed a sophisticated, dignified spokesman. Clearly, they're unaware of Mr. Jenkins' little incident at the Pelican Room."

How refreshingly distinctive.

DISTINCTIVE SINCE 1975

DISTINCTIVE SINCE 1830

DISTINCTIVE SINCE 1951

DISTINCTIVE SINCE

cocktails and its distinctive shape and exotic-sounding name made Tanqueray standout in the U.S., especially as it was the only green-bottled gin available in America at the time.

Construction of a new distillery began in 1951 and when completed in 1957 the Goswell Road Distillery included the rescued Old Tom still. The increased capacity was quickly filled as the US distributors drove the popularity of Tanqueray with a PR campaign that concentrated on California and its chicest bars. Celebrities such as Bob Hope, Frank Sinatra and Sammy Davis Jnr were reputed to enjoy Tanqueray.

From 1964 onwards, John Tanqueray, the great great-grandson of Charles Tanqueray, travelled around the world promoting the brand. Retiring in 1989, John was the last member of the Tanqueray family to work with the Tanqueray brand.

In 1989, to keep up with the growing demand for the brand, production of Tanqueray was moved from Goswell Road to Laindon in Basildon, Essex. The grain neutral spirit from which Tanqueray is distilled was, and still is, produced at one of the world's largest and most technically advanced distilleries at Cameron Bridge, Fife, Scotland. It seemed only logical to combine both rectification of the neutral alcohol and re-distillation with botanicals at the same site. Thus not ten years after the move to Laindon, Old Tom was once again moved, this time to its present day home, the gin still hall at Cameron Bridge.

THE CAMERONBRIDGE DISTILLERY
The Cameronbridge Distillery had been operating for several years before the famous whisky distiller John Haig

acquired it in 1824. Haig's cousin, Robert Stein, invented the first continuous still and Cameronbridge was the first distillery to produce grain whisky. The distillery takes its name from the bridge that crosses the River Leven on the distillery grounds. Once a mere ford, the present day bridge is much more substantial than the original but spans the river in exactly the same location. The river water is not used for production but it is used for cooling.

Cameronbridge is far from being a quaint picture postcard distillery and sprawls across a huge site with tank farms, tank filling stations and towering buildings that house tall column stills. However, the three large vintage copper pot stills used to make Tanqueray gin (and incidentally Tanqueray Stirling vodka) are beautiful examples of hand craftsmanship and once inside their dedicated still hall it is easy to forget you are in one of the largest distilleries in Europe. Wherever in the world it is sold, every bottle of Tanqueray is made in these stills with the hand-riveted 200 year old 'Old Tom' No. 4 Still always used for the final distillation of Tanqueray No. TEN.

PRODUCTION
The wheat neutral spirit on which Tanqueray gins are based is produced in the rectifiers housed in another part of Cameronbridge and is in fact the same base spirit used to make Smirnoff vodka, so extremely pure. Almost all other gin distillers buy in their grain neutral spirit from third party distillers and rectification at the same distillery gives the distillers of Tanqueray an even greater control over the consistency and quality of their base spirit.

Various brands of vodka and whisky are produced in other areas at Cameronbridge and the focus on one centre of distilling excellence means Tanqueray benefits from a large state of the art testing laboratory where the quality of botanicals and samples from various stages of production are carefully monitored.

The move from the Laindon Distillery which closed in 1998 (the site is now a business estate named Juniper Park) to Cameronbridge presented something of a challenge for Tanqueray's distillers as although the stills and other equipment were moved from London, the local water was different in character. Their solution was to use two different types of water in the gin's production. Water extracted from a deep bore hole on the distillery's grounds is blended with dem-ineralised water to mirror the character of London water. Interestingly, Tanqueray No. TEN is produced using only demineralised water.

Tanqueray's recipe has remained unchanged since 1832 and has three dominant botanicals: Tuscan juniper, angelica root and coriander, contributing to Tanqueuray's crisp, dry style with a rich juniper flavour. The fourth botanical, liquorice, is less obvious but no less important to the perfect balance of this blend of botanical flavours. The selection and care or these botanicals is crucial to the quality of the finished gin and test distillations are continuously undertaken in the onsite laboratory to monitor these.

Some distillers believe that the botanicals should be left for a period to steep in the neutral alcohol before commencing distillation. The folk at Tanqueray are in the other camp who start to distil immediately believing that a long period of maceration is either unnecessary or even detrimental as it 'stews' the botanicals.

As explained earlier, water plays an important role in the gin's final flavour. Its addition at this stage is also crucial to the distillation process. If water were not added and the botanicals distilled with just near pure alcohol (grain neutral spirit) when the distillation was completed the still would boil dry but with spent botanicals left burn onto the exposed steam heating coils at the foot of the still. Adding water means that all the alcohol can be distilled off still leaving water covering the steam coils and the botanicals can be run off with this water.

Most large scale gin distillers now make their gins using a 'multiple-shot' production method, whereby a recipe of botanicals several times stronger than the original recipe is macerated and distilled to produce a super concentrated gin. This is then diluted with neutral spirit to bring the proportion of botanicals to alcohol back to that of the original recipe. This multiple-shot method saves on still usage compared to the traditional 'one-shot' method, thus increasing production capacity and saving on energy costs. One-shot distillation is now extremely rare other than in boutique distilleries and Tanqueray is one of the last major gin brands still employing this method.

TANQUERAY SPECIAL DRY
47.3% alc./vol.
The name 'Special Dry' was introduced in 1950 and today is still applied to Tanqueray 47.3% alc./vol.

Appearance: Crystal clear. **Aroma:** Pungent, pine fresh piney juniper with faint lemon zest and light black pepper spice. **Taste:** More fresh juniper is closely followed by coriander and crystallised fruit with more subtle floral and rooty notes.
Aftertaste: Beautifully balanced and elegant with light peppery notes.
diffordsguide rating: ★ ★ ★ ★ ★ +

TANQUERAY EXPORT STRENGTH
43.1% alc./vol.
The Tanqueray Special Dry iconic bottle is used for this Tanqueray Export Strength introduced in 1999.
It is made to the same recipe but with a lower 43.1% alv./vol. strength.

Appearance: Crystal clear.
Aroma: Pungent pine, lavender and camphor juniper with faint lemon zest and liquorice. **Taste:** Clean and straightforward with strong juniper and pronounced rooty notes. **Aftertaste:** Lingering pine and camphor with a liquorice rootyness. Tanqueray 47.3% may suit G&Ts but this is the perfect strength.
diffordsguide rating: ★ ★ ★ ★ ★

TANQUERAY NO. TEN
47.3% alc./vol.
Launched in 2000, Tanqueray No. TEN is an ultra-premium gin based on the traditional four Tanqueray botanicals but with addition of Camomile flowers and

No. 4A STILL

THIS STILL HAS BEEN IN CONTINUOUS
USE SINCE THE REIGN OF GEORGE III

GORDON'S

fresh citrus fruit. Tanqueray No. TEN takes its name from the distillery's number 10 still, known as Tiny Ten. Dating back to the 30s, this small pot still was originally used as an experimental or trial-run still. Unlike its bigger brothers Tiny Ten is heated by a steam jacket as opposed to the steam coils found in the base of the larger stills.

Tiny Ten is used for the first distillation of Tanqueray No. TEN, which produces the citrus spirit known as the 'citrus heart' of No. TEN. Wheat grain neutral spirit is distilled with fresh hand chopped Florida oranges, Mexican limes and grapefruits to produce this essence. This use of fresh fruit rather than dried peels is most unusual and is thought to contribute Tanqueray No. TEN's fresh citrus-led style.

The second and final distillation takes place in the larger vintage 'Old Tom' No. 4 still. This is charged with the citrus heart previously distilled in Tiny Ten and wheat neutral spirit. Tanqueray's four traditional botanicals (juniper, coriander, angelica and liquorice) are added, along with camomile flowers and quartered fresh limes.

While the juniper, coriander, angelica and liquorice come from the same sources as those used in standard Tanqueray production, their proportions differ and many will be surprised to learn that there is a greater proportion of juniper in Tanqueray No. TEN than Tanqueray Special Dry.

Another important aspect of Tanqueray No. TEN's distillation is the low percentage of spirit retained as 'the cut' for the finished product. Typically (for example, with Special Dry) 90 per cent of the total spirit is captured as the cut, implying that around 10 per cent is discarded as 'heads' (the first spirit to run off the still) and 'tails' (the last spirit to run off the still). In contrast, during distillation of Tanqueray No. TEN, only around 60 per cent of the spirit makes the cut: 40 per cent is discarded.

This is because the all-important fresh citrus character is at its most intense and characterful within the first part of the run so a large percentage of the end of the run is discarded as tails. This also avoids the adverse flavours that can develop as botanicals 'stew' with spirit in the bottom of the still making their way into the final product. The cut leaves the still at 82% alc./vol. and blended with other batches to ensure a consistent product before being reduced to bottling strength with distilled water.

Appearance: Crystal clear. **Aroma:** Grapefruit and camomile are evident but so are complex spice and pine-sap juniper. **Taste:** Wonderfully rounded palate, incredibly so considering its heady alcoholic strength. Juniper is integrated with freshly squeezed lemon, orange and pink grapefruit juice while white pepper and coriander spice add depth. **Aftertaste:** Flavours from the palate continue through the long, almost creamy, sherbety finish with lingering black pepper and pine freshness.
diffordsguide rating: ★ ★ ★ ★ ★ +

Producer: Diageo, Cameronbridge Distillery, Cameron Bridge, Fife, Scotland.
www.tanqueray.com

"Charles Maxwell of Thames Distillers is the silent partner of a myriad gin brands – and that makes him something of an unsung hero in the drinks industry."

Thames Distillers

Clapham, London, England

London is where modern-day dry gin was created, hence the term 'London Dry Gin'. London was also birthplace to the great classic gin brands such as Tanqueray, Beefeater, Gordon's, Gilbey's and Booths. Consequently, many marketers want their new gin brands to be true 'London-made dry gins'. Of the dozen or so gin distilleries in the UK, less than a handful of those are in London. And only one, Thames Distillers, makes gin for third parties.

As the number of gin brands explodes, there are few UK gin distilleries for budding brand owners to turn to. In fact, just three facilities produce most of the gins to have emerged in recent years. These are G&J Greenall Distillery in Warrington, Langley Distillery near Birmingham, and the most prolific by far, Thames Distillers in Clapham, South London, which makes over 40 varieties of gin for more than 30 brands.

From Juniper Green to Portobello Road Gin, Ish, Sparrow and Oxley; from Swordsman, Jensen and Kingsbury to Gilpin's: all of these and more are made (technically 'rectified') here as part of the 200,000 cases that ship from SW4 every year.

Few of the bars on nearby Clapham High Street are aware that much of the gin they sell might come from just down the road. The Victorian terraces and tree-lined streets of this upmarket residential London suburb are not exactly the kind of place you'd expect to find a distillery, but Thames Distillers is discreetly tucked away in an anonymous industrial building at the end of a narrow lane by the side of a railway track. Thames is the perfect distillery for brand owners

wanting to create a new gin, as not only does it boast that all-important London address, it has two tiny stainless steel pot stills, Tom Thumb and Thumbelina. These produce batches as small as hundreds of cases, or the botanical recipe can be concentrated and the distillate stretched with neutral spirit (multi-shot) to make larger batches. The twin stills allow two entirely different gins to be made at the same time. An on-site bottling line means gin can be made and bottled here, allowing brands to be labelled 'distilled and bottled in London'. If all that were not already a gin marketer's dream, Thames is presided over by Charles Maxwell, the scion of a gin distilling dynasty that stretches back to the 17th century.

It is Charles who is personally approached by nascent gin distillers, be they from within the drinks industry or novices with a dream. It is he who advises whether their botanical ideas will make a good gin, then he tweaks their formulae to ensure they are up to scratch before putting them into production. Charles, and indeed Thames Distillers, is the silent partner – sometimes limited by contract from revealing being the true producer of a particular brand – and that makes him something of an unsung hero in the drinks industry.

"Some brands are happy to divulge that they work with us, but a lot prefer to give the illusion that they are the 'total' producer," he says. "That's the business model. Some gins we distil and bottle; others we ship in bulk, in concentrate, or at high strength to brands' own bottling lines.

"But all of our clients, particularly in Spain and

America, like the idea that it's distilled in London, a place where they can allude to the history of gin: we've been making gin since before The Mayflower set sail."

Less than ten years ago, before the new gin craze took root, life was rather different. Thames Distillers was making gin, but there was little creativity involved in what Charles calls 'standard' spirits, where the key factor was value for money. It was Hendrick's, Charles recalls, that changed everything. Its iconic botanicals, distinct bottle and quirky marketing strategy created the incentive for wider creativity: from then on, there was a new emphasis on flavour and less focus on volumes. With new brands coming to market Charles found he could suddenly charge more for his technical and creative expertise. "I thought it was all barking mad at first, but Hendrick's provided the jolt to the rest of the industry. Eight years ago we'd get a new approach only every few months: now we get one or two every week."

With that pressure on innovation, you'd be forgiven for thinking the botanical options for new gins might be running low. Not so, says Charles. He's a beneficiary to the fact that beyond juniper being the predominant flavour in gin, there are few rules. "Gin is still so far behind vodka in terms of the number of brands and flavours out there, but the botanical cupboard goes on forever. And if you don't want to make a London Dry Gin and choose to add things post distillation, there are even more options. I need to be sure we can properly clean the lines and tanks between runs, so I can be ruthless, but provided it's legal – we did have someone suggest cocaine once – we'll see if it can be done."

Today, Charles, now a spritely 60-years-old, produces four or five different gins each week. Production/distillation takes place three days out of five using both pot stills (excluding the separate still on site that's used by Oxley) and the bottling line runs five days a week.

Charles refuses to be drawn on whether he has a favourite gin among those he produces ("they're all favourites," he jokes) but he's clear on how he drinks it and, despite the soar-away craft gin market, he remains critical about the way gin is still often served. "I'm a distiller so I drink gin and water if I want to understand what's in it, but a well-made G&T if I want to relax. It upsets me if you want to guarantee a good G&T you still have to go to Spain. There, you find gin sommeliers with 8-10 gins who are able to tell you the difference between each one, you get a balloon glass, a good slug of gin and beautiful ice."

He acknowledges that his status as an 'unsung hero' does indeed resonate, though such is Thames Distillers' rising cachet that brands increasingly want Charles's presence felt more openly, with some carrying his signature on their labels. "Whether people know or not, I feel a real sense of pride walking into a bar and seeing our gins next to the big brands of Diageo, Pernod Ricard and William Grant. In Spain you might find a bar with 50 gin brands, and we'll produce ten of them – that's more than any other distiller in the world. In terms of number of brands we are the market leader."

Producer: Thames Distillers, Timbermill Way, Gauden Road, Clapham, London, England.
www.thamesdistillers.co.uk

Gin Brands

*175 and counting: a catalogue of the gin market from A. V. Wees to Zuidam,
taking in Europe, America and Australasia*

A.V. WEES AMSTERDAMSCHE OUDE GENEVER ★★★★☆

Alc./vol: 35% **Producer:** A. van Wees Distilleerderij De Ooievaar

This oude (old/traditional style) genever contains a high proportion of malt-wine and is has been matured for at least a year, and up to three years, in oak casks. It is made by the Van Wees family at their distillery in Amsterdam. It is presented in a traditional tall clay bottle. **Appearance**: Clear, pale straw yellow. **Aroma**: Nuts, olive oil and fresh hay with delicately spiced sandalwood, brioche and faint pear skin. **Taste**: Dry and fairly spicy – woody notes are slightly tannic. Cinnamon and clove spice, nutty oak and faint fruitiness (white grape/apple juice). **Aftertaste**: Dry clove spiced oak with peppery olive oil.

A.V. WEES THREE CORNER GIN RECOMMENDED ★★★★☆

Alc./vol: 42% **Producer:** A. van Wees Distilleerderij De Ooievaar

Established in 1782, 'A. van Wees Distilleerderij de Ooievaar' claims to be the last authentic distillery left in Amsterdam producing a range of Old Dutch genevers. Its 'Three Corner' dry gin is distilled with only two botanicals - juniper and lemon. **Appearance**: Crystal clear. **Aroma**: Clean nose with pine juniper to the fore supported by zesty lemon citrus and faint lavender. **Taste**: Beautifully clean, balanced, majestic and restrained in its delivery of piny juniper with a backbone of citrus zest. **Aftertaste**: Subtle with lightly tingling refreshing white pepper zing.

ADLER BERLIN DRY GIN RECOMMENDED ★★★★☆

Alc./vol: 42% **Producer:** Prussian Liquor Factory (Preussische Spirituosen)

Adler Gin, which incidentally translates from German as 'Eagle Gin', hence the illustration on the label, is based on a wheat distillate which is redistilled with the flavouring botanicals using vacuum distillation at temperatures below 80°C. **Appearance**: Translucent but with slight sediment in suspension. **Aroma**: Strong green cardamom immediately apparent with juniper and gingery coriander close behind. **Taste**: Robust palate where initial juniper hit is quickly chased by pleasing cardamom flavours with subtle candied ginger, lemon and sage, very faint floral notes. **Aftertaste**: Spicy pine and eucalyptus finish with lingering cracked red pepper corns.

ADNAMS COPPER HOUSE DISTILLED GIN EXCELLENT ★★★★★

Alc./vol: 40% **Producer:** Adnams Sole Bay Brewery & Copper House Distillery

Five of the botanicals which flavour this gin are very traditional (juniper berries, orris root, coriander seed, cardamom pod and sweet orange peel) while a sixth, hibiscus flower, adds contemporary floral flavours. **Appearance**: Clear, transparent. **Aroma**: Clean, zesty nose with orange zest competing with piny juniper for attention. **Taste**: Honest, classic old-school juniper led London dry gin palate but with zingy orange zest sitting above candied ginger, lemon and sage. **Aftertaste**: Hibiscus flavours are more obvious in the long lavender, black pepper and pine finish.

ADNAMS FIRST RATE GIN OUTSTANDING ★★★★★+

Alc./vol: 48% **Producer:** Adnams Sole Bay Brewery & Copper House Distillery

Based on spirit distilled from malted barley, wheat and oats by the brewer, First Rate is flavoured with 13 botanicals: juniper berries, orris root, coriander seeds, cardamom pods, cassia bark, vanilla pods, angelica root, caraway seeds, fennel seeds, thyme, liquorice, sweet orange and lemon peel. **Appearance**: Crystal clear. **Aroma**: A very complex and integrated nose with juniper, thyme, cardamom and orange zest being the most obvious aromas. **Taste**: Wonderfully clean and strongly flavoured palate with the balance between the juniper and the other botanicals well struck with juniper leading the charge with the other botanicals in tightly integrated formation behind. **Aftertaste**: Juniper is more prevalent in the long woody-citrus finish.

AVIATION GIN ★★★★☆

Alc./vol: 42% **Producer:** House Spirits Distillery

This gin is the result of an unusual collaboration between internationally known Seattle mixologist Ryan Magarian and the House Spirits Distillery in Portland, Oregon, run by partners Lee Medoff and Christian Krogstad, established in 2002 and responsible for the respected Medoyeff vodka. **Appearance:** Crystal clear. **Aroma:** Fresh with hints of pine forest, eucalyptus, anise and orange. **Taste:** Complex, integrated palate delivers the promised harmonious union of citrus, herbal, floral and spice **Aftertaste:** The juniper finally manages to rise above the other botanicals in the long, clean characterful finish.

BAYSWATER PREMIUM LONDON DRY GIN ★★★★☆

Alc./vol: 43% **Producer:** Thames Distillers Ltd

Based on wheat neutral spirit redistilled in a stainless steel pot still at London's Thames Distillers with nine botanicals: juniper berries, coriander seeds, angelica root, orris root, orange peel, lemon peel liquorice, cassia and nutmeg. Bayswater gin is finished with a black stopper and natural cork. **Appearance:** Crystal clear. **Aroma:** Pine and eucalyptus with orange zest, freshly sliced celery, nutmeg and liquorice. **Taste:** Very slightly sweet palate rounded by liquorice with juniper pine notes leading a well-integrated lightly spiced pack. **Aftertaste:** Invigorating pine and eucalyptus with lingering zesty lemon.

BEEFEATER 24 LONDON DRY GIN ★★★★★

Alc./vol: 45% **Producer:** Beefeater Distillery (James Burrough Ltd)

Flavoured with 12 botanicals including rare teas, Beefeater 24 takes its name from the 24-hour period the botanicals are steeped in alcohol prior to distillation. These include: hand-prepared grapefruit, bitter almond, orris root and Seville orange peel, Japanese Sencha tea and Chinese Green tea. **Appearance:** Crystal clear. **Aroma:** Delicate pine, lavender, tea and grapefruit zest. **Taste:** Soft, slightly sweet palate. Piny juniper leads with grapefruit, tea, liquorice and violet notes following. Top note of sweetened lemon zest and white pepper. **Aftertaste:** Tannins from the tea are evident in the long, pine-ey juniper fresh finish. All-in-all brilliantly rounded and balanced.

BEEFEATER BURROUGH'S RESERVE GIN ★★★★★

Alc./vol: 43% **Producer:** Beefeater Distillery (James Burrough Ltd)

Launched June 2012, Burrough's Reserve is distilled in a small 19th Century copper pot still and then rested in Jean de Lillet oak casks for a period prior to bottling. It is presented in an embossed bottle that has been individually labelled carrying its batch and bottle number. **Appearance:** Light straw yellow. **Aroma:** Oak aging appears to amplify the juniper with pungent pine, cedar wood, and eucalyptus with green herbal notes (sage and thyme), lemon oil, white pepper and subtle floral notes. **Taste:** Powerful dry spicy and slightly buttery oak with subtle herbal notes. Beefeater's signature citrus notes add freshness but are subdued by the dominant oak. **Aftertaste:** Long dry pine finish with slight smokiness. Personally I'd have taken out of oak a tad earlier but I bow to Desmond Payne's experience.

BEEFEATER LONDON DRY GIN ★★★★☆

Alc./vol: 40% **Producer:** Beefeater Distillery (James Burrough Ltd)

Named after the Yeoman Warders Who've guarded the Tower of London since appointed as personal bodyguards by King Henry VIII in 1485, they remain the Queens's official bodyguards at state occasions when they wear distinctive scarlet and gold state uniforms (instead of red and blue 'day' tunics). **Appearance:** Crystal clear. **Aroma:** Clean pine fresh juniper with a subtle lemon and orange zest. **Taste:** More orange notes emerge on the palate as do more subtle hints of parma violet and coriander. **Aftertaste:** Orange notes re-emerge the peppery, coriander finish.

Beefeater 24
Mi Lang Negroni

Glass: Old Fashioned
Garnish: Grapefruit Twist
Method: Stir over ice
35ml Oolong Infused Beefater 24
7.5ml Campari
7.5ml Aperol

BEEFEATER SUMMER EDITION LONDON DRY GIN  ★★★★★

Alc./vol: 40% **Producer:** Beefeater Distillery (James Burrough Ltd)

A limited edition seasonal line extension to classic Beefeater gin based on the original Beefeater botanical recipe with the addition of floral botanicals such as elderflower, hibiscus and blackcurrant. Launched May 2010, Beefeater Summer was created by Beefeater's master distiller, Desmond Payne. **Appearance:** Crystal clear. **Aroma:** Lavender bouquet of original Beefeater is replaced by floral aromas, particuarly hibiscus with berry notes also evident. **Taste:** Less citrussy than is usual for Beefeater with superbly intergrated flavours which present as a unified force making it hard to distinquish the individual contributions of the elderflower, hibiscus and blackcurrant that set this gin apart from original Beefeater. **Aftertaste:** Blackberry emerges in a reassuringly predominant pine-ey juniper finish. A master class in gin formulation by Desmond Payne.

BEEFEATER WINTER EDITION LONDON DRY GIN ★★★★⯪

Alc./vol: 40% **Producer:** Beefeater Distillery (James Burrough Ltd)

Launched October 2010, Beefeater's limited 'Winter Edition' follows its successful 'Summer Edition' (May 2010). Like the Summer Edition, this wintry gin is based on the original Beefeater botanical recipe with the addition of Christmassy botanicals such as cinnamon, nutmeg and pine shoots. **Appearance:** Clear, transparent. **Aroma:** Orange flesh and zest burst onto the nose with warm floral violet, cinnamon and nutmeg spice. **Taste:** Pine-ey juniper-led with barky spice and soapy violet. **Aftertaste:** Dry, barky spice lingers with pine and juniper.

BIERCEE GIN 'THESIS & ANTITHESIS' ★★★★⯪

Alc./vol: 44% **Producer:** Distillerie de Biercée

Launched in October 2012, Biercee Gin takes its name from its place of origin, the Biercée Distillery. The tall, square bottle is presented wrapped in a black and white diamond cardboard casing, a reference to the clothing of court jesters, mirroring the distillery's livery. **Appearance**: Crystal clear. **Aroma**: Fragrant and spicy with cumin, fresh coriander and piney juniper overtones of lavender and camphor. **Taste**: Cumin spice and naan bread-like coriander sit alongside piney juniper in this spice market of a gin. Despite the spice Biercee has a soft mouthfeel but is perhaps more Indian than Bulgium in style. **Aftertaste**: Cumin spice, piney juniper and white pepper spice.

BERKELEY SQUARE LONDON GIN ★★★★★

Alc./vol: 40% **Producer:** G&J Greenall Group Ltd

A distilled gin flavoured with traditional gin botanicals such as juniper, coriander, angelica and cubeb berries with basil, sage, French lavender and Kaffir lime leaves to produce a delicately spiced gin. **Appearance**: Crystal clear. **Aroma**: Deliciously aromatic nose with lime cordial, basil, crushed lavender, menthol eucalyptus and piney-freshness. **Taste**: Wonderfully balanced traditionally juniper led palate with a creamy mouthfeel. Obvious basil and sage influence. **Aftertaste**: Alpine-fresh finish with lingering lime, basil and sage.

BLADE CALIFORNIA GIN

Alc./vol: 40% **Producer:** Old World Spirits LLC

Blade Gin is based on 88 per cent wheat neutral spirit and 12 per cent California grape eau-de-vie. The producers also make a single-barrel aged 'Rusty Blade Gin'.

BLOOM GIN ★★★★☆

Alc./vol: 40% **Producer:** G&J Greenall Group Ltd

Bloom is the creation of Greenall's master distiller, Joanne Simcock, and is made using seven botanicals: juniper, coriander, angelica, cubeb, chamomile, honeysuckle and pomelo, a citrus fruit native to South East Asia and nicknamed Chinese Grapefruit. **Appearance:** Crystal clear **Aroma:** Floral Parma Violet nose. **Taste:** Parma Violet also predominates the palate with honeysuckle and pomelo providing apparent sweetness and possibly contribute to the silky mouth feel. Soft sweet tangerine and chamomile balance delicate piney juniper. **Aftertaste:** Floral, fruity finish – reminiscent of liquorice and Turkish Delight, with fresh black pepper and orange pine notes.

BLUE GIN ALL TIME ★★★★☆

Alc./vol: 43% **Producer:** Reisetbauer Qualitätsbrand Gmbh

Made by Hans Reisetbauer, the renowned Austrian eaux-de-vie distiller using 27 botanicals, which alongside juniper include lemon peel, angelica root, coriander seeds, turmeric and liquorice. The blend of alcohol and botanicals are left to macerate for 2-3 days before starting the third distillation. **Appearance:** (All Time 1.) Crystal clear. **Aroma:** Juniper pine nose with strong freshly turned soil/black gym shoes/anchovy-like aromas with cardamom, coriander, menthol eucalyptus spice and mandarin orange zest. **Taste:** Coriander seed comes through strongly on the juniper led palate with aniseed, white pepper, capsicum, pink grapefruit and a hint of liquorice and wormwood. **Aftertaste:** Spicy finish with cumin and juniper pine. Lingering pine bitterness.

BLUECOAT GIN ★★★★☆

Alc./vol: 47% **Producer:** Philadelphia Distilling LLC

Named after the Bluecoat militia that fought the American War of Independence, botanicals including organic juniper berries, American citrus peels, coriander and angelica root are distilled with third-party sourced grain neutral spirit in a copper pot still made in Scotland by Forsyths of Rothes. **Appearance:** Clear and transparent. **Aroma:** Clean, juniper and fresh coriander nose with alpine fresh piny, lemony aromas. **Taste:** Soft, very slightly sweet, peppermint fresh cleansing palate with pine, zesty lemony and liquorice. The high strength adds black pepper spirity notes. **Aftertaste:** Lemony, pine fresh finish with lingering sage, naan bread f and black pepper flavours.

BOË GIN

Alc./vol: 47% **Producer:** Deanston Distillery, Near Doune, Perthshire, Scotland, UK

Said to be based on the original Dutch gin/genever recipe, widely credited to Professor Sylvius de Bouve. He was a chemist, alchemist, renowned scholar and one of the founding professors of the oldest university in the Netherlands, Leiden University (founded in February 1575).

BOKMA EGTE OUDE FRIESCHE

Alc./vol: 38% **Producer:** Lucas Bols B.V.

A traditional 'oude' (literally, 'old') genever which has been cask-aged, Bokma was created by the Bokma family in 1826 in the Frisian capital of Leeuwarden. 'Bok' means a male goat, hence the goat emblem on the crest. Bokma's use of a square bottle dates from 1894.

BOKMA JONGE GRAANJENEVER ★★★★☆

Alc./vol: 35% **Producer:** Lucas Bols B.V.

This Dutch jenever was created by the Bokma family in 1826 in the Frisian capital of Leeuwarden, the skyline of which is featured on the label. This 'jonge' or light style of Bokma, based on a combination of juniper berries, coriander, peppercorns, angelica and liquorice, was introduced in in 1966. **Appearance:** Crystal clear. **Aroma:** Toasty oak with mineralality, cigarette ash, burnt rashers of bacon and delicate spice. **Taste:** Mellow palate with slight oiliness and notes of spiced poached pears, brazil nuts and hints of clove and cinnamon. **Aftertaste:** Toasty finish with subtle poached pear fruit, lingering clove and cinnamon spices.

BOKMA OUDE FRIESCHE GENEVER OUTSTANDING ★★★★★+

Alc./vol: 38% **Producer:** Lucas Bols B.V.

This 'oude' (literally, 'old') genever was created by the Bokma family in 1826 in the Frisian capital of Leeuwarden. 'Bok' means a male goat, hence the goat emblem on the crest. Bokma's unique square bottle dates from 1894 and is believed to predate other quadrilaterals such as Cointreau **Appearance:** Clear, pale straw yellow with a faint green tinge. **Aroma:** Nutty oily nose with fresh hay bales, olive oil and gentle warm cinnamon. **Taste:** Mellow and delicate with slight oily mouth feel. Light cinnamon spice, nutty brazil and hazelnut oiliness, a fruity touch of white grape juice, apple and faint tinned pineapple notes. **Aftertaste:** Cloves and spicy dry oak with lingering peppery olive oil.

BOLS BARREL AGED GENEVER EXCELLENT ★★★★★

Alc./vol: 42% **Producer:** Lucas Bols B.V.

Made according to a 19th century recipe, a base of 50 per cent malt-wine, triple-distilled in a pot still from rye, wheat and corn is blended with traditional genever botanicals including juniper, hops, cloves, anise, liquorice and ginger. The blend is then aged for 18 months in Limousin oak casks. **Appearance:** Clear, pale golden. **Aroma:** Pungent wholemeal bready juniper with nutty cream of soda and tinned peach slices. **Taste:** Peach stones, macadamia nuts and rye bread with warm clove, mace and subtle juniper. **Aftertaste:** Toasty, assertive finish with lingering oily tropical fruitiness.

BOLS CORENWYN 10 JAAR GELAGERD EXCELLENT ★★★★★

Alc./vol: 40% **Producer:** Lucas Bols B.V.

Corenwyn '10 Jaar Gelagerde', meaning 'aged for ten years' is made in very limited quantities due to its requiring ten years' maturation. Even at Bols where large stocks of aged malt-wine are held, stock of such old malt-wine is very limited. **Appearance:** (bottle No. 000416) Clear, dark golden amber with bright golden highlights. **Aroma:** Madeira, cigar, lanolin and vanilla with a drop of linseed oil. **Taste:** Starts sweet with nut oils and faint juniper. Cracked black pepper spice quickly emerges with pine, eucalyptus, vanilla and faint liquorice. **Aftertaste:** Long delicately spiced woody juniper.

BOLS CORENWYN 2 JAAR ★★★★☆

Alc./vol: 38% **Producer:** Lucas Bols B.V.

Bols Corenwyn is aged for two years and packaged in an individually numbered, brick-orange coloured clay bottle finished with a white and red ribbon. **Appearance:** (Bottle No. 030010) Clear, pale golden yellow. **Aroma:** Malty sweet corn with new leather, macadamia nut and linseed oil. **Taste:** Dry, malty, spicy palate with pine juniper and faint woody tannins. **Aftertaste:** Long, malty, grainy finish with lingering pine spice.

BOLS CORENWYN 4 JAAR ★★★★⯪
RECOMMENDED

Alc./vol: 40% **Producer:** Lucas Bols B.V.

Bols Corenwyn '4 Jaar Gelagerd', meaning 'aged for four years' is presented in an individually numbered gun-metal-grey coloured clay bottle with a beige and black ribbon. **Appearance:** (Bottle No. 009309) Clear, buttery yellow with a hint of green. **Aroma:** Linseed oil, new wood shavings, straw hay bales, cashew nuts and just snuffed candle smoke. **Taste:** Smoothed by vanilla and woody oiliness but with enlivening pine spice. **Aftertaste:** Lightly spicy oaky finish with lingering pine fresh juniper.

BOLS CORENWYN 6 JAAR GELAGERD ★★★★★+
OUTSTANDING

Alc./vol: 40% **Producer:** Lucas Bols B.V.

Corenwyn '6 Jaar Gelagerde', meaning 'aged for six years'. Only the maturation of this variant of Bols Corenwyn takes place in two types of oak casks; both French Limousin and American oak. **Appearance:** (bottle No. 035099) Clear, buttery yellow with a hint of green. **Aroma:** Sweet herbal nose with vanilla, tree bark, ground coriander and thyme. **Taste:** Silky, slight oily mouth feel, yet dry, spicy and herbal with juniper and light woodiness. **Aftertaste:** Angelica, ground coriander and nutty balsawood finish with lingering pine flavours.

BOLS GENEVER ★★★★⯪
RECOMMENDED

Alc./vol: 42% **Producer:** Lucas Bols B.V.

Flavoured with a whisky-like triple grain distillate made of corn, wheat and rye, which the Dutch call maltwine. This flavoursome distillate is blended with a juniper-berry distillate and a separate botanical distillate, including coriander, caraway and aniseed. The recipe contains over 50 per cent malt-wine **Appearance:** Crystal clear. **Aroma:** Pine forest juniper odours over a nutty malty ready new make spirit base (malt whisky prior to aging) with delicate floral jasmine tea aromas. **Taste:** Resinous pine and eucalyptus juniper with complex zingy spice, rounded by nutty bready flavours. **Aftertaste:** Slightly bitter, bready, burnt nutty toast.

BOLS GENEVER 21 ★★★★☆

Alc./vol: 40% **Producer:** Lucas Bols B.V.

Dutch distiller Bols worked with the famous street wear store Patta's creative director, Vincent van de Waal, to create a special edition bottle to launch their new Bols Genever 21. This has less malt wine and slightly more sugar. The bottle features the hand of the designer. **Appearance:** Crystal clear. **Aroma:** Lightly malty with distinctive but subtle genever. **Taste:** Ever so slightly sweet but balanced with a refreshing peppery spice. Nutty bready malt wine is evident but lightly so and the spice botanicals are far more restrained when compared to Bols standard genever. **Aftertaste:** Spicy, fading with oily bready malt notes.

BOLS ZEER OUDE (ZO) GENEVER ★★★★☆

Alc./vol: 37.5% **Producer:** Lucas Bols B.V.

A long established brand of Oude Genever sold in traditional clay bottles.

BOMBAY SAPPHIRE 250TH ANNIVERSARY LIMITED EDITION

Alc./vol: 40% **Producer:** G&J Greenall Group Ltd

A limited-edition bottle released in 2010 to mark the 250th anniversary of Bombay Original's recipe which back in 1761 was used to make 'Warrington Gin' (not the Bombay Sapphire brand or recipe, which was only created in 1960).

BOMBAY SAPPHIRE DISTILLED LONDON DRY GIN (40%) ★★★★☆

Alc./vol: 40% **Producer:** The Bombay Spirits Company

Flavoured with ten botanicals: juniper berries from Tuscany, coriander seeds, angelica root, liquorice, Italian orris, cassia bark, Spanish almonds and lemon peel, Cubeb berries from Java and West African Grains of Paradise. Unusually, Bombay Sapphire is distilled using the vapour infusion method. **Appearance:** Crystal clear. **Aroma:** Fresh, complex nose with juniper, lemon zest and lemon meringue pie filling with pepper and Indian spice. **Taste:** Initially delicate, light and slightly sweet palate with juniper, lemon zest and coriander opens to reveal yet more lemon zest and strong peppery spiced notes. **Aftertaste:** Delicate lavender notes from the piney juniper put up a valiant fight against a mixed pepper assault and a touch of chilli heat.

BOMBAY SAPPHIRE EAST GIN

Alc./vol: 47% **Producer:** The Bombay Spirits Company

Launched September 2011, Bombay Sapphire East is the first Bombay Sapphire extension since the brand was launched 25 years earlier. This 'eastern' variant is distinctive due to the use of Thai lemongrass and Vietnamese black peppercorns and was created by Master of Botanicals, Ivano Tonutti. **Appearance:** Crystal clear. **Aroma:** Wonderfully aromatic and floral with pungent cracked black pepper spice. Complex scents of parma violet, lavender, camphor, balsa wood-like orris root and freshly cut celery (turns stewed vegetal is left for a prolonged period in the glass). **Taste:** Clean and crisp with zesty citrus, lemongrass, juniper and zingy cracked black pepper. Silky mouthfeel despite the peppery bite which dominates the palate. **Aftertaste:** Long, lingering lemongrass, black pepper and lavender influenced juniper.

BOMBAY SAPPHIRE LAVERSTOKE MILL LIMITED EDITION ★★★★☆

Alc./vol: 49% **Producer:** The Bombay Spirits Company

This Bombay Sapphire limited edition bottle was launched in Autumn 2013 to celebrate the opening of Bacardi's Laverstoke Mill Distillery. **Appearance:** Crystal clear. **Aroma:** Surprisingly subdued. The high alcohol content appears to lock-in botanical aromas. Piney juniper emerges with lemony notes akin to lemon meringue pie filling with red pepper corns. A splash of water releases musky nutty scents from the angelica root and fragrant aromas from the coriander seeds **Taste:** Sampled neat this high-strength gin has a surprisingly mild alcohol attack. Piney juniper and coriander sing out with a perceived slight sweetness subduing lemon and black pepper notes. Perversely, the addition of water appears to amplify the peppery spiced notes. **Aftertaste:** Pine and lavender juniper notes with lingering cracked black pepper.

BOODLES BRITISH GIN [RECOMMENDED] ★★★★☆

Alc./vol: 45.2% **Producer:** Beefeater Distillery (James Burrough Ltd)

Dating back to 1847 and named after Boodle's gentlemen's club in London's St. James's, founded in 1762 and originally run by Edward Boodle, Boodles Gin (without the apostrophe) is now bottled in and only available only in the United Sates. Unusually it contains no citrus botanicals. **Appearance:** Crystal clear. **Aroma:** Woody, bark aromas suggest lavish use of angelica root with floral lavender, candied ginger and sage. **Taste:** Slightly sweet, clean and floral. As no citrus botanicals are used, the hint of lemon zest apparent on the palate may come from generous use of coriander seeds. Fruity and herbal with sweet spices. **Aftertaste:** Citrusy with lingering herbal astringency.

BOORD'S LONDON DRY GIN  ★★★★⯪

Alc./vol: 40% **Producer:** Made in USA by unknown producer

Boord was founded in 1726 and was famous for its brand of Old Tom gin with its distinctive Cat & Barrel trademark. The company's interests were acquired by Booth's and Boord's became an export gin, mainly to the USA, where it is still made and sold.

BOOTH'S DISTILLED LONDON DRY GIN ★★★★⯪

Alc./vol: 45% **Producer:** Diageo Americas Supply Inc.

The Booth family started distilling in 1740 when they built a distillery in London's Clerkenwell. Although now made in Illinois, this date is referenced on Booth's modern label which also retains the brand red lion logo, confirming Booth's to be the oldest gin brand still in existence. **Appearance:** Clear, transparent. **Aroma:** Clean with juniper pine, lavender and camphor. Subtle notes of sage, celery and chewing gum (Dentine). Subdued citrus notes. **Taste:** Classic juniper led London Dry Gin palate with hints of liquorice but little in the way of citrus evident. **Aftertaste:** Dry piney juniper and orris. A well-made good value traditional styled gin.

BRECON SPECIAL RESERVE DRY GIN ★★★★☆

Alc./vol: 40% **Producer:** Penderyn Distillery (The Welsh Whisky Company)

Based on third party-produced grain neutral spirit, redistilled in Penderyn Distillery's own copper pot still with juniper berries, orange peel, cassia bark, liquorice root, cinnamon bark, angelica root, ground nutmeg, coriander seeds, lemon peel and oris root. **Appearance:** Crystal clear. **Aroma:** Complex yet very traditionally styled juniper-led nose with aromas of sage, fresh celery, sweet Parma Violets and cold-stewed Lady Grey tea. **Taste:** Citrus and liquorice flavours emerge in a palate bursting with flavour, and still juniper-led. **Aftertaste:** Long, slightly bitter cinnamon and cracked black pepper finish with lingering juniper pine and liquorice.

BROCKMANS ★⯪☆☆☆

Alc./vol: 40% **Producer:** G&J Greenall Group Ltd

The producers of Brockman take a traditional distillate made by distilling neutral spirits with fairly classic gin botanicals and then (in our opinion) ruin it by cold compounding a berry essence. Why did they add that fruit essence rather than a simple apostrophe? Shame! (Launched in 2010) **Appearance:** Crystal clear. **Aroma:** Dark berry/blueberry fruit dominates the nose with 'gin' aromas almost totally overpowered. **Taste:** Oh dear! Traditionalists expecting a 'gin' will be disappointed and if, like me, horrified by what I liken to an artificial blueberry flavoured palate with juniper struggling to assert its presence. **Aftertaste:** The aggressive finish is at least a little more gin-like than the palate.

BROKER'S GIN ★★★★⯪

Alc./vol: 40% **Producer:** Langley Distillery (Alcohols Limited)

Launched in 1998, Broker's was created by brothers Martin and Andy Dawson. It is based on 100% wheat neutral sprit and flavoured with ten botanicals: juniper, coriander, orris, nutmeg, cassia bark, cinnamon, liquorice, angelica root, orange peel and lemon peel. **Appearance:** Crystal clear. **Aroma:** Classically appealing, clean juniper nose with coriander, zesty citrus and mild black pepper spice. **Taste:** Traditionally styled with juniper pine freshness, strong orange and lemon zestyness, coriander and pepper spice with sweet Parma Violet notes. **Aftertaste:** Resiny pine finish with lingering cracked black pepper spice.

BROOKLYN GIN

Alc./vol: 40% **Producer:** Warwick Valley Winery & Distillery

Brooklyn gin (not to be confused with Breuckelen gin – but that's another legal battle) is made by Joe Santos, an ex-Bacardi marketeer who grew up in New Jersey. He makes his gin with 11 botanicals, five of them fresh citrus peels, at Warwick Valley Winery & Distillery in Warwick, New York State.

BULLDOG GIN

Alc./vol: 40% **Producer:** Unknown producer

Contract-distilled in England using a traditional pot still but with untraditional botanicals such as dragon eye (longan), poppy and lotus leaves. More conventional of the 12 botanicals include: lemon peel, almond, cassia, lavender, orris, liquorice, angelica, coriander and, of course, juniper. **Appearance:** Crystal clear. **Aroma:** Mellow nose with floral, woody aromas reminiscent of shrubbery with candle wax, musky, nutty angelica and lime zest. **Taste:** Pleasingly dry yet soft palate with juniper rightly to the fore. **Aftertaste:** Well-balanced botanical elements give character and structure. Lingering nutty angelica.

BURNETT'S GIN (WHITE SATIN)

Alc./vol: 40% **Producer:** Heaven Hill Distilleries, Inc, Bardstown, Kentucky, USA

Since the break-up of Seagram, who acquired Burnett's White Satin in 1963, this brand has been around the block. In 2002 the American firm Heaven Hill purchased worldwide production and distribution rights (excluding Japan) and dropped the 'White Satin' from the name.

CADENHEAD'S OLD RAJ RED LABEL

Alc./vol: 46% **Producer:** William Cadenhead Ltd

Old Raj gin is made with a gin essence prepared by steeping juniper, coriander seeds, angelica root, orris root, cassia, almond powder, lemon peel and orange peel in a mixture of alcohol and water for 36 hours, then distilling the results in a small pot still. **Appearance:** Clear, faint straw green yellow hue. **Aroma:** Floral herbaceous nose with saffron, eucalyptus, candied ginger, lemon and sage. **Taste:** Lightly spicy, saffron and juniper palate with cracked black pepper and grapefruit bitterness. **Aftertaste:** Spicy, citrus finish with a pleasant, toothpaste-like freshness.

CALVERT GIN

Alc./vol: 40% **Producer:** Made in USA by undisclosed producer

Launched in 1964, this gins origins are connected to Calvert whiskey which was produced by the Calvert Distillers Company in Relay, Maryland, USA. The Calvert name was in memory of Lord Calvert, the first governor of Maryland.

CAORUNN SMALL BATCH SCOTTISH GIN

  ★★★★★

Alc./vol: 41.8% **Producer:** Caorunn Distillery

Caorunn, pronounced 'ka-roon', is the Gaelic word for rowan berry which along with dandelion, bog myrtle, heather and Coul Blush apple comprise the 5 Celtic botanicals of the 11 botanicals used to flavour this proudly Scottish gin. The number of botanicals are reflected in the pentagon-shaped bottle **Appearance**: Crystal clear. **Aroma**: Citrusy and floral with spicy pine-fresh juniper. **Taste**: Fresh and superbly clean and balanced with good juniper notes, zesty citrus, delicate spice and floral flavours. **Aftertaste**: Long, cleansing, lightly spiced piny juniper finish which fades with cracked black pepper.

CASCADE MOUNTAIN GIN ★★☆☆☆

Alc./vol: 47.5% **Producer:** Bendistillery

Cascade Mountain Gin is flavoured by the maceration of botanicals rather than distillation, hence this gin's faint yellow hue. Fresh herbs and spice, rather than dried, are used. These include handpicked juniper berries from the central Oregon high desert plateau. **Appearance:** Clear, light pale straw yellow. **Aroma:** (batch No. 211) Clean, fresh pine forest juniper rich nose with lemon pie citrus and delicate all-spice. **Taste:** Herbal spicy palate, perhaps more reminiscent of a Czech absinthe than most gins. Dry resinous pine notes build to hot black pepper. **Aftertaste:** Hot pepper spice finish.

CHASE WILLIAMS ELEGANT CRISP GIN ★★★★☆

Alc./vol: 48% **Producer:** Chase Distillery

William Chase's farm-made apple vodka is the base for this gin. Eleven botanicals are used: juniper, coriander seeds, angelica seeds, angelica root, liquorice root, orris root, orange and lemon peel, hops, dried elderflower and fresh Bramley apples cut into eighths. **Appearance:** Crystal clear. **Aroma:** Clean, subtle nose with good piny juniper aromas and zesty citrus notes. **Taste:** (reduced to approx. 43%) Leads with spicy hop and piney juniper with more subtle floral elderflower and spiced apple. Spicy and barky in style rather than being light and zingy but very full flavoured and strong enough to stand up to tonic. **Aftertaste:** Spicy finish with bursts of dry liquorice and a pleasingly spicyness.

CHURCHILL LONDON DRY GIN

Alc./vol: 40% **Producer:** Deanston Distillery, Near Doune, Perthshire, Scotland, UK

This London dry gin dates back to 1878 and is now made by Burn Stewart at its Deanston Single Malt Whisky Distillery, near the village of Doune, Perthshire. Churchill's botanical recipe includes juniper berries, coriander, orris and lemon.

CITADELLE GIN

 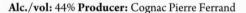 ★★★★☆

Alc./vol: 44% **Producer:** Cognac Pierre Ferrand

Based on French wheat neutral spirit and 19 botanicals: French juniper, orris, French violet root, coriander, almonds, Spanish lemon peel, Mexican orange peel, angelica, cardamom, nutmeg, cassia bark, cinnamon, fennel, grains of paradise, cubeb, Chinese liquorice, cumin, French anise and savory. **Appearance:** Crystal clear. **Aroma:** Juniper-led fresh, leafy nose with fragrant coriander, honeysuckle, peppery grains of paradise and fruity orange and mango aromas. **Taste:** Fresh, clean off dry, piney juniper, citrusy palate with quickly emerging cracked black pepper notes. **Aftertaste:** Clean, spicy peppered finish with good juniper notes and orange zest.

Caorunn Apple Three Ways

Glass: Martini
Garnish: Red apple peel
Method: 50ml Caorunn Gin
10ml bitter cider reduction
(Reduce 500ml cider with 5ml Angostura
and 10ml Peychaud on a medium hob for 5
minutes, take off heat, add skin of 3 red apples,
cool and strain.)

CITADELLE RÉSERVE GIN 2010  ★★★★★+

Alc./vol: 44% **Producer:** Cognac Pierre Ferrand

The third of Citadelle's annually released oak aged gins. Citadelle Reserve is distilled using the same 19 botanicals as Citadelle gin but aged for four months in Pierre Ferrand Cognac barrels. It is available in limited quantities. Each bottle is vintage dated and individually numbered. **Appearance:** Clear, pale yellow/green straw. **Aroma:** Delicate juniper, faint lemon thyme citrus and lightly buttery old oak wardrobe with floral aromas, practically violet. **Taste:** Soft mouth feel. Elegant juniper, creamy zesty lemon, vanilla cream, burnt pastry and dry delicate oak and spice. **Aftertaste:** Long-lasting and round finish with lingering oak, lemon zest and a medley of juniper floral spice.

CITADELLE RÉSERVE GIN 2010 ★★★★★+

Alc./vol: 44% **Producer:** Cognac Pierre Ferrand

The third of Citadelle's annually released oak aged gins. Citadelle Reserve is distilled using the same 19 botanicals as Citadelle gin but aged for four months in Pierre Ferrand Cognac barrels. It is available in limited quantities. Each bottle is vintage dated and individually numbered. **Appearance:** Clear, pale yellow/green straw. **Aroma:** Delicate juniper, faint lemon thyme citrus and lightly buttery old oak wardrobe with floral aromas, practically violet. **Taste:** Soft mouth feel. Elegant juniper, creamy zesty lemon, vanilla cream, burnt pastry and dry delicate oak and spice. **Aftertaste:** Long-lasting and round finish with lingering oak, lemon zest and a medley of juniper floral spice.

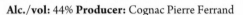

CITY OF LONDON DRY GIN ★★★★✭

Alc./vol: 40% **Producer:** City of London Distillery (C.O.L.D.) Ltd

Distilled by Jamie Baxter in two copper pot stills in the heart of the City of London with seven botanicals: juniper berries, angelica, liquorice, coriander seeds and fresh oranges, lemons and pink grapefruit. Hand-bottled and bottle labelled with batch and bottle number. **Appearance:** (batch 01, bottle No. 305) Clear but with small white particles in suspension. **Aroma:** Pungent rooty juniper nose with zesty pink-grapefruit, orange and lemon. Subtle notes of celery, sage and parma violet. **Taste:** Clean, characterful classic London Dry Gin with attractive parma violet orris and rooty liquorice notes and rounded citrusy spice. **Aftertaste:** Lingering rootyness, piney juniper and subtle peppery spice.

COMB 9 GIN ★★★★✭

Thought to be the world's only gin distilled from honey. Production of this gin starts with honey wine made from fermented orange blossom honey. This is distilled to make the gins base spirit and this is redistilled with the botanicals which flavour the gin. **Appearance:** Crystal clear. **Aroma:** Piney juniper, camphor and lavender with angelica and cinnamon spice (the later perhaps from cassia. Pungent and spicy yet regal nose. **Taste:** Dry and clean with upfront juniper and generous herbal spice – perhaps a tad too generous. (Unusually the concentrated flavours of this gin might benefit from diluting with additional neutral spirit before hydrating to bottling strength. There again it stands up well to tonic.) **Aftertaste:** Pronounced lavender and pine in a long punchy finish. Stands out for being distilled from fermented honey and not third-party produced grain neutral spirit.

CORK DRY (RED LABEL)

Alc./vol: 37.5% **Producer:** Irish Distillers Fox & Geese

Cork Dry Gin was first distilled in 1793 at the Watercourse Distillery, with the recipe transcribed in 1798 by apprentice distiller, William Coldwell. This now compounded gin is still made in Cork and popular in Ireland. **Appearance:** Clear, transparent. **Aroma:** Tropical fruit and toasted bread – reminiscent of a bag of boiled sweets with little in the way of juniper. **Taste:** The peppery palate also has a touch of the tropics, accompanied by subdued juniper and barky botanical notes. **Aftertaste:** Juniper is more evident in the jagged finish.

CORSAIR ARTISAN GIN 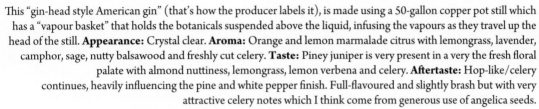 ★★★★⯪

Alc./vol: 44% **Producer:** Corsair Artisan Distillery

This "gin-head style American gin" (that's how the producer labels it), is made using a 50-gallon copper pot still which has a "vapour basket" that holds the botanicals suspended above the liquid, infusing the vapours as they travel up the head of the still. **Appearance:** Crystal clear. **Aroma:** Orange and lemon marmalade citrus with lemongrass, lavender, camphor, sage, nutty balsawood and freshly cut celery. **Taste:** Piney juniper is very present in a very the fresh floral palate with almond nuttiness, lemongrass, lemon verbena and celery. **Aftertaste:** Hop-like/celery continues, heavily influencing the pine and white pepper finish. Full-flavoured and slightly brash but with very attractive celery notes which I think come from generous use of angelica seeds.

CROWN JEWEL PEERLESS PREMIUM GIN  ★★★★⯪

Alc./vol: 50% **Producer:** Beefeater Distillery (James Burrough Ltd)

Developed for the market then known as Duty Free and launched in 1993, this sister brand to Beefeater is named after the Crown Jewels – on display at the Tower of London, which the Beefeaters guard. **Appearance:** Clear, transparent. **Aroma:** Pronounced citrusy note to a balanced nose with bursts of pine fresh juniper, Parma Violets and gentle spice. **Taste:** More citrusy than regular Beefeater, Crown Jewel bursts onto the palate yet is well rounded and dry with plenty of juniper plus hints of parma violets, candied citrus peel and zingy white pepper. **Aftertaste:** Refreshing and cleansing pine finish fades with white pepper tingle.

DAMRAK GIN ★★★★☆

Alc./vol: 40% **Producer:** Lucas Bols B.V.

Thanks to sea level changes and development, Damrak is now a paved square in the centre of Amsterdam but was originally Amsterdam's first harbour. From the early 1600s until the 19th century, Damrak was a major port for the ships of the Dutch East India. **Appearance:** Crystal clear. **Aroma:** Orange sherbet / spicy orange nose with little juniper. **Taste:** Tightly complex palate dominated by orange zest with underlying juniper and dry, piny spice. **Aftertaste:** The juniper flavour is somewhat overwhelmed by the other botanicals, so Damrak tastes very unlike traditional gins.

DARNLEY'S VIEW SPICED GIN ★★★⯪☆

Alc./vol: 42.7% **Producer:** Thames Distillers Ltd

Darnley's View Spiced Gin is based on neutral wheat spirit and is distilled in a small stainless steel pot still at Thames Distillers in London with ten botanicals: Juniper, Cinnamon, Nutmeg, Cassia, Grains of Paradise, Ginger, Cumin, Cloves, Coriander Seed and Angelica Root. **Appearance:** (batch No. 1568) Crystal clear. **Aroma:** Pungent cumin seed spice dominates. Akin to a garam masala influenced London dry gin – only a tad heavy on the garam masala. **Taste:** Traditional London dry gin flavours bravely stand against almost overwhelming garam masala spice to the extent that Darnley's predominantly juniper gin credentials may be questioned by some. **Aftertaste:** Pine needle, cracked black pepper (Grains of Paradise) and garam masala spice

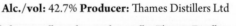

DARNLEY'S VIEW LONDON DRY GIN ★★★★⯪

Alc./vol: 40% **Producer:** Thames Distillers Ltd

Produced for the Wemyss family, whisky merchants whose historic family seat is Wemyss Castle, Scotland. Back in 1565, Mary Queen of Scots first caught sight of her future husband, Lord Darnley through the courtyard window of the Wemyss Castle. This gin is named in recognition of the event. **Appearance:** Crystal clear. **Aroma:** Juniper-led nose has warm white pepper with strong coriander and sage aromas with good lemon notes. **Taste:** Initially classic London gin palate. As the citrus falls away so the elderflower emerges followed by warm ginger. Creamy mouth feel throughout. **Aftertaste:** Round smooth and warm finish. Surprising delicate and lacking that forceful pepper found of the nose.

DE KUYPER CITROEN JENEVER ★★★★☆

Alc./vol: 30% **Producer:** De Kuyper Royal Distillers

A citrus jenever from De Kuyper distilled with sun-dried Spanish lemon peel in an original copper pot still. **Appearance:** Clear, bright buttercup yellow with slight green tinge. **Aroma:** Citrus fresh - somewhat akin to citrus scented washing up liquid (but not in an unattractive way). **Taste:** Clean, fresh sherbety, off-dry, lemon zest with notes of liquorice and icing sugar. **Aftertaste:** Faint peppery spice and lingering zesty dusted with icing sugar.

DEATH'S DOOR GIN ★★★★★+

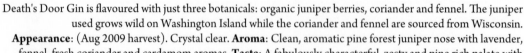

Alc./vol: 47% **Producer:** Death's Door Spirits

Death's Door Gin is flavoured with just three botanicals: organic juniper berries, coriander and fennel. The juniper used grows wild on Washington Island while the coriander and fennel are sourced from Wisconsin. **Appearance**: (Aug 2009 harvest). Crystal clear. **Aroma**: Clean, aromatic pine forest juniper nose with lavender, fennel, fresh coriander and cardamom aromas. **Taste**: A fabulously characterful, zesty and pine rich palate with liquorice, fennel, coriander and oily spice. **Aftertaste**: Long, harmonious finish. (I have given Death's Door a well-deserved extra high rating for being distilled from grain rather than third-party supplied neutral spirit).

DESERT JUNIPER GIN ★★★★☆

Alc./vol: 41% **Producer:** Bendistillery

First released in late 1998, Desert Juniper is made by Bendistillery in batches of around 500 gallons and filtered through crushed volcanic lava rock up to ten times before being bottled. The juniper berries used are harvested locally in Oregon from one of the world's largest juniper tree forests. **Appearance:** (Batch 132) Clear with very faint lime green/straw yellow hue. **Aroma:** There's a whiff of sauna to the restrained fresh cedar wood, citrus and coriander nose. **Taste:** Slightly sweet, oily, woody, nutty palate with very faint pine resin influenced juniper. More a botanical spirit than a 'traditional' gin. **Aftertaste:** Lingering woody, nutty, sawdust flavours.

DH KRAHN GIN ★★★★☆

Alc./vol: 40% **Producer:** Essential Spirits

D. H. Krahn Gin is contract distilled by Essential Spirits in Silicon Valley, California for a New York-based company established by a couple of former Cornell classmates, Dave Hughes and Scott Krahn, who have pursued what started as a class project after graduation. **Appearance:** Crystal clear. **Aroma:** Juniper to the fore with pine, lavender and camphor with lemongrass, woody angelica and Parma Violets and earth (orris). **Taste:** Clean citrus and lemongrass palate with juniper pine notes and spicy ginger bursting through. **Aftertaste:** Dry, bark, pine and citrus zest finish.

DODD'S GIN ★★★★★

Alc./vol: 49.9% **Producer:** The London Distillery Company Ltd

Most of the botanicals are steeped and distilled in Christina, a traditional 140 litre capacity copper pot still, but more delicate botanicals are distilled in a cold distillation still called 'Little Albion'. The two distillates are married for several weeks before being bottled and hand-labelled. **Appearance**: Crystal clear. **Aroma**: Nutty, rooty pine and balsawood with black tea leaves and cardamom spice. A splash of water releases fresh green leafy aromas. **Taste**: At smidgen under 50% this gin packs a flavoursome punch. As with the nose, the addition of water amplifies green flavours which combine well with piney juniper, subtle black tea and enlivening cardamom. **Aftertaste**: Green leafy notes linger with white tea, pine and mixed peppery spice. Both strength of flavour and alcoholic strength make this a G&T rather than a cocktail gin.

NEW YORK DISTILLING CO. DOROTHY PARKER AMERICAN GIN ★★★★✦

RECOMMENDED

Alc./vol: 44% **Producer:** New York Distilling Company

The informative back label quotes Dorothy Parker, "I like to drink a martini, Two at the very most. After three I'm under the table, After four I'm under the host." Name after this gin lover, Dorothy Parker American Gin's botanicals include: juniper, elderberries, citrus, cinnamon and hibiscus. **Appearance:** Crystal clear. **Aroma:** Wonderfully clean and fragrant with juniper presented lavender and camphor rather than pungent pine. Lime cordial and floral aromas with delicate spice. Water releases notes of nutty mushroom-like angelica root. **Taste:** Initial sweetness is quickly countered by a cleansing peppery bite which appears to bind all the other more delicate floral and spicy flavours together in a balanced, well-integrated palate. **Aftertaste:** Juniper remains dominant but is well tamed throughout.

DOWNSLOPE OULD TOM GIN ★★★★☆

Alc./vol: 40% **Producer:** Downslope Distilling Inc

Downslope's Ould Tom Gin is historical interpretation of a late-1800s-style of gin. It is based on a distillate made from fermented Maui cane juice which is distilled in a pot still and then twice distilled in a column still. The seven botanicals used include juniper, Vietnamese cinnamon and star anise **Appearance:** Clear, pale golden. **Aroma:** Oily, slightly grappa-like, toasted cinnamon bagel nose with eucalyptus and alpine spruce forest after rain. **Taste:** Pine flavoured cinnamon bagel with those slightly grappa-like notes from the nose. Has genuine notes of a traditional Dutch genever. **Aftertaste:** Cinnamon, liquorice finish with piney star anise. An interesting bridge between various gin styles but perhaps more genever than old tom.

EDINBURGH GIN ★★★☆☆

Alc./vol: 43% **Producer:** Langley Distillery (Alcohols Limited)

Edinburgh Gin is part distilled and part cold-compounded with Scottish juniper and other local botanicals such as heather, pine and milk thistle. It is based on grain neutral spirit from Invergordon distillery redistilled with nine classic gin botanicals in a copper pot still at Langley Distillery. **Appearance:** Crystal clear. **Aroma:** Up-front juniper, piney heather nose, with cracked black pepper, nutmeg, almond and thyme. **Taste:** Piney juniper to the fore, nutmeg spiced palate with almond. Things hot up as black pepper heat emerges and builds. **Aftertaste:** Overly combative resinous pine finish.

ETHEREAL GIN BATCH NO. 2 (PINK LABEL) ★★★☆☆

Alc./vol: 43% **Producer:** Berkshire Mountain Distillers Inc.

Ethereal Gin's recipe changes with each limited edition batch, as does the colour of the label. The first batch was lime green and this second batch is a very tasteful pink. **Appearance:** Crystal clear. **Aroma:** A fragrant nose with strong eucalyptus, menthol, angelica and liquorice aromas. **Taste:** The pungent pine-ey juniper, angelica and rose palate turns prickly with black pepper before softening again with floral flavours. **Aftertaste:** Pine, eucalyptus and pepper return with vengeance in the lingering finish.

ETHEREAL GIN BATCH NO. 4 (LIME GREEN LABEL) ★★★★☆

Alc./vol: 43% **Producer:** Berkshire Mountain Distillers Inc.

Appearance: Crystal clear. **Aroma:** Eucalyptus, zesty lemon and sage nose with parma violets, cardamom and curry leaf. **Taste:** Clean, eucalyptus and citrus palate with aggressive cracked black pepper spice, pronounced coriander seed, fresh celery and chewing gum (Dentine). **Aftertaste:** Eucalyptus finish fades with lingering dry lemon oil flavours.

FIFTY POUNDS GIN ★★★★★

Alc./vol: 43.5% **Producer:** Thames Distillers Ltd

The inspiration for this handsomely packaged gin's name comes from the 1736 Gin Act which practically prohibited gin sales by imposing a two gallon minimum unit of sale and swingeing £1 per gallon duty. It also required gin retailers to purchase a £50 annual licence (equivalent to a year's salary). **Appearance:** [Batch No. 01/09] Clear with a very slight yellow tinge. **Aroma:** Juniper rich, lemon zesty nose with sage and fresh celery aromas. **Taste:** Slightly sweet, juniper, orange and lemon citrus led palate with fresh eucalyptus, sage spice and liquorice. **Aftertaste:** Sweet peppermint notes emerge in the juniper, mandarin orange zest and eucalyptus finish.

FINSBURY 47 PLATINUM ★★★★☆

Alc./vol: 47% **Producer:** Langley Distillery (Alcohols Limited)

More than ten botanicals, including juniper berries, coriander seeds, lemon and orange peels, are used in the distillation of this London Dry gin. **Appearance:** Crystal clear. **Aroma:** Liquorice and resinous pine nose with fresh coriander and cassia. **Taste:** Initially slightly sweet palate with the juniper rightly to the fore supported by citrus and the distinctive Parma Violets, earth and cold stewed tea notes of orris. Cracked black pepper builds to counter any initial sweetness. **Aftertaste:** Somewhat bitter, lingering liquorice and juniper flavours with cracked black pepper reaching a crescendo.

FINSBURY LONDON DRY GIN (37.5%) ★★★★☆

Alc./vol: 37.5% **Producer:** Langley Distillery (Alcohols Limited)

The Finsbury Gin brand name was founded by Joseph Bishop back in 1740 and is possibly a reference to Clerkenwell springs which was once the centre of London's gin industry and part of the old London Borough of Finsbury. Today Finsbury Gin is owned by a German company, Borco International. **Appearance:** Crystal clear. **Aroma:** Aromatic nose has a whiff of lemon meringue pie-filling and coriander. **Taste:** Robustly flavoured oily citrus palate with lemon sherbet, liquorice, and coriander supporting juniper. **Aftertaste:** Slightly bitter citrus finish.

FINSBURY LONDON DRY GIN (60%) ★★★★☆

Alc./vol: 60% **Producer:** Langley Distillery (Alcohols Limited)

The Finsbury Gin brand name was founded by Joseph Bishop back in 1740 and is possibly a reference to Clerkenwell springs which was once the centre of London's gin industry and part of the old London Borough of Finsbury. Today Finsbury Gin is owned by a German company, Borco International. **Appearance**: Crystal clear. **Aroma**: Cracked black pepper spirit aromas dominate until dilution (to approx. 40%) reveals generous coriander, woody juniper and citrus. **Taste**: Clean, juniper palate with cleansing coriander seeds (candied ginger, lemon and sage taste) , citrus and Angelica root (musky, nutty). **Aftertaste**: Lingering juniper coupled with its sheer strength of alcohol.

FORD'S GIN ★★★★★+

Alc./vol: 45% **Producer:** Thames Distillers Ltd

Simon Ford who developed this gin with Charles Maxwell of Thames Distillers. It is flavoured with 9 botanicals (juniper, coriander seeds, orris, jasmine, angelica, cassia, bitter orange, lemon and grapefruit peels) steeped for 15 hours before distillation in 500 litre stainless steel pot stills. **Appearance:** Crystal clear. **Aroma:** Clean pungent lavender and camphor from the high juniper content with celery, parma violets and citrus. **Taste**: Juniper and fresh floral notes compete with zesty citrus for attention with just enough spice. Very soft mouth feel, especially given the high alcohol strength. **Aftertaste:** Classic London dry with all the flavours found in the nose and palate presenting themselves in a long lingering finish.

FOXDENTON 48% LONDON DRY GIN ★★★★☆

Alc./vol: 48% **Producer:** Thames Distillers Ltd

The Foxdenton Estate, after which this gin is named, is run by Nicholas Radclyffe – the descendent of a military family that first acquired the Foxdenton estate through marriage in 1367. Like so many others, Nick asked Charles Maxwell at the Thames Distillery to development a Foxdenton Gin. **Appearance:** Crystal clear. **Aroma:** (diluted to approx. 43%) Fresh, clean, traditional London dry juniper nose with heavy naan bread-like coriander seed and angelica. **Taste:** Citrus lime zest burst leads to an equally traditional, clean palate with orris root providing distinctive earthy parma violet flavours. **Aftertaste:** Finishes dry with lingering pine juniper and fresh hay.

G'VINE FLORAISON ★★★★☆

Alc./vol: 40% **Producer:** EuroWineGate

G'Vine Floraison Gin is based on grape neutral spirit which is used to make five separate botanical infused spirits. The first is made by macerating fleurs de vigne – the green flowers of the Ugni Blanc vine; the others are made from more traditional fresh gin botanicals. **Appearance:** (bot No. 05X07405) Crystal clear. **Aroma:** Floral pot-pourri with zesty lime notes – almost lime cordial – and a hint of cardamom. **Taste:** Hints of rosewater, lime zest, cardamom and liquorice alongside some relatively subdued juniper. **Aftertaste:** Ginger builds and lasts through a long, dry lime zesty finish with liquorice still shouting from the wings.

G'VINE NOUAISON ★★★★★

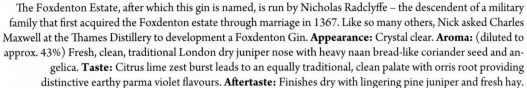 EXCELLENT

Alc./vol: 43.9% **Producer:** EuroWineGate

Based on grape spirit rather than the more usual grain spirits and flavoured with the petals of vine flowers alongside more traditional gin botanicals. 'Nouaison' is a French term for the blossoming of a vine flower. **Appearance:** (bot N0. 08B1460) Crystal clear **Aroma:** Floral, mineral nose with aromas of juniper, coriander and lime zest with fainter hints of fresh root ginger and rose water. **Taste:** On the huge palate, piney juniper notes rightly predominate with fresh coriander right up there and lime zest close behind. Spicy notes of nutmeg, ginger and sweet liquorice follow with floral flavours. **Aftertaste:** Nouaison is bigger and spicier than G'Vine's Floraison making it more suited to traditionalist gin drinkers such as myself.

GABRIEL BOUDIER SAFFRON GIN ★★★☆☆

Alc./vol: 40% **Producer:** Gabriel Boudier

Distilled in Dijon by Gabriel Boudier apparently using nine botanicals (although we only know of eight): juniper, coriander, lemon, orange peel, angelica seeds, iris, fennel and the eponymous saffron, which considering this gin's colour we presume is steeped after distillation. **Appearance:** Clear, rust orange. **Aroma:** Soft rubber, car tyre-like nose with pine forest and saffron. **Taste:** Dry, palate with strong bitter orange and pine-like juniper flavours vying with the saffron and spices – a fight rather than a harmonious existence. **Aftertaste:** Dry, bitter orange and saffron finish. Also almost makes our 'ver-gin' classification (verging on being a real gin).

GALE FORCE GIN ★★★☆☆

Alc./vol: 44% **Producer:** Triple Eight Distillery LLC

Gale Force gin is made at the Triple Eight Distillery, a micro-distillery founded in 1997 by Dean and Melissa Long on Nantucket Island, near Boston. The distillery is named after its water source, well No. 888. **Appearance:** Transparent and clear. **Aroma:** Lacklustre nose with mild barky juniper lemon pie filling citrus aromas. **Taste:** Juniper and citrus compete for attention with cracked black peppery spice on the palate. **Aftertaste:** Dry cracked black pepper dominates the finish.

GERANIUM LONDON DRY GIN

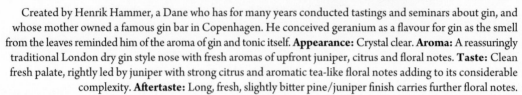

Alc./vol: 44% **Producer:** Unknown producer

Created by Henrik Hammer, a Dane who has for many years conducted tastings and seminars about gin, and whose mother owned a famous gin bar in Copenhagen. He conceived geranium as a flavour for gin as the smell from the leaves reminded him of the aroma of gin and tonic itself. **Appearance:** Crystal clear. **Aroma:** A reassuringly traditional London dry gin style nose with fresh aromas of upfront juniper, citrus and floral notes. **Taste:** Clean fresh palate, rightly led by juniper with strong citrus and aromatic tea-like floral notes adding to its considerable complexity. **Aftertaste:** Long, fresh, slightly bitter pine/juniper finish carries further floral notes.

GILBEY'S SPECIAL DRY GIN

Alc./vol: 37.5% **Producer:** Jim Beam Brands

The dragon-like creature featured on Gilbey's label is a Wyvern, a mythical winged animal often seen in medieval heraldry. Gilbey's gin is owned by Diageo but is produced and sold under a long-term licence by Jim Beam Brands. It is flavoured with 12 botanicals. **Appearance:** Clear, transparent. **Aroma:** Citrus and juniper led nose, akin to pine and lemon meringue pie filling, with herbal, spicy, rooty notes. **Taste:** Minerally palate more dominated by lemon citrus than juniper – although the two seem to be in battle rather than in harmony. Rooty, herbal notes emerge. **Aftertaste:** Citrus finish is reminiscent of packed pasteurised lemon juice rather than fresh zest.

GILPIN'S WESTMORLAND EXTRA DRY GIN

Alc./vol: 47% **Producer:** Thames Distillers

Gilpin's is distilled at Thames Distillers in London using wheat neutral spirit redistilled with eight botanicals: juniper berries, sage, borage, lemon peel, lime peel, bitter orange, coriander seeds and angelica root. **Appearance:** (year 2011, batch No. 11/0001, bottle No. 2106) Crystal clear. **Aroma:** Fresh, green pine forest with sage, thyme and faint whiffs of swimming pool changing rooms (in an agreeable way) with. **Taste:** Bitter resinous pine with sage, peppery basil, coriander, fresh flat leaf parsley and chewing gum (Dentine). **Aftertaste:** Lingering bitter sappy pine.

GIN MARE

Alc./vol: 42.7% **Producer:** Gin Mare at Destilerías Miquel Guansé

Pronounced: 'Mar-ray' and made in a 19th century chapel on the outskirts of Barcelona in the small Spanish fishing town on the Costa Dourada (literally 'golden coast'). **Appearance:** Crystal clear. **Aroma:** Spicy nose with herbaceous notes reminiscent of a humid pine forest filled with tomato plants and subtle rosemary and black olive aromas. **Taste:** Boldly flavoured palate bursts open with juniper and fresh coriander before turning bitter with spicy notes of thyme, rosemary and basil (as promised on the label). **Aftertaste:** Slightly bitter finish has green olive notes with cardamom and basil. A gin offering genuinely different flavours.

GIN RIVES TRIDESTILADA SPECIAL

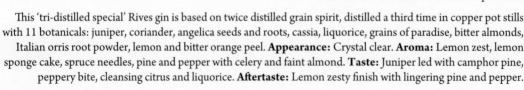

Alc./vol: 40% **Producer:** Unknown producer

This 'tri-distilled special' Rives gin is based on twice distilled grain spirit, distilled a third time in copper pot stills with 11 botanicals: juniper, coriander, angelica seeds and roots, cassia, liquorice, grains of paradise, bitter almonds, Italian orris root powder, lemon and bitter orange peel. **Appearance:** Crystal clear. **Aroma:** Lemon zest, lemon sponge cake, spruce needles, pine and pepper with celery and faint almond. **Taste:** Juniper led with camphor pine, peppery bite, cleansing citrus and liquorice. **Aftertaste:** Lemon zesty finish with lingering pine and pepper.

GINEBRA S. MIGUEL RED ★★☆☆☆

Alc./vol: 40% **Producer:** Ginebra San Miguel Inc.

Known in the Philippines (this gin's domestic market) as GSM, Ginebra S. Miguel is the world's best-selling gin brand. A fact all the more incredible as, if you're not from the Philippines, then you've probably not even heard of it, yet alone tried a GSM&T made with it. **Appearance:** Crystal clear. **Aroma:** Subdued nose with little discernible juniper but faint high alcohol spirit notes – possibly butanone. **Taste:** Slightly sweet palate with a mildly syrupy mouthfeel (glycerine perhaps?). While slightly hidden on the nose, juniper is very apparent on the palate – almost one-dimensionally so, with cracked black pepper spirit being the only other notable flavour. **Aftertaste:** Not unpleasant juniper finish with a perceived creaminess but lacking complexity.

GLOAG'S LONDON DRY GIN EXCELLENT ★★★★★

Alc./vol: 40% **Producer:** The Edrington Group Ltd

Launched in 1996 by The Edrington Group, makers of The Famous Grouse Scotch this gin is named after Matthew Gloag, the man who created Famous Grouse. An extended steeping period is used to extract the flavour from the 11 botanicals, which include sweet orange peel, nutmeg and grains of paradise. **Appearance:** Crystal clear. **Aroma:** Citrusy nose with mandarin orange zestyness and celery-like aromas (perhaps angelica seeds). **Taste:** Fresh, crisp palate with balanced juniper, citrus/orangey ripeness, liquorice, angelica, nutmeg, and refreshing citrus acidity. **Aftertaste:** Dry, citrusy finish with lingering pine and camphor juniper.

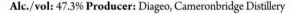

GORDON'S THE ORIGINAL LONDON DRY (UK 47.3%) RECOMMENDED ★★★★☆

Alc./vol: 47.3% **Producer:** Diageo, Cameronbridge Distillery

Until around 1900 only green glass could be produced in volume, so Gordon's green and white colour palette had remained effectively unchanged. The clear bottle and yellow 'export' label was created in celebration of a large, prestigious Australian export order placed in 1907. **Appearance:** Clear, transparent. **Aroma:** Pine, lavender and camphor from juniper dominate with lemon zest and black pepper. **Taste:** The flavours found in Gordon's are amplified by strength. The juniper-led palate features spicy, lemon zest notes and a peppery edge, while rooty notes combine with fresh peppermint, zingy lemon zest, a touch of liquorice and white pepper. **Aftertaste:** Pine-ey juniper and candied lemon zest.

GORDON'S LONDON DRY GIN (USA 40%)

Alc./vol: 40% **Producer:** Diageo Americas Supply Inc.

When Prohibition was repealed in 1933, Gordon's owners, Tanqueray Gordon, established a huge distillery and bottling plant in New Jersey. Another followed in Illinois in 1965 and a third hit California in 1971.

GORDON'S SPECIAL LONDON DRY (UK 40%) RECOMMENDED ★★★★☆

Alc./vol: 40% **Producer:** Diageo, Cameronbridge Distillery

This yellow label Gordon's was created for the export market. Contrary to popular belief it is only the bottle and the strength that differ to regular Gordon's gin. The same recipe and botanicals are used to make both gins. **Appearance:** Clear, transparent. **Aroma:** Pine-fresh juniper with lavender, camphor, lemon sherbet, celery and white pepper spice. **Taste:** Classic juniper led London Dry Gin palate with hints of liquorice and faint lemon citrus. **Aftertaste:** Dry pine-ey juniper and orris.

GORDON'S THE ORIGINAL SPECIAL DRY (UK 37.5%) ★★★☆☆

Alc./vol: 37.5% **Producer:** Cameronbridge Grain Distillery

Gordon's is the UK's leading gin brand and one of the ten best-selling spirits worldwide: on average, ten bottles of Gordon's are sold every minute. It has been made to the same recipe since 1769 (now using a multi-shot method in Scotland) when Alexander Gordon set up his business in London. **Appearance:** Clear, transparent. **Aroma:** Hops and spruce needles, lemon and sage with faint almond and liquorice. **Taste:** Juniper-led palate with some spicy, lemon zest notes and a peppery edge, plus peppermint and liquorice freshness with a faint sweetness. **Aftertaste:** Rootier notes come through in a long, zingy, peppery finish with juniper and lemon zest.

GREENALL'S ORIGINAL LONDON DRY GIN ★★★★½

RECOMMENDED

Alc./vol: 40% **Producer:** G&J Greenall, Warrington, Cheshire

Greenall's is made to Dakin's original 1761 recipe using eight botanicals - juniper berries, coriander, lemon peel, angelica, orris, liquorice, cassia bark and bitter almonds. These are macerated in wheat neutral spirit and purified water in a pot still for at least 24 hours prior to distillation. **Appearance:** Crystal clear. **Aroma:** Clean, coriander, juniper and angelica roots nutty, forest floor notes. Subdued citrus notes. **Taste:** Very classic London dry clean palate with surprisingly creamy mouthfeel. Juniper leads with liquorice, parma violet and cracked black pepper. **Aftertaste:** Nutty, balsa wood notes emerge in the finish where previously subdued citrus also shines. Lingering peppery minty freshness.

GREENHOOK GINSMITHS AMERICAN DRY GIN ★★★★☆

Alc./vol: 47% **Producer:** Greenhook Ginsmiths

Made in Brooklyn, New York by Steven DeAngelo using a copper pot still which operates under reduced pressure (due to vacuum pump) so distils at a lower temperature. Botanicals used include juniper, elderflowers, German chamomile, Ceylon cinnamon, blue ginger, oris root, orange and lemon peel. **Appearance:** Crystal clear. **Aroma:** Fragrant juniper and fresh coriander with parma violet. **Taste:** Fresh and clean, dry piney juniper and chamomile with earthy orris root and forward spice. **Aftertaste:** Juniper lingers with warming ginger, cinnamon spice and chamomile.

GREYLOCK GIN ★★★★☆

Alc./vol: 40% **Producer:** Berkshire Mountain Distillers Inc.

Berkshire Mountain Distillers says its Greylock Gin "is handcrafted in small batches. Our proprietary blend of seven botanicals, packed in to a gin head suspended over a pot still, infuses the distillate with its unique essence." **Appearance:** Crystal clear. **Aroma:** Bold, fresh, green, pine forest juniper rich nose with eucalyptus and menthol. **Taste:** Clean, juniper rich with liquorice, citrus zest and herbal complexity. **Aftertaste:** Dry with lingering liquorice flavours.

HAMMER & SON OLD ENGLISH GIN ★★★★★+

OUTSTANDING

Alc./vol: 44% **Producer:** Langley Distillery (Alcohols Limited)

As the name suggests, this gin sets out to replicate an original style of English gin, a slightly sweetened distilled gin which many people refer to as Old Tom. Old English Gin is distilled at Langley Distillery using a John Dore copper pot still called Angela, the oldest such gin still in use today **Appearance:** Crystal clear. **Aroma:** Classic musky, nutty angelica aromas of damp wood and mushrooms lead the nose with pine fresh juniper. Rubbery liquorice, cassia, earthy-clean hamster cage orris root and relatively faint citrus aromas. **Taste:** Superbly rounded palate with juniper just rising to the fore with the other 10 botanicals presented as a uniform front. The sugar content is hard to discern other than by the soft mouth feel. **Aftertaste:** Long, slightly hot pepper, lingering juniper finish with citrus notes more pronounced than on the palate or nose.

HARTEVELT PRIMA JONGE JENEVER ★★★☆☆

Alc./vol: 35% **Producer:** Lucas Bols B.V.

Now owned by Bols, the Hartevelt brand of jenever was established in 1734 and has its origins in Leiden. Hartevelt Fine Young Genever has a mild juniper-character malted wine and is based on molasses alcohol. **Appearance:** Crystal clear. **Aroma:** Toasty bread with light fresh pine forest aromas. **Taste:** Passive, juniper led palate with faint maltyness and very delicate spice. **Aftertaste:** Citrus notes emerge in a subdued finish with faint carbolic soap like notes. Hard criticize but lacks any real appeal.

HAYMAN'S LONDON DRY GIN ★★★★☆

Alc./vol: 40% **Producer:** Thames Distillers Ltd

Distilled with seven botanicals – juniper, French angelica roots, French coriander seeds, liquorice, Italian orris root, Spanish orange and lemon peel – which are steeped in the pot still for 24 hours prior to distillation. **Appearance**: Crystal clear. **Aroma**: Crystallised lemon zest and orange peel with aromatic lavender and camphor rich juniper. Delicate rooty earthy notes with freshly cut celery. **Taste**: Piney juniper with dry, slightly bitter orris root and zesty citrus – practically lime zest (although this is not a botanical used in this gin). Complex and bone dry. **Aftertaste**: Slightly bitter rooty notes continue through the rooty juniper finish.

HAYMAN'S OLD TOM GIN ★★★★☆

Alc./vol: 40% **Producer:** Thames Distillers Ltd

Launched in November 2007, Hayman's Old Tom is a modern-day version of the sweet gins of old. It is distilled in London from grain neutral spirit and flavoured with juniper, orange and lemon peel and seven other additional secret botanicals. Hayman's Old Tom is lightly sweetened by the addition of sugar. **Appearance:** Crystal clear. **Aroma:** Clean fresh juniper and orange zest nose. **Taste:** Juniper led, clean, slightly sweet palate. Juniper is very much to the fore but backed by citrus notes and subtle spice. **Aftertaste**: Clean, cracked black pepper lingers throughout the long finish.

HAYMAN'S 1850 RESERVE DISTILLED GIN ★★★★★

Alc./vol: 40% **Producer:** Thames Distillers Ltd

Said to be distilled to a recipe dating from the 1850s and then cask rested for 3-4 weeks in ex-Scotch whisky casks. Hayman's 1850 Reserve Gin is distilled in small batches of 5,000 bottles with each bottle carrying the batch and individual bottle number. **Appearance:** (batch No. 00-001, Bot No. 0855) Crystal clear. No colour from oak ageing. **Aroma**: Clean attractive and aromatic nose with generous pine forest-like juniper and fresh coriander. **Taste**: Reassuringly traditional, pine-fresh juniper and coriander palate with earthy Parma Violet (orris root?), liquorice and gentle dry spice. **Aftertaste**: Cleansing spice continues in the finish with lingering dry oaky bitterness.

HENDRICK'S GIN ★★★★☆

Alc./vol: 41.4% **Producer:** Girvan Grain Distillery

This "most unusual gin" has been brilliantly marketed as a quintessentially British product, associated with cucumber sandwiches and rose gardens, whilst simultaneously being proudly Scottish in its origins. **Appearance:** Crystal clear. **Aroma:** Hints of pine, eucalyptus and lime marmalade combine with juniper and spicy floral fragrances in a fresh, complex nose. **Taste:** Slightly sweet and silky smooth, with a burst of juniper and citrus set against fresh green flavours. This is followed by cumin, cracked black pepper and salty liquorice back notes. **Aftertaste**: Long and lingering with floral hints and a quinine and juniper bitterness.

HERNO GIN ★★★★☆

Alc./vol: 40.5% **Producer:** Hernö Brenneri AB

Launched in December 2012, Hernö is batch distilled in a 250 litre Carl copper still called Kierstin using organic neutral wheat spirit. This base spirit is diluted with well water and redistilled to ensure purity before the eight botanicals are steeped in the spirit and then redistilled. **Appearance**: (batch 14, bottle 66/1320) Crystal clear. **Aroma**: Coriander linalool oil with pine sap and lavender. Faint note of nubuck leather. **Taste**: Fresh and spicy with vigorous coriander (ginger, lemon and sage) and chilli spice/black peppery heat. **Aftertaste**: Chilli-like hot spicy coriander finish.

HERNO NAVY STRENGTH GIN ★★★★☆

Alc./vol: 57% **Producer:** Hernö Brenneri AB

Launched in April 2013, Hernö Navy Strength is batch distilled in a 250 litre Carl copper still called Kierstin using organic neutral wheat spirit. This base spirit is diluted with well water and redistilled to ensure purity before the eight botanicals are steeped in the spirit and then redistilled. **Appearance**: (batch 2, bottle 138/216) crystal clear. **Aroma**: Coriander with vanilla-like notes sings out over the pepper prickle of the high strength alcohol. Water releases a burst of pine, lavender and lemon zest. **Taste**: Peppery heat. Water reveals generous coriander, floral lavender, vanilla and nubuck leathery oily notes. **Aftertaste**: Oily peppery coriander finish.

HOXTON GIN ★★☆☆☆

Alc./vol: 43% **Producer:** Gabriel Boudier

Developed by Gerry Calabrese of London's Hoxton Pony bar, Hoxton Gin is flavoured with coconut, grapefruit, juniper, iris, tarragon and ginger – steeped for five days before a single distillation in a copper pot still. Purists argue that juniper isn't the dominant flavour so this is not a 'real' gin. **Appearance**: Crystal clear. **Aroma:** Reminiscent of vanilla cream soda, lime cordial and coconut liqueur with a waft of eucalyptus. **Taste:** Even with a splash of water I find the palate bitter and hot with astringent bitter grapefruit, ginger and pine notes, partially smoothed by vanilla. **Aftertaste**: Lingering bitter grapefruit, ginger and resinous pine and eucalyptus notes.

HUNTERS CHESHIRE GIN ★★★★☆

Alc./vol: 43.3% **Producer:** Langley Distillery (Alcohols Limited)

A distilled gin made at Langley Distillery, England. The botanical recipe is a secret but is known to contain juniper berries, coriander seeds, lemon and sweet orange peel. The botanicals are steeped in neutral spirit for an undisclosed period prior to distillation in a John Dore pot still. **Appearance**: Crystal clear. **Aroma**: Candied lime zest, piney juniper and musky, nutty, balsawood-like angelica root with delicate floral aromas. Faint cinnamon spice. **Taste**: Well poised and delicate but with punchy juniper. Note of honeyed elderflower sweetness balancing generous zesty citrus. **Aftertaste**: Lingering juniper and dried floral notes - potpourri.

IMAGIN... STOCKHOLM DRY GIN ★★☆☆☆

Alc./vol: 40% **Producer:** Unknown producer

This Swedish gin is flavoured with thirteen botanicals. **Appearance**: Clear with slight blue tinge. **Aroma**: Zesty citrus – reminiscent of a lemon cleaning product and orange soda pops with peach flavoured boiled sweets. **Taste**: Juniper is much more evident on the pasteurised citrus juice zesty palate with boiled sweet flavours. **Aftertaste**: Dry zesty lime and orange with lingering juniper.

IMPERATOR BOROVIČKA ORIGINAL SLOVAK JUNIPER BRAND ★★★☆☆

Alc./vol: 42% **Producer:** Imperator Ltd

Borovička, or 'juniper brandy', is the Slovakian equivalent to England's London dry gin. The producer, Imperator Ltd, was established in 1994.
Appearance: Crystal clear. Aroma: Pine scented bathroom cleaner-like with fresh pungent green pine needle-like juniper aromas. Taste: Fresh breath inducing lemon zest and fresh pine needle - lacks complexity and subtly. Aftertaste: Herbal, pine with lingering pine and peppermint flavours.

ISH GIN ★★★★☆

Alc./vol: 40% **Producer:** The Poshmakers

Ish Gin is batch distilled using eleven botanicals: juniper, coriander seed, angelica root, almond, orris root, nutmeg, cinnamon, cassia, liquorice, lemon and orange peel. These are macerated in grain neutral spirit for 24 hours prior to distillation. **Appearance:** Crystal clear. **Aroma:** Heavy juniper nose with delicate coriander and a slight soapy (carbolic) aroma. **Taste:** Hefty juniper palate with prickly pepper heat, bitter orange oils and gentle parma violet (iris) sweetness. **Aftertaste:** Finish is a continuation of the palate with lasting juniper, piney bitterness. Despite the cringe-making marketing, a decent gin.

J.H. HENKES STARBRAND AROMATIC SCHIEDAM SCHNAPPS [RECOMMENDED] ★★★★⅃

Alc./vol: 40% **Producer:** Unknown producer

The square bottle's long rectangular label declares 'Aromatic Schiedam Schnapps' but the tiny print at the bottom indicates that this is, indeed, a style of jenever. Henkes has been made for over 200 years and is highly regarded in Nigeria where it is used at births, marriages and deaths ceremonies. **Appearance:** Crystal clear. **Aroma:** Fragrant oily hay and toasted nuts with faint freshly baked apple pie. **Taste:** Mellow with oily brazil nuttiness and rich notes of meat stock, baked apples, cinnamon, nutmeg and cloves. The juniper flavour is somewhat masked by the other strong botanicals. **Aftertaste:** Brasil nuts and lingering Christmas spice.

JENSEN'S LONDON DISTILLED OLD TOM GIN [RECOMMENDED] ★★★★⅃

Alc./vol: 43% **Producer:** Thames Distillers Ltd

This is real Old Tom, replicating the style of original 'sweet' gins from the late 18th and early 19th centuries, not just a bog standard London dry with added sugar. Jensen's Old Tom is made to a 1840s recipe, and is naturally sweetened with larger quantities of sweet botanicals such as liquorice. **Appearance:** (1st bottling) Crystal clear.
Aroma: Eucalyptus and piney juniper with woody liquorice, parma violet and earthy cold stewed tea with zesty orange and a soapy hint of almond. **Taste:** Strongly eucalyptus influenced palate with green vegetal notes and woody liquorice. This is far from tasting sweet – it's not that kind of Old Tom – it is in fact dry with the merest perception of sweetness. **Aftertaste:** Eucalyptus and piney juniper with lingering vegetal notes.

JENSEN'S DRY BERMONDSEY GIN [OUTSTANDING] ★★★★★+

Alc./vol: 43% **Producer:** Thames Distillers Ltd

Bermondsey Gin is made to a very traditional style: it is a true London distilled dry gin made only using the botanicals found in gins from the 1800s. Bermondsey Gin does not include cucumber, rose, grains of paradise or any of the other 'contemporary' botanicals. **Appearance:** (version 1.1) Crystal clear. **Aroma:** Clean piney juniper with lavender and Parma Violet, generous coriander, orange and lemon zest. **Taste:** Clean dry palate with pine fresh juniper to the fore with coriander and strong hints of parma violet from the orris, liquorice and nutty almond notes. **Aftertaste:** Liquorice starts sweet and dries throughout the long pine-ey finish.

JUNIPER GREEN ORGANIC GIN

Alc./vol: 37.5% **Producer:** Thames Distillers Ltd

The world's first organic London Dry Gin, Juniper Green is distilled in the Thames Distillery, Clapham, London using 100% organic botanicals (juniper, coriander, angelica root and savoy), certified organic by the Soil Association.

JUNIPERO GIN 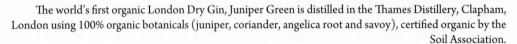 ★★★★⯪

Alc./vol: 49.3% **Producer:** Anchor Brewing/Distilling Company

Junipero is made using a tiny copper pot still which was installed in a corner of the Anchor Steam Brewery in San Francisco in 1993. After experimentation with a range of differe

KENSINGTON LONDON DRY

Alc./vol: 47.2% **Producer:** Unknown producer

Kensington gin stands out for a range of reasons, not just because it is made in Scotland yet branded with a very upscale London name. The outstanding thing about this gin is that it is aged in new American oak casks imported from Kentucky.

KETEL 1 JONGE AMBACHTELUKE GRAANJENEVER ★★★★★

Alc./vol: 35% **Producer:** Nolet Distillery

The Ketel 1 name is recognisable, due to the Nolet's successful Ketel One Vodka, named, like this jenever, for their coal-fired No.1 pot still. This jonge jenever is based on a blend of wheat, rye and maize spirit rested in 217 litre French oak casks for a year and flavoured with 14 botanicals. **Appearance:** Crystal clear. **Aroma:** Crusty apple pie pastry with fresh pear skin and poached pears with faint cloves and star anise. **Taste:** Superbly clean, very slightly sweet and mellow with light oily brazil nuts, overripe bananas, poached pears and roasted apples. **Aftertaste:** Delicately spiced, toasted cereal grain and backed apple.

LARIOS 12 BOTANICALS PREMIUM GIN

Alc./vol: 40% **Producer:** Larios Pernod Ricard S.A.

Larios 12 Botanicals Premium Gin is flavoured with, yes, 12 botanicals in five separate distillations: wild juniper, coriander, nutmeg, angelica root, Mediterranean lemon, orange, tangerine, mandarin, clementine, grapefruit, lime and orange blossom.

LANGLEY'S NO.8 DISTILLED LONDON GIN 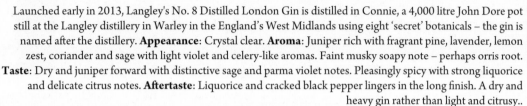 RECOMMENDED ★★★★⯪

Alc./vol: 41.7% **Producer:** Langley Distillery (Alcohols Limited)

Launched early in 2013, Langley's No. 8 Distilled London Gin is distilled in Connie, a 4,000 litre John Dore pot still at the Langley distillery in Warley in the England's West Midlands using eight 'secret' botanicals – the gin is named after the distillery. **Appearance**: Crystal clear. **Aroma**: Juniper rich with fragrant pine, lavender, lemon zest, coriander and sage with light violet and celery-like aromas. Faint musky soapy note – perhaps orris root. **Taste**: Dry and juniper forward with distinctive sage and parma violet notes. Pleasingly spicy with strong liquorice and delicate citrus notes. **Aftertaste**: Liquorice and cracked black pepper lingers in the long finish. A dry and heavy gin rather than light and citrusy..

LARIOS DRY GIN ★★★⯪☆

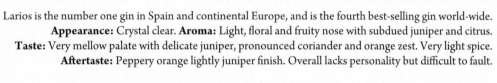 

Alc./vol: 37.5% **Producer:** Larios Pernod Ricard S.A.

Larios is the number one gin in Spain and continental Europe, and is the fourth best-selling gin world-wide. **Appearance**: Crystal clear. **Aroma**: Light, floral and fruity nose with subdued juniper and citrus. **Taste**: Very mellow palate with delicate juniper, pronounced coriander and orange zest. Very light spice. **Aftertaste**: Peppery orange lightly juniper finish. Overall lacks personality but difficult to fault.

LEBENSSTERN LONDON DRY GIN RECOMMENDED ★★★★⯪

Alc./vol: 43% **Producer:** Freihof Distillery

This London dry gin is made at the Freihof Distillery in Austria, famous for its fruit eaux-de-vie, especially for Lebensstern bar above Berlin's Cafe Einstein. **Appearance**: Crystal clear. **Aroma**: Alpine elderflower, pear skin, eucalyptus and pine. **Taste**: Pear and elderflower are very evident initially before pine notes of juniper cut with palate drying cracked black pepper and orange zest. **Aftertaste**: Floral and fruity notes are practically lost in a classic juniper and pepper gin finish.

LEOPOLD'S GIN

Alc./vol: 40% **Producer:** Leopold Bros. Distillery

Launched in 2002, Leopold's American Small Batch Gin is made by distilling each of the six botanicals (juniper, orris root, cardamom, coriander and hand-zested Valencia Oranges and Pummelos) separately and then blending the six distillates together to make this hand-bottled, labelled and numbered gin.

LIGHTHOUSE GIN ★★★⯪☆

Alc./vol: 42% **Producer:** Greytown Fine Distillates

Made using dried kawa kawa leaves which are unique to New Zealand as well as fresh zest from New Zealand-grown navel oranges and Yen Ben lemons. The rest of the nine botanicals are more traditional. **Appearance**: Crystal clear. **Aroma**: Clean pine and citrus (particularly lemon zest) dominate the nose with whiffs of violet. **Taste**: Very dry, slightly oily palate has strong lemon citrus, eucalyptus, pine notes, hints of floral violet and a somewhat earthy note. **Aftertaste**: Raspingly dry citrus finish with lingering pine and pepper.

LOYAAL ZEER OUDE GENEVER ★★★★☆

Alc./vol: 42% **Producer:** A. van Wees Distilleerderij De Ooievaar

Made at Distilleerderij De Ooievaar, which translates as 'The Stork Distillery', hence the stork on the label. Loyaal Zeer Oude is based on malt-wine distilled from seven different types of malted barley and corn, aged for an average of three years. **Appearance:** Clear, faint yellow green tinge. **Aroma:** New-make spirit-like cereal with oily fresh hay and brioche. **Taste:** Dry and fairly spicy (cinnamon and clove) with lovely cereal notes and slight nuttiness. **Aftertaste:** Wholemeal bread with clove spice, dry oak and cracked black pepper heat.

MARTIN MILLER'S GIN ★★★☆☆

Alc./vol: 40% **Producer:** Langley Distillery (Alcohols Limited)

Named after and minority owned by Martin Miller, creator of the *Miller's Antiques* price guides. Formerly labelled as a 'London Dry Gin', regulations forbidding flavouring to be added to a London Dry Gin after distillation necessitated this classification to be omitted from the new taller bottle. **Appearance:** Crystal clear **Aroma:** Very aromatic pronounced zesty orange nose with woody juniper, liquorice and light spice. **Taste:** Like the nose, orange zest appears to dominate the palate with underlying freshly cracked black pepper spice, juniper and vegetal flavours (perhaps from the added cucumber essence. A touch of added sugar is suspected). **Aftertaste:** Black pepper heat leads and ends the slightly bitter finish with coriander and citrus shine also coming to the fore.

MARTIN MILLER'S WESTBOURNE STRENGTH

Alc./vol: 45.2% **Producer:** Langley Distillery (Alcohols Limited)

This Westbourne Strength line extension is named for Miller's original base in Westbourne Grove, West London. It has a higher alcoholic strength than Miller's Reformed.

MASCARÓ 9 GIN ★★★★★

Alc./vol: 40% **Producer:** Antonio Mascaró S. L.

This Spanish gin is made from just one botanical – juniper. This is the only 100 per cent juniper gin we know of and that alone makes it interesting, but the fact it is a product with real heritage adds to its appeal. **Appearance:** Crystal clear. **Aroma:** A clean eucalyptus nose with a light pepper tingle – surprisingly delicate. **Taste:** Clean, dry and fairly soft palate with fresh eucalyptus and pine juniper uncompromised or complicated by other botanicals. **Aftertaste:** Pine and white pepper dry, lingering finish. Proof that simple can be beautiful.

MONKEY 47 SCHWARZWALD DRY GIN ★★★★☆

Alc./vol: 47% **Producer:** Black Forest Distillers

The Monkey 47 story begins with Wing Commander Montgomery ('Monty') Collins of the Royal Air Force. He was one of those old-school British eccentrics – a watch-lover, cricket enthusiast, globe trotter and general maverick. **Appearance:** (batch 01, bot No. 0572, bottled 05/2010) Crystal clear **Aroma:** Lime zest/lime cordial are immediately apparent on the nose and are made even fresher with eucalyptus and pine forest aromas. **Taste:** Clean, invigorating zesty palate with lime still very evident, but with good herbal notes and juniper presence. **Aftertaste:** Citrus and pine flavours also dominate the finish.

NEW AMSTERDAM NO.485 STRAIGHT GIN ★★★★☆

Alc./vol: 40% **Producer:** Modesto Distillery

As any schoolboy knows, New York City was originally called New Amsterdam and for those a little slow to make the connection with this gin's name, the image of the Empire State building printed on reverse of back label is visible through the gin and the clear front label as an aide-mémoire. **Appearance:** Crystal clear. **Aroma:** Sweet floral, candied orange and lemon peel nose with celery-like fragrant, slightly floral notes from the angelica. **Taste:** Initially arguably more a orange citrus botanical spirit that a gin at all. However, juniper eventually makes a subtle appearance, if a little outgunned by peppery spice. **Aftertaste:** Orange zest and cracked black pepper finish. Close to making our 'ver-gin' classification (verging on being a real gin).

NO. 209 GIN ⬛OUTSTANDING⬛ ★★★★★★+

Alc./vol: 46% **Producer:** Distillery No. 209

209 is distilled on a pier over the water in San Francisco's docks from 11 botanicals including bergamot orange peel from Southern Italy and more usual gin botanicals such as Guatemalan cardamom, Chinese cassia, coriander, Angelica root and, of course, Italian juniper berries. **Appearance:** Crystal clear. **Aroma:** Fresh lavender and juniper nose with green cardamom spice. **Taste:** Very slightly sweet, bergamot and rosewater palate with strong juniper. Appealing soft slightly soapyness with freshening lemon and orange citrus. The high alc./vol. contributes weight and invigorating peppery notes. **Aftertaste:** Floral lavender notes ride a peppery juniper wave.

NO.3 LONDON DRY GIN ★★★★☆

Alc./vol: 46% **Producer:** De Kuyper Royal Distillers

No.3 refers to the address in St James' Street, London, the home of wine and spirit merchants, Berry Bros. & Rudd since 1698. The inspiration for the key on the bottle came when the packaging designers were rummaging through the shop and found the key to The Parlour, one of the shop's oldest rooms. **Appearance:** Crystal clear. **Aroma:** Grapefruit and orange zest led fresh with good piny juniper and cardamom. **Taste:** Zingy clean palate explodes with grapefruit and orange oil freshness, dried by pine-fresh juniper and bursts of spice (coriander and cardamom). **Aftertaste:**

NOLET'S SILVER DRY GIN ★★★★☆

Alc./vol: 47.6% **Producer:** Nolet Distillery

Made from wheat and flavoured with traditional botanicals including citrus, orris root, liquorice and, of course, juniper alongside contemporary ingredients such as white peach, raspberry and Turkish rose. The more contemporary botanicals are introduced as essences made by a French flavour house. **Appearance:** Crystal clear. **Aroma:** A splash of water opens a perfumed floral rose petal/Turkish delight, sweet cherryade nose with subtle herbal and fruit aromas. **Taste:** Similarly rose petal/Turkish delight-influenced palate has raspberry, prickly black pepper and a drying blast of piney juniper and earthy orris root. **Aftertaste:** Long finish brings interplay between fruity, floral, rooty, piney and peppery flavours. Distinctly different but some traditionalist gin fans may find this a little too 'feminine' and contemporary.

NOLET'S THE RESERVE DRY GIN (GOLD LABEL)

Alc./vol: 52.3% **Producer:** Nolet Distillery

Nolet's Reserve Gin is the personal creation of Carolus Nolet Sr. and he alone approves each batch before bottling. The botanicals used include saffron from the Middle East and cerbena picked in North Africa.

OLIFANT JONGE GRAANJENEVER ★★★★☆

Alc./vol: 35% **Producer:** Wenneker Distilleries

The Olifant (Elephant) brand of genever dates from 1841 when the of J.J Melchers Wz Distillery in Schiedam started exporting Olifant Gin to the Dutch African colonies. So the dockworkers would recognise their barrels and to overcome the language barrier they were branded with an Elephant logo. **Appearance:** Clear, transparent. **Aroma:** Subdued, subtle juniper and green tea with faint cedar and nuts. **Taste:** Not as flavourful as some other jonge jenevers, Olifant's palate features cedary, nutty notes, alongside juniper, black olives, green tea and spice. **Aftertaste:** Slight oily and nutty with lingering piney juniper and spice.

OXLEY CLASSIC ENGLISH DRY GIN ★★★★★ RECOMMENDED

Alc./vol: 47% **Producer:** Thames Distillers Ltd

This 'cold distilled' gin is flavoured with 14 botanicals ('Recipe 38'): juniper, meadowsweet (an English herb), cocoa, coriander, angelica root, cassia bark, grains of paradise, liquorice, nutmeg, iris root, vanilla beans and fresh hand-peeled citrus peels: lemon, orange and grapefruit zest. **Appearance:** (bottle No. B03796) Crystal clear. **Aroma:** Superbly clean, fresh nose with very mild piney juniper and generous freshly zested citrus, particularly orange. **Taste:** Bursts alive with sweet zesty orange citrus, moderate juniper and herbal complexity. Pink grapefruit emerges and then dominates. **Aftertaste:** Zesty, pronounced juniper finish with lingering liquorice. Not as rounded as some gins but then they're not as fresh and zesty.

PALMERS PREMIUM DISTILLED LONDON DRY GIN ★★★★☆

Alc./vol: 40% **Producer:** Langley Distillery (Alcohols Limited)

This gin, made with 10 botanicals according to a recipe that's more than 350-years-old, is owned and made by W H Palmer Group, a family-owned company which owns and operates the Langley Distillery near Birmingham, England where numerous other gins are also distilled under contact. **Appearance:** Crystal clear. **Aroma:** Subdued nose with pine forest juniper, almond and zesty lemon aromas. **Taste:** Clean, muted, zesty citrus and juniper led palate with nutty angelica root, subtle spice and lightly tingling black pepper. **Aftertaste:** Long, clean, mouth cleansing citrus and black pepper finish.

PERIGAN'S CANNABIS-FLAVOURED GIN ★☆☆☆☆

Alc./vol: 37.5% **Producer:** Beveland SA.

According to the bottle, "Perigan's Cannabis Gin is a blend of the purest gin with a subtle hint of cannabis" and based on "100% pure grain spirit". We understand that hemp is not a botanical ingredient and that the cannabis flavouring, along with colouring, are added after distillation. **Appearance:** Clear, aquamarine. **Aroma:** Aggressive, pine, juniper and spearmint chewing gum-like, very spiritous nose. **Taste:** Herbal, aggressive sweet mint, bitter palate with unpleasant pine and cinnamon spice. **Aftertaste:** Somewhat nasty, long lingering herbal, cinnamon finish.

NEW YORK DISTILLING CO. PERRY'S TOT NAVY STRENGTH GIN ★★★★★ EXCELLENT

Alc./vol: 57% **Producer:** New York Distilling Company

This gins use of the term 'Navy Strength' and its high 57% alc./vol. strength references the historical 'proof' strength for alcohol, derived as being the strength at which gunpowder would still light when doused with the alcohol. 'Tot', a British measure for alcohol also nods to Navy strength roots **Appearance**: Crystal clear. **Aroma:** Pungent spruce and lavender jump from an alluring nose with nutty balsa wood-like angelica, parma violets, cold stewed tea and zesty citrus. **Taste**: The high strength appears to lock this gins flavours together which explode in the mouth with clean peppery spirit attack. Like its Dorothy Parker sibling, Perry's Tot has classic London Dry cues with delicate juniper and judiciously added extra contemporary complexity. **Aftertaste**: Nutty juniper and spice finish.

PINK 47 LONDON DRY GIN ★★★★☆

Alc./vol: 47%

Pink 47 is named after the Khavaraya pink diamond which also influences the design of its multi-faceted, screen printed bottle. London Dry in style and flavoured with 12 botanicals. **Appearance**: Crystal clear. **Aroma**: Peppery spice (Grains of Paradise use suspected) with earthy angelica and candied ginger, lemon and sage notes from the coriander. **Taste**: Dry, spicy (enliveningly so) juniper led with pleasant, but subtle, parma violet notes - we suspect from Orris Root. **Aftertaste**: Pleasing, peppery spice and pine juniper.

PLYMOUTH GIN NAVY STRENGTH  ★★★★★+

Alc./vol: 57% **Producer:** Black Friars Distillery (Coates & Co Ltd)

By 1850 Coates & Co, the makers of Plymouth gin, were supplying over 1,000 casks of Navy strength gin to the British Royal Navy each year. Naval officers would mix it with Angostura aromatic bitters and lime juice for 'medicinal' purposes. **Appearance:** Crystal clear. **Aroma:** The addition of a little water releases a wonderfully floral, citrus nose with strong notes of lavender, camphor and pine. **Taste:** Supercharged Plymouth in both flavour and strength. The wonderfully flavoursome palate includes more floral notes with rounded lemon and sage coriander, lemon zest and clean juniper notes. **Aftertaste:** Pine freshness dominates with spicy naan bread and lingering citrus zest.

PLYMOUTH GIN ORIGINAL STRENGTH  ★★★★★

Alc./vol: 41.2% **Producer:** Black Friars Distillery (Coates & Co Ltd)

Plymouth is made in a 7,000 litre copper pot still which has been in regular use at the distillery for over 150 years. The seven botanicals used in order of dominance are: juniper, coriander, lemon peel, sweet orange peel, sweet angelica, orris root and cardamom. No bitter botanicals are used. **Appearance:** Crystal Clear. **Aroma:** Juniper notes of pine, lavender and camphor with lemon zest, sage and eucalyptus. **Taste:** Fresh zingy juniper with zesty lemony bite and orange ripeness; character and interest are enhanced by more subtle rooty notes with fresh coriander and mild white pepper spice. **Aftertaste:** Refreshing pine freshness lingers with subtle white pepper and liquorice-like rootyness.

POLO CLUB EXTRA

Alc./vol: 43% **Producer:** Deanston Distillery

Polo Club Extra London dry gin was launched in 1997 and was distilled by Burns Stewart in traditional copper stills at its Deanston Distillery. It was sold in a square decanter-shaped bottle with embossed side panels.

PORTOBELLO ROAD NO.171 LONDON DRY GIN ★★★★☆

Alc./vol: 42% **Producer:** Thames Distillers Ltd

Above the infamous Portobello Star bar at 171 Portobello Road you'll find Ged Feltham and Jake Burger's Ginstitute. London's second smallest museum and home to the city's smallest working copper pot still, the amusingly named 'Coppernicus', in which Portobello Road No. 171 was first conceived. **Appearance:** (bottle No. 358) Crystal clear. **Aroma:** Elegant, floral nose with junipery lavender and camphor. Generous use of orris root imparts its characteristic parma violet and clean hamster cage while citrus aromas are subdued. **Taste:** Juniper is centre stage but not screaming, while citrus is way down the billing. As London gins go, Portobello is on the spicy side, but it's a 'warm interest adding', rather than a 'hot pepper' spice, with nutmeg and cinnamon (from cassia bark) with savoury celery-like notes (angelica root). **Aftertaste:** Lingering liquorice and nutmeg finish.

RANSOM OLD TOM GIN ★★★★☆

Alc./vol: 44% **Producer:** Ransom Wines and Spirits

The recipe for Ransom Old Tom was developed in collaboration with the rightly revered historian and author David Wondrich, and is designed as a gin to recreate vintage cocktails dating from the mid- to late-1800s. **Appearance:** (Batch 007, bottle No.1270) Clear, golden amber. **Aroma:** Spicy pine forest and flamed orange zest nose with aromas of freshly split sappy pine, eucalyptus, dark honey, cardamom, star anise, angelica and bitter lavender. **Taste:** A dry, huge but balanced palate delivers the flavours present in the nose but far more elegantly than the nose might suggest with pine and orange zest to the fore. **Aftertaste:** Orange bitters, rye dryness with distinct woody, smoky and dry orange zest finish.

REISETBAUER BLUE GIN VINTAGE ★★★★★

Alc./vol: 43% **Producer:** Reisetbauer Qualitätsbrand Gmbh

Made by Hans Reisetbauer, the renowned Austrian eaux-de-vie distiller, this is in fact a clear gin in a clear bottle – not blue as the name suggests. Reisetbauer distils this gin with more than 20 botanicals and releases a vintage batch each year – so inherently slightly different each year. **Appearance:** (Vintage 2008) Crystal clear. **Aroma:** Good juniper citrusy nose with Satsuma skin. **Taste:** Citrus joins the juniper with Satsuma, grapefruit and lemon followed by herbaceous notes. **Aftertaste:** White pepper and woody coriander influenced spicy finish.

RIGHT GIN ★★★☆☆

Alc./vol: 40% **Producer:** Right Gin Company

Launched in Las Vegas in May 2007, Right Gin is based on corn neutral spirit produced using a five-column process redistilled with eight botanicals: juniper, coriander, cardamom, lemon, bergamot, lime, bitter orange and Sarawak black pepper from Borneo. **Appearance:** Crystal clear. **Aroma:** Zesty orange and lemon nose with bursts of bergamot and eucalyptus rich cardamom. **Taste:** Equally zesty palate with slight sweetness and prickly heat from the Sarawak black pepper. **Aftertaste:** Long Sarawak black pepper prickly heat with lingering bitterness.

ROAST LONDON DRY GIN ★★★★☆

Alc./vol: 46% **Producer:** Thames Distillers Ltd

Distilled by Thames Distillers exclusively for London's Roast Restaurant and bottled in Perth this London dry gin was launched in May 2013. The key botanical used are juniper, coriander, angelica root and savoury. **Appearance:** Crystal clear. **Aroma:** A faint note of old-fashioned toy gun caps and match box lighting strip pervades a juniper-led classic London dry gin-styled nose. **Taste:** Sweet angelica root leads a juniper forward palate with coriander - lemon and sage. **Aftertaste:** Nutty piny juniper with freshening spice.

RUTTE & ZN 12 OUDE GRAAN JENEVER ★★★★★

Alc./vol: 38% **Producer:** Distillery Rutte & ZN

Composed of two-fifths malt-wine, juniper berries, herbs and spices blended with three-fifths neutral grain alcohol and then mellowed by aging in oak cakss for 12 years. **Appearance:** Crystal clear. **Aroma:** Stewed rhubarb nose with praline and cream ice-cream, butterscotch and honeyed wood chips. **Taste:** Graceful lightly oily palate with delicate yet assertive oak, nuts, juniper and gentle cracked black pepper tingle. **Aftertaste:** Slightly reminiscent of a mature grain whisky. Nutty, juniper finish with gentle spice.

RUTTE & ZN 5 OUDE GRAN JENEVER ★★★★☆

Alc./vol: 38% **Producer:** Distillery Rutte & ZN

Composed of two-fifths malt-wine, juniper berries, herbs and spices blended with three-fifths neutral grain alcohol and then mellowed by aging for five years in oak casks. **Appearance:** Crystal clear. **Aroma:** Toasted cereal nose with oiled just sawn white wood, fresh hay bales and dried apple peels. **Taste:** Slight sweetness and oily mouthfeel to a nutty juniper palate with aloe. **Aftertaste:** Bitter, nut oil finish with lingering toasted nutty oily flavours.

RUTTE & ZN PARADYSWYN JENEVER ⬛OUTSTANDING⬛ ★★★★★+

Alc./vol: 37.9% **Producer:** Distillery Rutte & ZN

Paradyswyn is Dutch for 'paradise'. The most premium product available from Rutte & ZN, this is based on a blend of malt-wine aged between 10 and 30 years in French oak casks. Paradyswyn Jenever is best drunk at room temperature as a digestive after meals. **Appearance:** Crystal clear. **Aroma:** Peachy, green banana and boatyard varnish nose with muscovado sugar, pilau rice and straw. **Taste:** Candied, buttery, oily, nutty flavour sensation with peach, tropical fruit, flaky pastry and vanilla. **Aftertaste:** Light, delicate buttery croissant finish with coconut and delicate spice.

RUTTE & ZN ZEEUWIER JENEVER ★★★☆☆

Alc./vol: 35% **Producer:** Distillery Rutte & ZN

Zeeuwier is a jonge jenever best drunk cold with shell fish, oysters, sushi and seafood. **Appearance:** Crystal clear. **Aroma:** Grainy malty nose with slight oiled nubuck leather, burnt cream and stale fruit cake. **Taste:** Leather, lightly influenced, dull juniper palate with oily cold dry toast and nutty flavours. **Aftertaste:** Slightly bitter, dry nutty spicy finish.

SACRED GIN ★★★⯪☆

Alc./vol: 40% **Producer:** Sacred Spirits Co Ltd

Sacred Gin is what led distiller Ian Hart into being an award-winning micro distiller. He continues to use reduced-pressure distillation to separately distil each of the 12 botanicals (in English wheat spirit), which include juniper, cardamom, nutmeg and Boswellia Sacra (aka Frankincense). **Appearance:** Crystal clear. **Aroma:** Subdued, pine-fresh juniper-led nose with delicate violet and estery aromas. **Taste:** Dry, piney juniper, pilau rice and peppery spiced palate. **Aftertaste:** Long spicy finish with lingering pine, juniper, red pepper corns.

SACRED JUNIPER ORGANIC BOTANICAL DISTILLATE ⬛OUTSTANDING⬛ ★★★★★+

Alc./vol: 40% **Producer:** Sacred Spirits Co Ltd

Flavoured by steeping organic Bulgarian Juniperus Communis berries in English wheat spirit and then delicately low-pressure distilling at low temperatures. **Appearance:** Crystal clear. **Aroma:** Fresh, clean, slightly 'green', pine forest nose with white pepper spice. **Taste:** Equally fresh, clean herbal palate with citrus bursts. Like having your mouth spring cleaned with and sprayed with pine-fresh cleaner. The polar opposite to soapy water, this is the kind of cleansing you'll come back for more of. **Aftertaste:** Lingering dill, green, fresh-breath finish with black pepper spice. A great gin.

SACRED TATE LONDON DRY GIN ★★★★☆

Alc./vol: 40% **Producer:** Sacred Spirits Co Ltd

Reduced pressure (vacuum) distiller Ian Hart worked with the art gallery's own cocktail aficionado, Alex Stevenson, to produce this special edition Tate London Dry Gin. This has a high proportion of cardamom, angelica and liquorice. Each batch is limited to just 250 individually numbered bottles. **Appearance:** (batch a, bottle No. 137 of 250) Crystal clear. **Aroma:** Pungent freshly crushed cardamom seeds dominate delicate nutty damp wood and eucalyptus. **Taste:** Fabulously crisp, clean and fresh with more cardamom, black pepper spice and eucalyptus/pine juniper fighting for attention. **Aftertaste:** Palate cleansing fresh breath finish with lingering cardamom, black pepper and juniper. This may technically be a 'London Dry Gin' but its flavour profile is far from what the term classically suggests.

SARTICIOUS GIN ★★★★☆

Alc./vol: 47% **Producer:** Unknown producer

The word 'sarticious' is a made-up word that, while not recognised as part of the English language, the makers of this gin assert means 'well-dressed and desirable'. Botanicals used to flavour Sarticious include juniper, organic orange, coriander, cardamom, cinnamon and pepper. **Appearance:** Crystal clear. **Aroma:** Powerful, wet Christmas tree, orange zest and fresh coriander leaf nose. **Taste:** Potent palate with woody piny juniper, fresh coriander, zesty lemon and orange citrus, fiery cracked black pepper. **Aftertaste:** Long finish starts with bursts of red chilli pepper heat and subsides to reveal a vegetal, piny base.

SCHINKENHÄGER

Alc./vol: 40% **Producer:** Unknown producer

The König family were producing a type of gin in the village of Steinhagen in the early 17th century. They are still involved in the production of this juniper-flavoured German schnapps, which is triple distilled from a blend of rye and wheat, and bottled in a traditional clay bottle.

SEAGRAM'S EXTRA DRY ★★★⯪☆

Alc./vol: 40% **Producer:** Lawrenceburg Distillers Indiana LLC

Seagram's gin is made from American grain neutral spirit flavoured with botanicals using a low temperature vacuum distillation process. Besides the obligatory juniper berries, the botanical recipe includes Sri Lankan cardamom, Vietnamese cassia, Spanish orange peel, Czech coriander and angelica. **Appearance:** Clear, transparent. **Aroma:** Candied citrus and juniper. **Taste:** Slightly sweet, sherbety palate with prickly spice and floral notes. **Aftertaste:** Long, dry, spicy finish. The spicy gin in the bumpy bottle."

SEAGRAM'S DISTILLER'S RESERVE

Alc./vol: 51% **Producer:** Lawrenceburg Distillers Indiana LLC

First launched in May 2006, Seagram's Distiller's Reserve Gin differs from the standard Seagram's Extra Dry in its higher alcoholic strength and due to its being blended from casks of aging gin personally selected by Seagram's master distiller.

SEAGRAM'S LIME TWISTED GIN ★★★★☆

Alc./vol: 40% **Producer:** Joseph E Seagram & Sons Limited

This lime-flavoured gin is based on Seagram's Extra Dry Gin and comes in the same distinctive crinkly bottles embossed with seashells and starfish. **Appearance:** Clear, transparent. **Aroma:** Fresh zesty lime and lime cordial with pine-ey juniper. **Taste:** Soft mouth feel and slightly sweet (suspiciously so – suspect sugar added) with convincing fresh lime flavours rather than the citrus meringue often found in other citrus flavoured white spirits. **Aftertaste:** Fades like it started, with lime cordial with pine-ey juniper. Gimlet anyone?

SIPSMITH LONDON DRY GIN EXCELLENT ★★★★★

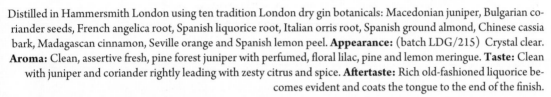

Alc./vol: 41.6% **Producer:** Sipsmith Distillery

Distilled in Hammersmith London using ten tradition London dry gin botanicals: Macedonian juniper, Bulgarian coriander seeds, French angelica root, Spanish liquorice root, Italian orris root, Spanish ground almond, Chinese cassia bark, Madagascan cinnamon, Seville orange and Spanish lemon peel. **Appearance:** (batch LDG/215) Crystal clear. **Aroma:** Clean, assertive fresh, pine forest juniper with perfumed, floral lilac, pine and lemon meringue. **Taste:** Clean with juniper and coriander rightly leading with zesty citrus and spice. **Aftertaste:** Rich old-fashioned liquorice becomes evident and coats the tongue to the end of the finish.

SIX O'CLOCK GIN ★★★★☆

Alc./vol: 43% **Producer:** Bramley & Gage

Named after the time when drinking becomes socially acceptable (guess the folk at B&G don't partake in Three-Martini Lunches) and made with juniper and six other botanicals including orange peel and elderflower. Designed to complement the makers own Six O'Clock Tonic. **Appearance:** Crystal clear. **Aroma:** Clean nose bursts with pine and camphor juniper and mandarin orange zest. Faint floral parma violet and liquorice. **Taste:** Huge whack of refreshing, slightly bitter, pine-ey juniper and orange oils - so much so that it is hard to identify the elderflower and other botanicals. **Aftertaste:** Stewed tea tannins and juniper with faint almond-like nuttiness.

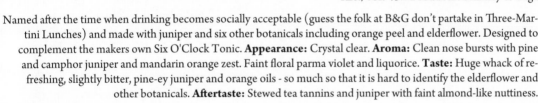

SLOANE'S ORIGINAL DRY GIN ★★★★☆

Alc./vol: 40% **Producer:** Toorank Distilleries

Named after Sir Hans Sloane (1660-1753), a Royal physician and botanist, whose botanical collection formed the foundation of what is now the Natural History Museum, Sloane's gin reflects a small part of his collection of botanicals. **Appearance:** Crystal clear. **Aroma:** Clean, aromatic but delicate nose with fragrant citrus notes rising over coriander and pine-ey juniper. **Taste:** Clean, very soft and well balanced palate with juniper very evident but not dominating citrus, cardamom and coriander. Liquorice and vanilla add discernable sweeten and enhance the parma violet and tea flavours of the bitter orris root. **Aftertaste:** The finish is much drier than the palate with lasting juniper, citrus and liquorice flavours. We loved this gin neat so tried it in both a Dry Martini and G&T. Sadly we found it just too soft to stand up to 1:5 vermouth and a double G&T.

SMOOTH AMBLER BARREL AGED GIN ★★★★☆

Alc./vol: 49.5% **Producer:** Smooth Ambler Spirits

Smooth Ambler's Barrel-Aged Gin is made using the same botanical distillate as their Greenbrier Gin, but is a 50/50 blend of the Greenbrier spirit aged in new oak and refill ex-bourbon barrels which are filled 60% alc./vol. **Appearance:** Clear, light golden. **Aroma:** Delightfully aromatic, orange marmalade boiling on the stove, dried tropical fruit, hot-cross-buns dusted with cinnamon and warm clove spice. **Taste:** Bitter sweet, tangy orange marmalade with lemon verbena and overtones of pine and camphor from the juniper. Spicey notes include candied ginger, hops, cinnamon and clove spice. **Aftertaste:** Dry oaky pine finish with marmalade citrus.

SOUTHBANK GIN (FORMERLY PARLIAMENT GIN)

Alc./vol: 37.5% **Producer:** Thames Distillers Ltd

Distilled at the Thames Distillery in Clapham London which is part-owned by Hayman Distillers, the owners of this gin brand. Christopher Hayman, Chairman of Hayman Distillers, is the great grandson of James Burrough who is famous for creating Beefeater Gin.

SPARROW LONDON DRY GIN ★★★★☆

Alc./vol: 41.6% **Producer:** Thames Distillers Ltd

Conceived and distilled in South London (another gin from Thames Distillery), bottles of Sparrow are graced with the image of Ginger, apparently there to bestow good luck. Artist Jules Langran gave her just a hint of stocking top and a tattoo of a flying sparrow with a heart wrapped in blue ribbon. **Appearance:** Crystal clear. **Aroma:** Juniper and zesty citrus with musky-nutty, window putty-like angelica and almond aromas. **Taste:** Clean, pine-ey juniper-led palate with prickly cracked black pepper, bitter citrus zest and ginger attack. **Aftertaste:** Long pine and citrus finish.

SQUIRES GIN ★★★☆☆

Alc./vol: 37.5% **Producer:** Thames Distillers Ltd

Squires Gin is named after Squire Thomas Pope of Dorset and was originally made by his descendants, the Pope of Eldridge Pope Brewery in Dorchester, England. Whitbread acquired the brand which is now distilled by Thames Distillers, bottled by Invergordon and sold by Waverly TBS as a value brand. **Appearance:** Clear, transparent. **Aroma:** Classic juniper, coriander and angelica nose with lemon zest and Parma Violets (perhaps orris root). **Taste:** Juniper comes to the fore backed by classic London dry flavours but perhaps a tad heavy on the angelica root. Little perceptible citrus. **Aftertaste:** Disappointing bitter, rooty finish.

SW4 LONDON DRY ★★★★☆

Alc./vol: 40% **Producer:** Thames Distillers Ltd

SW4 is made using 12 botanicals: juniper berries, coriander seeds, angelica, cinnamon, orange peel, orris powder, nutmeg, savory, cassia, almond, lemon peel and liquorice. The name plays on that fact it is distilled by Thames Distillers in Clapham, London, which has a postcode of SW4. **Appearance:** Crystal clear. **Aroma:** Angelica root's musky, nutty, damp wood, mushroom aromas are very evident on the nose. **Taste:** Fresh pine forest juniper plays a leading role dry, slightly bitter, peppery spiced palate with lavender and camphor. Orris root's Parma Violet and cold stewed tea with citrusy lemon peel. **Aftertaste:** Dry, woody pine finish with lingering orris notes.

TANQUERAY EXPORT STRENGTH (43.1) 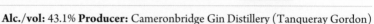 ★★★★★

Alc./vol: 43.1% **Producer:** Cameronbridge Gin Distillery (Tanqueray Gordon)

Packaged in the same iconic bottle and almost identically labelled to the original 47.3% Tanqueray Special Dry 'Export Strength', this lower 43.1% strength was introduced in 1999 and is made to the original Tanqueray recipe. This is the perfect strength for cocktails so is our Tanqueray of choice. **Appearance:** Crystal clear. **Aroma:** Pine fresh juniper led with subtle lemon zest and faint rootyness. **Taste:** Piney juniper, cedar, lemon zest and coriander with crystallised fruit and subtle floral and rooty notes. **Aftertaste:** Beautifully balanced and elegant with light peppery notes and lingering piny juniper.

TANQUERAY EXPORT STRENGTH (47.3) SPECIAL DRY `OUTSTANDING` ★★★★★+

Alc./vol: 47.3% **Producer:** Cameronbridge Gin Distillery (Tanqueray Gordon)

Until 1947, Tanqueray was sold in many different shaped bottles. The design we recognise today was inspired by a 1920s range of Tanqueray pre-mixed cocktails sold in bottles designed to resemble a cocktail shaker. **Appearance:** Crystal clear. **Aroma:** Pine fresh juniper with subtle zesty lemon, faint rootyness and black pepper prickle. **Taste:** Clean and pine fresh with juniper bursting forth, closely followed by lemon zest, coriander and rooty notes. The 47.3% strength contributes enlivening cracked black pepper spirity notes. **Aftertaste:** Beautifully balanced and elegant with light peppery notes and lingering piny juniper.

TANQUERAY MALACCA GIN ★★★★☆

Alc./vol: 40% **Producer:** Cameronbridge Gin Distillery (Tanqueray Gordon)

This softly spiced version of Tanqueray gin was originally developed in 1839 for the Far East and is named after the Straits of Malacca, a narrow waterway separating the Malaysia Peninsula and the Indonesian island of Sumatra, in turn named after the area's 15th century ruler, the Malacca Sultanate. **Appearance:** (bottle N0. TC 93899) Crystal clear. **Aroma:** Aromatic pink grapefruit zest and lemon meringue pie filling with delicate spice and piney juniper. **Taste:** Citrusy boiled sweets and juniper. Coriander bursts forth in the mid-palate with lemon zestyness. Faint sweetness with deleicate nutmeg, clove and gingery warmth. **Aftertaste:** Candied grapefruit with delicate ginger, nutmeg, clove and cracked pepper corn spice.

TANQUERAY NO. TEN GIN `OUTSTANDING` ★★★★★+

Alc./vol:% **Producer:** Cameronbridge Gin Distillery (Tanqueray Gordon)

Launched in 2000, Tanqueray No. Ten Gin is based on the traditional Tanqueray botanical recipe but with unusual extras such as camomile and fresh grapefruit. It takes its name from the distillery's number 10 still, known as Tiny Ten. **Appearance:** Crystal clear. **Aroma:** Spruce-like juniper, pink grapefruit and camomile with complex spice. **Taste:** Wonderfully rounded palate is incredibly silky considering its heady alcoholic strength. Juniper is integrated with freshly squeezed lemon, orange and zesty pink grapefruit while white pepper and coriander spice add depth. **Aftertaste:** All these flavours continue through the long, almost creamy, sherbety finish.

TANQUERAY RANGPUR GIN ★★★★☆

Alc./vol: 41.3% **Producer:** Cameronbridge Gin Distillery (Tanqueray Gordon)

Copy: Launched in the US in 2006, Rangpur is based in the traditional Tanqueray botanical recipe with the addition of ginger, bay leaves and most notably rangpur limes from India which surprisingly have orange coloured skins. Whatever would Charles Tanqueray say? **Appearance:** Crystal clear. **Aroma:** Wonderfully fresh with lime juice, lime zest and juniper. **Taste:** Slightly sweet (to the extent that added sugar is suspected). Lime dominates to the detriment of the other botanicals, although juniper wins the battle to shine through with peppery ginger heat adding balance. **Aftertaste:** Pleasantly fresh zesty lime finish. It is as though Diageo have set out to make a premixed Tanqueray Gimlet. A long way from what I would expect of the Tanqueray brand. Gimlet anyone?

THE BOTANIST ISLAY DRY GIN `OUTSTANDING` ★★★★★+

Alc./vol: 46% **Producer:** Bruichladdich Distillery

Distilled by Bruichladdich on Islay with nine traditional botanicals (wild Islay juniper berries, cassia bark, angelica root, coriander seed, cinnamon bark, lemon and orange peel, liquorice root and oris root), augmented with 22 native Islay botanicals in a copper pot-still nicknamed 'Ugly Betty'. **Appearance:** Crystal clear. **Aroma:** Incredibly pungent, resiny pine, juniper and eucalyptus-led with subtle parma violets, heather, candied ginger and sage. **Taste:** Dry, juniper with sappy pine dominating but with an integrated herbal complexity and faint liquorice sweetness. **Aftertaste:** Junipery pine dominance continues in the clean finish with faint lingering parma violets and liquorice. A robust gin.

THE DORCHESTER OLD TOM 2007 [RECOMMENDED] ★★★★⯪

Alc./vol: 40% **Producer:** William Grant

Specially made for the Dorchester Hotel by William Grant as their interpretation of the historic style of old English Old Tom gin. **Appearance:** Crystal clear. **Aroma:** Juniper and orange zest with camphor and lavender. **Taste:** Lightly sweet palate (just the merest hint of sugar) with pine-ey juniper and integrated orange zest and lavender. Despite the hint of sweetness when held the taste becomes slightly bitter as resiny pine from the juniper has a hop-like effect. **Aftertaste:** Pine-ey fresh juniper and warming cracked black pepper spice with lingering orange zest oils.

THE DUKE MUNICH DRY GIN ★★★⯪☆

Alc./vol: 45% **Producer:** Persephone Destillerie

Founded in 2009, The Duke is an organic gin created in small batches – batch numbers are written on each bottle. Seemingly nothing to do with John Wayne. **Appearance:** (IN: 05/2009/II) Crystal clear. **Aroma:** Aggressive eucalyptus/juniper nose with green pine needles, cracked coriander seeds and violet blossom. **Taste:** Slightly sweet palma violet and juniper palate with a soft mouthfeel – in fact soft in flavour as well. **Aftertaste:** Sweet, floral finish with lasting violet and sweet liquorice.

THE LONDON NO.1 GIN (ORIGINAL BLUE GIN) ★★★★☆

Alc./vol: 47% **Producer:** Thames Distillers

This turquoise-blue gin is marketed as "The Original Blue Gin" and is distilled at Thames Distillers with English grain neutral spirit and 12 botanicals: juniper, liquorice, orris root, cinnamon, almond, bergamot, savory, coriander, angelica root, cassia, lemon peel and orange peel. **Appearance:** Clear, very pale turquoise-blue. **Aroma:** The force of 47% alc./vol. is evident on a pungent, camphor and citrus nose with overripe banana, hop-like celery, chewing gum (Dentine), cinnamon and soapy nutty aromas. **Taste:** Zingy pine, citrus and black pepper palate screams for tonic water. **Aftertaste:** Peppery pine, eucalyptus and chewing gum finish.

THE ORIGINAL BOMBAY DRY GIN (40%) ★★★★☆

Alc./vol: 40% **Producer:** The Bombay Spirits Company

As the name would suggest, this is the original Bombay gin, predating the now better-known Bombay Sapphire. It was designed by American entrepreneur Allan Subin, who was inspired by one of the oldest known English dry gin recipes, created by Thomas Dakin in 1761. It launched in the USA in 1960.

THE ORIGINAL BOMBAY DRY GIN (43%) [OUTSTANDING] ★★★★★+

Alc./vol: 43% **Producer:** The Bombay Spirits Company

As the name would suggest, this is the original Bombay gin, predating the now better-known Bombay Sapphire. It was designed by American entrepreneur Allan Subin, who was inspired by one of the oldest known English dry gin recipes, created by Thomas Dakin in 1761. It launched in the USA in 1960. **Appearance:** Crystal clear. **Aroma:** Coriander, juniper and citrus with hints of Olbas oil tablets. **Taste:** Juniper, citrus and coriander flavours predominate with liquorice, Parma Violet and an underlying rootiness. Superbly structured. **Aftertaste:** Lingering juniper freshness with liquorice and Parma Violets.

TUB GIN ★★★★☆

Alc./vol: 40% **Producer:** Peach Street Distillers

This gin from Colorado is flavoured with juniper berries, coriander, angelica, oris root, liquorice, lemon peel, lime peel and cassia bark and "a few other things we found lying around the place". Judging by Tub Gin's website and marketing materials we presume it is aimed at America's gun lobby. **Appearance:** Crystal clear. **Aroma:** Zesty orange marmalade, lemon meringue pie filling, pine and camphor with musky sage, eucalyptus and Dentine chewing gum-like aromas. **Taste:** Citrus forward style but with supporting piney juniper and well-judged cleansing prickly spice. **Aftertaste:** Clean zesty finish with faint lingering notes of piney junper and peppery spice.

TWO BIRDS COUNTRYSIDE LONDON DRY GIN ★★★★★

Alc./vol: 40% **Producer:** Union Distillers Ltd

Two Birds Gin is produced in batches of 100 bottles from a 25 litre pot still bespoke handmade copper still in Market Harborough, Leicestershire England. The recipe and even the number of botanicals used is not disclosed. **Appearance:** Crystal clear. **Aroma:** Lavender, camphor and overripe banana juniper notes lead fresh sage and coriander. **Taste:** The overripe banana note, which I assume is from the juniper, is particularly strong, softening and sweetening the dry pine notes in a very attractive way. **Aftertaste:** Classic juniper and spice finish.

VAN WEES DE OOIEVAAR ROGGENAER 3 JAAR ★★★★☆

Alc./vol: 40% **Producer:** A. van Wees Distilleerderij De Ooievaar

Distilled from 100 per cent fermented rye and aged on in oak casks for at least three years – basically a Dutch 100 per cent rye whiskey. **Appearance:** Clear, faint yellow green tinge. **Aroma:** New-make spirit-like cereal with oily Ryvita crispbread and faint lemon zest. **Taste:** Clean and soft toasted cereal. Much lighter and softer than might be expected from a three old rye distillate, seeming soothed by oily notes with rye spice attractive rather than aggressive. **Aftertaste:** Black pepper and Ryvita.

VAN WEES ROGGENAER SPECIAL RESERVE 15 JAAR ★★★★☆

Alc./vol: 40% **Producer:** A. van Wees Distilleerderij De Ooievaar

This 100 per cent rye spirit has been aged for 15 years in oak and is the very old brother of Van Wees' three-year-old Roggenaer. Presented in a short clay bottle with a green wax stalk seal on top. **Appearance:** Clear, straw yellow with a faint green hint. **Aroma:** Balsa wood, anise, coriander, mint and linseed oil. **Taste:** Lightly spiced with pronounced clove and herbal notes. **Aftertaste:** Complex herbal notes emerge in the long lightly spiced finish.

VAN WEES ZEER OUDE (VERY OLD GENEVER) 15 JAAR ★★★☆☆

Alc./vol: 42% **Producer:** A. van Wees Distilleerderij De Ooievaar

This zeer oude (very old) genever from Van Wees has been matured for 15 years in oak casks at its Amsterdam distillery. Presented in a tall clay bottle. **Appearance:** (bottle 00656) Clear, light mustard yellow. **Aroma:** Oily herbal nose with light oak and acorns. **Taste:** Surprisingly herbaceous, vegetal palate with dry oak and faint pine. Hint of leathery tobacco leaf. **Aftertaste:** Lingering herbal notes but fades with black pepper spice and faint stewed vegetables

VICTORIA GIN ★★★☆☆

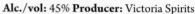
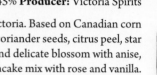

Alc./vol: 45% **Producer:** Victoria Spirits

Distilled in a German made pot still, the bottle features a young, radiant Queen Victoria. Based on Canadian corn neutral spirit, the ten botanicals flavouring this gin include juniper, angelica root, coriander seeds, citrus peel, star anise and rose petals. **Appearance**: Crystal clear. **Aroma**: Vanilla, fried donuts and delicate blossom with anise, angelica and coriander. **Taste**: Slightly sweet and generously spiced pancake mix with rose and vanilla. **Aftertaste**: Aggressively spiced finish with vanilla fudge. Very far from a traditionally styled gin.

..

WHITLEY NEILL LONDON DRY ★★★★☆

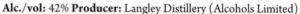

Alc./vol: 42% **Producer:** Langley Distillery (Alcohols Limited)

Johnny Neill, a fourth generation member of the Greenall Whitley distilling family, was inspired by his wife's South African homeland when creating this distilled gin. Hence, the use of two African botanicals, fruit of the baobab 'tree of life' and Cape gooseberry, with seven more traditional botanicals **Appearance**: Crystal clear. **Aroma:** Pine fresh juniper leads a tropical fruit and zesty lemon nose. **Taste:** Dry, juniper-led palate with lemon and orange sherbet plus hints of creamy mango spiced with cracked black pepper. **Aftertaste:** The tropical fruit emerges again in the long peppered finish. Very clean and fresh throughout.

WILLIAMS CHASE SINGLE BOTANICAL GIN/CHASE JUNIPER EXCELLENT ★★★★★

Alc./vol: 40% **Producer:** Chase Distillery

Is it a single botanical gin? Or is it a juniper flavoured vodka? The answer – it's both. So appropriately one side of the bottle is labelled "Limited Edition Chase Juniper Vodka" while the other side is labelled "Williams Chase Single Botanical Gin. Perhaps it's just bi-polar? **Appearance**: (First batch, bottle no 908 of 1000) Crystal clear. **Aroma**: Clean and fresh – even freshening, leathery eucalyptus with delicate piney spice. **Taste**: Clean, eucalyptus, lavender, camphor, pine and faint overripe banana garnished with mild black pepper. **Aftertaste**: Pine and cleansing cracked black pepper.

.

XORIGUER MAHÓN GIN RECOMMENDED ★★★★☆

Alc./vol: 38% **Producer:** M. Pons Justo SA

Pronounced 'sho-ri-gair' and produced on the island of Menorca, Xoriguer is one of only two gins in the world with its own EU Designation of Origin. Gin has been distilled at Mahón since the 18th century when the island was under British control and the port was an important naval base. **Appearance**: Crystal clear. **Aroma**: A very floral, almost perfumed oily orange zest and orange flower nose with delicate juniper. **Taste**: The grape character of the base alcohol comes through on the spicy, aromatic palate. The flavour profile is more reminiscent of Morocco: hints of real Turkish Delight mingle with generous juniper, aniseed, camomile, lemon zest and almond. Xoriguer is a little rough round the edges but in a pleasingly, characterful way. **Aftertaste**: Long, lingering, breath freshening juniper and orange zest finish.

ZUIDAM DRY GIN EXCELLENT ★★★★★

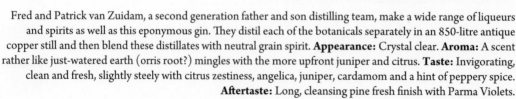

Alc./vol: 44.5% **Producer:** Zuidam Distillers BV

Fred and Patrick van Zuidam, a second generation father and son distilling team, make a wide range of liqueurs and spirits as well as this eponymous gin. They distil each of the botanicals separately in an 850-litre antique copper still and then blend these distillates with neutral grain spirit. **Appearance**: Crystal clear. **Aroma:** A scent rather like just-watered earth (orris root?) mingles with the more upfront juniper and citrus. **Taste**: Invigorating, clean and fresh, slightly steely with citrus zestiness, angelica, juniper, cardamom and a hint of peppery spice. **Aftertaste**: Long, cleansing pine fresh finish with Parma Violets.